Adolf H   **2 NOV 2011** to be the most evil political leader of twentieth-century   draws on his background and involvement in the rise of National Socialism, the government of the Third Reich, his leadership of the Second World War in Germany and his psychology to discuss the Führer's credentials as a revolutionary.

This volume examines:

- the general characteristics of revolutions and revolutionaries
- Hitler as agitator, dictator, deceiver and warlord
- Hitler's architectural and artistic ambitions
- Hitler's mind and personality

Hitler investigates what it was that motivated this national leader to achieve such monstrosities that still cast a shadow over Europe today.

Martyn Housden is Lecturer in Modern and Contemporary European History at the University of Bradford. He is author of *Helmut Nicolai and Nazi Ideology* (Macmillan, 1992) and *Resistance and Conformity in the Third Reich* (Routledge, 1997).

ROUTLEDGE SOURCES IN HISTORY
Series Editor
David Welch, University of Kent

OTHER TITLES IN THE SERIES
The Suez Crisis
Anthony Gorst and Lewis Johnman

Resistance and Conformity in the Third Reich
Martyn Housden

The Russian Revolution 1917–1921
Ronald Kowalski

The Fascist Experience in Italy
John Pollard

The Rise and Fall of the Soviet Union
Richard Sakwa

FORTHCOMING
The Third Republic in France, 1870–1940: Conflicts and Continuities
William Fortescue

The German Experience
Anthony McElligott

The Cold War
George Conyne

Hitler

Study of a Revolutionary?

Martyn Housden

London and New York

First published 2000
by Routledge
11 New Fetter Lane, London EC4P 4EE

Simultaneously published in the USA and Canada
by Routledge
29 West 35th Street, New York, NY 10001

Routledge is an imprint of the Taylor & Francis Group

Typeset in Galliard and Gill by Keystroke, Jacaranda Lodge, Wolverhampton
Printed and bound in Great Britain by Biddles Ltd, Guildford and King's Lynn

British Library Cataloguing in Publication Data
A catalogue record for this book is available from the British Library

Library of Congress Cataloging in Publication Data
Housden, Martyn, 1962–
    Hitler : study of a revolutionary? / Martyn Housden.
        p.   cm. — (Routledge sources in history)
    Includes bibliographical references and index.
    1. Hitler, Adolf, 1889–1945. 2. National socialism. 3. Statesmen—
Germany—Biography. 4. Germany—Politics and government—1918–1933.
5. Germany—Politics and government—1933–1945. I. Title. II. Series.
DD247.H5 H68 2000
943.086'092—dc21
    [B]   99-058191

ISBN 0–415–16359–5 (pbk)
ISBN 0–415–16358–7 (hbk)

For EFVH and DWH

Contents

Series editor's preface   ix

Acknowledgements   xi

1   Revolutions and revolutionaries   1

2   Ideologue   17

3   Agitator   42

4   Dictator   66

5   Deceiver   92

6   Warlord   117

7   Artist and Architect   143

8   Mind   166

9   Conclusion – study of a revolutionary?   187

Timeline   199

Further reading   201

Bibliography   204

Index   218

Series editor's preface

Sources in History is a new series responding to the continued shift of emphasis in the teaching of history in schools and universities towards the use of primary sources and the testing of historical skills. By using documentary evidence, the series is intended to reflect the skills historians have to master when challenged by problems of evidence, interpretation and presentation.

A distinctive feature of *Sources in History* will be the manner in which the content, style and significance of documents is analysed. The commentary and the sources are not discrete, but rather merge to become part of a continuous and integrated narrative. After reading each volume a student should be well versed in the historiographical problems which sources present. In short, the series aims to provide texts which will allow students to achieve facility in 'thinking historically' and place them in a stronger position to test their historical skills. Wherever possible the intention has been to retain the integrity of a document and not simply to present a 'gobbet', which can be misleading. Documentary evidence thus forces the student to confront a series of questions which professional historians also have to grapple with. Such questions can be summarised as follows:

1 What type of source is the document?
- Is it a written source or an oral or visual source?
- What, in your estimation, is its importance?
- Did it, for example, have an effect on events or the decision-making process?
2 Who wrote the document?
- A person, a group, or a government?
- If it was a person, what was their position?
- What basic attitudes might have affected the nature of the information and language used?
3 When was the document written?
- The date, and even the time, might be significant.
- You may need to understand when the document was written in order to understand its context.
- Are there any special problems in understanding the document as contemporaries would have understood it?
4 Why was the document written?
- For what purpose(s) did the document come into existence, and for whom was it intended?

- Was the document 'author-initiated' or was it commissioned for somebody? If the document was ordered by someone, the author could possibly have 'tailored' his piece.
5   What was written?
- This is the obvious question, but never be afraid to state the obvious.
- Remember, it may prove more revealing to ask the question: what was *not* written?
- That is, read between the lines. In order to do this you will need to ask what other references (to persons, events, other documents, etc.) need to be explained before the document can be fully understood.

Sources in History is intended to reflect the individual voice of the volume author(s) with the aim of bringing the central themes of specific topics into sharper focus. Each volume will consist of an authoritative introduction to the topic; chapters will discuss the historical significance of the sources, and the final chapter will provide an up-to-date synthesis of the historiographical debate. Authors will also provide an annotated bibliography and suggestions for further reading. These books will become contributions to the historical debate in their own right.

Any study of Adolf Hitler is hampered by the lack of definitive evidence about crucial areas of his life (for example, his relationship to the origins of the Holocaust). There is also the problem of what to do with the knowledge we do have. The judges at the Nuremberg war crimes tribunals defined his politics conclusively as criminal, but it falls to historians to give this criminality meaning. The task requires that Adolf Hitler be located in the sweep of recent history. By discussing Hitler's credentials as a revolutionary, Martyn Housden helps establish the place of this most perverse of all politicians in the maelstrom of early twentieth-century Europe. In doing so, there emerges a paradox: Hitler was a product of his times, but he was determined to surpass its rules and limitations. So was he a revolutionary who bears comparison to the likes of Lenin and Stalin? And at what point must comparison stop? This study has the merit of posing such fundamental questions as these, while still managing to evoke in vivid colours the life and character of a man whose consequences still impact upon the world today.

David Welch
Canterbury 2000

Acknowledgements

Any book grows out of a complicated background of influences. In addition to writing about Adolf Hitler I have been involved in research projects about Hans Frank and the history of international security in connection with the Baltic States. These projects certainly have influenced what has been written here. As a result I must acknowledge the generous financial support of the British Academy, the Nuffield Foundation and the British Council. This study would be much the poorer without their help. The editor of the Sources in History series, David Welch, offered good advice on an earlier draft of this book. It is all the better for his intervention.

The following publishers have been kind enough to give permission for more lengthy extracts from their wares to be reproduced: Weidenfeld and Nicolson for extracts from A. Speer, *Inside the Third Reich*, 1971; Simon and Schuster for extracts from A. Speer, *Inside the Third Reich*, 1971. Oxford University Press for the Royal Institute of International Affairs, London for extracts from N.H. Baynes (ed.), *The Speeches of Adolf Hitler, Volumes 1 and 2*, 1942; and Houghton Mifflin for extracts from A. Kubizek, *The Young Hitler I Knew*, 1954.

The Wiener Library, London should also be acknowledged for help and supplying all the photographs used as documents in this book.

Every effort has been made either to trace ownership of copyright and adhere to publishing conventions. We will be glad to make any suitable arrangements with copyright holders whom it has not been possible to contact.

As a final word here, it is only right to acknowledge the help of my copy editor, Michael Fitch, and the team at Routledge (past and present), all of whom brought the project to completion.

Revolutions and revolutionaries

1

Document 1.1 Peculiar Greatness

Source: Wiener Library Folder: Hitler, Parades
© *Heinrich Hoffmann*

Adolf Hitler had 'peculiar greatness' (Fest, 1973, p. 3). Document 1.1 makes it clear enough. In this image drawn from the mid-1920s he tries to strike an authoritative pose. His face is severe, he is almost standing 'at attention', he is flanked by uniformed SA men; and yet Hitler is wearing the traditional Bavarian costume of loden jacket and shorts. The impression is, indeed, 'peculiar'. It challenges us to understand this enigmatic individual. Over the years his figure has evoked rejoicing, hysteria, hope of salvation, not to say revulsion, hatred and downright fear. Appropriately Adolf Hitler was a man of many parts. He established the ideology which underpinned the National Socialist movement. In the beer halls of Munich, he agitated tirelessly on behalf of his particular political message. He became first the leader of the National Socialist German Workers' Party (NSDAP) and then of the whole German nation. Through a process of consistent deceit, he orchestrated the country's foreign policy. From 1939 onwards he determined ever more closely the nation's war effort. Through it all, he remained fixated on the idea that he was involved in an artistic undertaking. Adolf Hitler was all of these things: agitator, ideologue, dictator, deceiver, warlord and artist. This brief study takes its chapter structure from the manifold roles he adopted in an existence which, although it often seems to have lasted longer, spanned just 56 years. An additional psychoanalytical chapter explores how his mind worked. Each of these individual themes is clear enough, but even together they may miss the most important feature of his life.

Was Adolf Hitler a revolutionary who sought to bring about fundamental change to Germany and Europe? The question is absolutely central to an understanding of his place in history (Bracher, 1976, p. 199). Important recent studies have promoted the idea that National Socialism and Communism should be counted equally revolutionary movements and that Hitler and the Communist leaders were equally revolutionaries. Take Alan Bullock's study *Hitler and Stalin. Parallel Lives* (Bullock, 1991). In terms of personality, both dictators believed they were destined to play a formative part in history and were perfectly prepared to devote themselves completely to a higher cause to achieve this. Regarding political activity, both evidenced a singleness of aim combined with complete tactical flexibility and shared a passion to dominate all around them. To Bullock's mind, the pair expressed paranoia in comparable measure, and both managed to focus this against a single category of enemies. For Stalin the target became the kulaks, for Hitler it was the Jews. The crimes committed by the two means they share responsibilities without parallel (Bullock, 1991, pp. 393, 395, 396, 466 and 1075). The impression from over a thousand pages of Bullock's text has to be that Hitler and Stalin were very similar types of person.

Rainer Zitelmann's work is less well-known to English-language audiences. His most important study, *Hitler. Selbstverständnis eines Revolutionärs (Hitler. The Way a Revolutionary Understood Himself)* was first published in the 1980s but came out in a new edition in the late 1990s (Zitelmann, 1998). The author argues at length that Hitler held highly ambivalent attitudes towards Communists. Although he was at odds completely with their ideology, he admired their dedication, achievements and highly effective use of the spoken word to rally popular support. As a result, after the *Machtergreifung* (the seizure of power) Hitler advertised for Communists to switch loyalties. As he put it in October 1935, if a Communist 'comes to reason and returns to his people, he is heartily welcome' in the NSDAP. Speaking to the Bulgarian regent in March 1944, Hitler boasted that the National Socialist movement had managed to absorb completely the Communists in Germany – except for criminal elements, which he had been compelled to stamp out (Zitelmann, 1998, pp. 467–9). Zitelmann has concluded that National Socialism and Communism were in many ways so similar that they offered each other direct political competition. Because National Socialism could not tolerate this, it was forced in the end to eradicate Communism. Zitelmann says National Socialism was 'an alternative competing revolutionary movement which did not have the annihilation of Marxism as its main goal'. It was forced to eradicate Marxism *precisely on account of* the proximity to it' (Zitelmann, 1998, p. 475).

According to Zitelmann, this ambivalence towards Communism was reflected in Hitler's attitude to Stalin. While the German rejected entirely the Soviet's ideology, he revered his means. There was even fellow feeling between dictators. Zitelmann believes Hitler regarded Stalin as a reflection of himself. He was the creator of a modernising dictatorship which was prepared to pursue its ends using even the most brutal means. Increasingly Hitler regarded the Stalinist method as an ideal which had to be applied in Germany as the only means to beat the Soviet Union in the war of existence (Zitelmann, 1998, pp. 479–80). Hitler applauded the way Stalin had prepared his army for conflict by a merciless process of liquidations and wished he had shared such a degree of determination and rigour in excluding representatives of the traditional élites from positions of power in the Third Reich. In upshot he actually regretted a failure to revolutionise society to the extent Stalin had achieved in Russia. As evidence of such a way of thinking, reference can be made to Hitler's *Testament*. The following extract, written in February 1945, underlines the Führer's sadness that he had been unable to transform Germany's leadership cadre more thoroughly.

Document 1.2 Petty Bourgeois Reactionaries

Since we lacked men moulded in the shape of our ideal, we had perforce to make what use we could of those whom we had. The result had been obvious. Thanks to this discrepancy between conception and realization, the war policy of a revolutionary state like the Third Reich has of necessity been the policy of petty bourgeois reactionaries. Our generals and diplomats, with a few, rare exceptions, are men of another age; and their methods of waging war and of conducting our foreign policy also belong to an age that is passed. This is just as true of those who serve us in all good faith as it is of the rest of them. The former serve us ill through lack either of aptitude or enthusiasm, and the latter do so deliberately and of malice aforethought.

Source: F. Genoud (ed.), The Testament of Adolf Hitler, *1959, pp. 59–60*

Zitelmann also argues that during the Weimar period, and just like his Communist counterparts, Hitler believed he had a revolutionary calling to overthrow a corrupt, lethargic bourgeois state. As Hitler put it in October 1920, 'Our party must bear a revolutionary character, because the condition of "peace and order" means only the preservation of the current pig-sty' (Zitelmann, 1998, p. 82). Hitler hated parliamentarianism so much that, during Summer 1921, he even left the NSDAP for a brief time when some of its other leaders began exploring, amongst other things, the possibility of electoral participation. In July 1921 Hitler denied that democracy could solve the nation's problems: it had to be done by a revolutionary movement (Zitelmann, 1998, p. 82). He put it particularly clearly in February 1922, 'We don't want to go into the parliaments. . . . Whoever proceeds into a bog dies there' (Zitelmann, 1998, p. 82). Zitelmann produces evidence that even at this early point Hitler conceived revolutionary change in the most extensive of ways. He spoke as follows in May 1921.

Document 1.3 State, Economy and Morality

What is a revolution? It is the violent alteration of an existing order by a minority supported and possibly made by the will of the majority of the people. . . . What can be improved by a revolution? 1. The form of the state if the existing one justifies this act by a deficiency. 2. The economy of a people, but only in a slow, careful reforming of the existing operation of the economy . . . ; and 3. a revolution, all in all, is only sustainable by the renewal of the moral force of a people through the exclusion of habitual moral and economic corruption.

Source: R. Zitelmann, Hitler, *1998, p. 69*

Zitelmann shows how Hitler interpreted his coming to power in Germany as a revolutionary event. The Führer once described it as the closure of one age and the opening of another, like the coming of Christianity, the triumph of Islam or the Reformation; on another occasion he said it was one of the 'greatest trans-formations which have ever happened on the earth' (Zitelmann, 1998, pp. 103–4). In fact Hitler liked to describe the changes he brought to Germany in fundamental yet *benign* ways. He emphasised it had been a 'legal' revolution. On 23 March 1933 Hitler told the Reichstag, 'Hardly ever has a revolution on such a large scale been carried out in so disciplined and bloodless a fashion as this renaissance of the German people in the last few weeks' (Zitelmann, 1998, p. 209). That October he made the same point at greater length.

Document 1.4 Free from Excesses

When has there ever been a revolution so free from excesses (Greuel) as ours? In the days when there was revolution in Germany there was greater order than in many countries where there was no revolution. . . . Even if there were excesses, we could still stand comparison with the excesses of revolutions amongst other peoples. It is true we have to barricade the streets, but not because the people wants to stone the government, but because the people wants to express to the Government its jubilation. I go any day amongst the people without a cordon of police. People can always know where I am and where I am going. I have not the least fear that the people may attack me: on the contrary my greatest anxiety is that perhaps a small child might be crushed before my motor.

And if I compare the excesses of the French Revolution I can only say: We at least have established no guillotine, we have not created any Vendée in Germany. Even with the worst elements we have only kept them apart from the nation. Unfortunately the rest of the world declines to take them from us; we would so gladly put them at their disposal.

Source: N.H. Baynes, The Speeches of Adolf Hitler, Vol. 1, *1942, p. 210*

At first sight, it is easy to make a case that Adolf Hitler was a revolutionary, so why has the proposition not been explored more fully in the past? The answer requires an explanation of prior popular trends of thinking about the way history and society work. Some of these actually led to the belief that Hitler was the complete antithesis of a revolutionary. In this connection there is just no escape from Marxism.

Karl Marx and Friedrich Engels conceptualised revolution as the driving force of history. As explained in *The Communist Manifesto*, the history of society was the history of class struggle (Marx and Engels, 1985, p. 79). The world was said to be divided into social groups with different and conflicting economic interests. In capitalist society the bourgeoisie (factory owners and employers) was engaged in the exploitation of the proletarians (the workers). Competition between members of the bourgeoisie for profit made the exploitation ever more merciless such that the conditions of life of the workers become ever worse (Marx, 1959, p. 270). With nowhere left to turn, the proletarians began to form a class of revolutionaries which in time would overthrow bourgeois capitalist society. In its place something new and Communistic would be forged. Marx and Engels explained the creation of proletarian revolutionaries well.

Document 1.5 Grave-Diggers

Hitherto, every form of society has been based, as we have already seen, on the antagonism of oppressing and oppressed classes. . . . The modern labourer . . . instead of rising with the progress of industry, sinks deeper and deeper below the conditions of existence of his own class. He becomes a pauper, and pauperism develops more rapidly than population and wealth. And here it becomes evident, that the bourgeoisie is unfit any longer to be the ruling class in society, and to impose its conditions of existence upon society as an overriding law. It is unfit to rule because it is

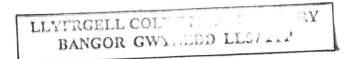

incompetent to assure an existence to its slave within his slavery, because it has to feed him, instead of being fed by him. Society can no longer live under this bourgeoisie, in other words, its existence is no longer compatible with society.

The essential condition for the existence, and for the sway of the bourgeois class, is the formation and augmentation of capital; the condition for capital is wage labour. Wage labour rests exclusively on competition between the labourers. The advance of industry, whose involuntary promoter is the bourgeoisie, replaces the isolation of the labourers, due to competition, by their revolutionary combination, due to association. The development of Modern Industry, therefore, cuts from under its feet the very foundation on which the bourgeoisie produces and appropriates products. What the bourgeoisie therefore produces, is its own grave-diggers. Its fall and the victory of the proletariat are equally inevitable.

Source: K. Marx and F. Engels, The Communist Manifesto, *1985, pp. 93–4*

In the brave new Communist world, land ownership would be abolished, there would be a progressive system of income tax, there would be no rights of inheritance, anti-Communists would not be allowed to own property, the state would manage all credit, it would control the means of communication and factory production, everyone would be equally liable to labour duties, the division between agricultural and manufacturing production would be overcome, and there would be free education for all (Marx and Engels, 1985, pp. 104–5). For Marx and Engels, true revolutionaries were members of the exploited working classes fighting for Communist ideals.

According to orthodox Marxists, when fascism (and in this category they included National Socialism) arose, it was in opposition to the growing proletarian revolutionary process. Hitler and his followers were deemed counter-revolutionary: they operated on behalf of vested capitalist interests (the bourgeoisie) and applied revolutionary means to pre-empt or divert the truly revolutionary, proletarian upsurge that was identified in Germany in the 1920s (Calvert, 1970, p. 137). National Socialism was said to comprise members of the petit bourgeoisie, slum-proletarians and demoralised workers who were funded and directed by finance-capital to smash truly working-class organisations and to defeat the proletarian revolution which was believed to be growing out of the economic chaos of especially the late 1920s and early 1930s (Palme Dutt, 1934, pp. 80–2). The Communist International of 1933 described fascism most famously.

Document 1.6 The 13th Communist International Plenum

1. Fascism is the open, terrorist dictatorship of the most reactionary, most chauvinist and most imperialist elements of finance capital. Fascism tries to secure a mass basis for monopolist capital among the petty bourgeoisie,

appealing to the peasantry, artisans, office employees and civil servants who have been thrown out of their normal course of life, and particularly to the declassed elements in the big cities, also trying to penetrate into the working class.

The growth of fascism and its coming to power in Germany and in a number of other capitalist countries means:

(a) that the revolutionary crisis and the indignation of the broad masses against the rule of capital are growing;
(b) that the capitalists are no longer able to maintain their dictatorship by the old methods of parliamentarianism and of bourgeois democracy in general;
(c) that, moreover, the methods of parliamentarianism and bourgeois democracy in general are becoming a hindrance to the capitalists both in their internal politics (the struggle against the proletariat) and in their foreign politics (war for the imperialist redistribution of the world);
(d) that in view of this, capital is compelled to pass to open terrorist dictatorship within the country and to unrestrained chauvinism in foreign politics, which represents direct preparation for imperialist wars.

Source: Roger Griffin (ed.), International Fascism, *1998, p. 60*

R. Palme Dutt was a Marxist observer writing in western Europe in the 1930s. He understood the origins of fascism in terms of counter-revolutionary circumstances and the needs of the bourgeoisie (Palme Dutt, 1934, pp. 75–7).

Document 1.7 R. Palme Dutt

Fascism, in fact, is no peculiar, independent doctrine and system arising in opposition to existing capitalist society. Fascism, on the contrary, is the most complete and consistent working out, in certain conditions of extreme decay, of the most typical tendencies and policies of modern capitalism.

What are these characteristics which are common, subject to a difference in degree, to all modern capitalism and to Fascism? The most outstanding of these characteristics may be summarised as follows:

1. The basic aim of the maintenance of capitalism in the face of the revolution which the advance of productive techniques and of class antagonisms threatens.
2. The consequent intensification of the capitalist dictatorship.
3. The limitation and repression of the independent working-class movement, and building up of a system of organised class co-operation.
4. The revolt against, and increasing supersession of, parliamentary democracy.
5. The extending State monopolist organisation of industry and finance.

6. The closer concentration of each imperialist bloc into a single economic-political unit.
7. The advance to war as the necessary accompaniment of the increasing imperialist antagonisms.

Source: R. Palme Dutt, Fascism and Social Revolution, *1934, pp.72–3*

Palme Dutt believed representatives of big business throughout Europe supported fascism: for example, Owen Young, Mond, Detering and, of course within Germany, Thyssen and Krupp. Hitler and his followers were believed to be nothing but the 'catspaws' of people such as these. They were a means to the oppression of society's real revolutionaries; they were agents acting against the sort of social change which was much needed.

The idea that Hitler and his followers were the exact opposite of revolutionaries was adopted as official policy by the Communist regimes of eastern Europe after 1945. One standard East German textbook argued that following the Wall Street crash of October 1929, and the electoral success of the National Socialist party in September 1930, Germany's industrialists began to take notice of the organisation. From this time on, leading capitalists sent representatives to party meetings to influence the formulation of party policy in favour of their own interests (Herrmann et al., 1988, p. 345). Industrialists went out of their way to cultivate friendships with those who surrounded Hitler in an attempt to influence the leader of Germany's most significant new political force. The same East German book pointed out that in November 1932 a petition supporting Hitler was sent to President Hindenburg. It was agreed by the Ruhr magnates Vögler, Reusch and Springorum. It was signed by Thyssen and notable bankers, potash industrialists, export business people and estate owners (Hermann et al., 1988, p. 347). The following passage is taken from the same East German textbook and gives a flavour of the material applied in Marxist historical analysis. It discusses the way the interests of Nazism and big business were said to have become enmeshed as the party tried to re-establish itself during the late 1920s.

Document 1.8 The Counter-Revolutionaries

The surface [of the Weimar Republic] shone in pluralistic fashion, imitating a society that was half-way pacified, but beneath it fascism, pressed to rock bottom, could gather new strengths. Nazi number two, Gregor Strasser and other fascist functionaries, who were devoting themselves to building up the NSDAP [Nationalsozialistische Arbeiter Partei Deutschlands – the National Socialist German Workers' Party] in northern Germany after the failed beer hall putsch, succeeded in forging contacts with influential big industrialists, namely at the head of heavy industry in Rhineland-Westphalia. This élite, which traditionally adopted rabble-rousing positions and which was interested to a considerable extent in future armaments business, could influence the strategy formation of monopoly capital in more weighty fashion than other interest groups, because it dominated the energy and raw materials market and had organised its branch of the economy most tightly. In 1926 Hitler found an entrance to the clubs and luxury villas of the Ruhr magnates through the north German Nazi big-wigs, and he was able to convince his hosts without difficulty that his goals were also their own: the rooting out of Marxism, the introduction of the unlimited 'leadership principle' into the economy and politics, the conquest of territories for raw materials, sales and settlement, and the annihilation of Soviet power. The Schwerin industrialists, who had considerable power, got involved too. At the same time they were used to offering support to rival reactionary troops [i.e. more traditional forces that were anti-Socialist and against the Weimar Republic] and at first only supported fascism hesitantly, because on the one hand it had not proved it was also capable of delivering the goods, and on the other hand because it awakened the fear that its followers, who were fed on pseudo-socialist slogans, could, in the hours they had to prove themselves, shove the demagogic leaders to one side and storm against the capitalist order.

. . . Of special importance – to name but one example – was the engagement of the senior figure of Ruhr industry, Emil Kirdorf, one of the Pan-Germans, who in 1927, and quite covertly, established a kind of committee of big industrialists for promoting the Nazis. He became a member of the NSDAP himself and, even after he left the party in 1928 due to anti-capitalist statements by several junior Nazi leaders, he remained closely associated with Hitler. The number of big capitalists interested in fascism grew constantly so that from the second half of the twenties ever more significant amounts of money flowed to the NSDAP with which new local organisations and newspapers could be founded, propaganda campaigns implemented and the terroristic SA expanded.

Source: J. Hermann et al., Deutsche Geschichte in 10 Kapiteln, *1988, pp. 343–4*

Marxism cast a long shadow over even non-Marxist literature. Very recently indeed one commentator still defined fascism as the ultimate expression of 'reactionary counter-revolutionary thought' – albeit directed against the Enlightenment rather than capitalism (Neocleous, 1997, p. 74). But Marxism's approach was untenable. In terms of theory, the whole Marxist model of history has fallen into disrepute. Economic development need not be viewed as the sole driving force of social and political change. Capitalist economics may create tensions in society, but there is no inevitability about these becoming so grave as to create general revolutionary conditions. People have their behaviour shaped by pressures other than just economic ones and they can be motivated to pursue goals which they regard as worthy but which have very little in common with Marxist principles. In other words, to be revolutionary is not just a matter of being a proletarian Communist, and so a fascist need not be his or her complete opposite. In upshot, to try to maintain the categories of 'revolutionary' and 'counter-revolutionary' is anachronistic, confusing and misleading (Weber, 1976, p. 488). There is no need for National Socialists to be understood as agents only trying to forestall the sort of social and political changes theorised by Marx and Engels.

There are empirical problems about Marxism's claims too. Although there were German industrialists who supported Hitler and who tried to harmonise Nazi interests with their own, not all representatives of big business were uniformly against the Republic. They were not a coherent class acting as the 'paymaster' of Hitler and his gang (Hiden, 1996, pp. 121–2). After an exhaustive study of the relationship between the industrialists and Hitler, H.A.Turner concluded that depicting him 'as just another lackey of capitalism . . . amounted to a reckless trivialization of a lethal political phenomenon' (Turner, 1985a, p. 357). It is no good blaming capitalism for National Socialism.

Under the circumstances, while accepting we can learn much from their highly impressive work, there is no need to follow too closely the examples of Bullock or Zitelmann and limit discussion of Hitler's possible revolutionary credentials to comparison with Communist cases from history. For all the similarities that can be identified either between Hitler and Stalin or between their political movements, there were big differences. Unlike Hitler, Stalin did not preach racial and national intolerance openly. In public he spoke of friendship and equality between peoples (Mercalowa, 1996, p. 205; Grosser, 1993, p. 95). Hitler's use of pseudo-religious terminology found no comparison in Stalin's speeches and hints at a type of charisma only associated with the Führer (Geiss 1996, p. 170; Kershaw, 1996a, p. 188). Hitler enjoyed the loyalty of his subordinates, Stalin motivated support through arbitrary terror. Hitler never brought Germany to a position of autarky, in Russia Stalin began to achieve it. While Hitler created war and attempted the conquest of Europe, Stalin had the more 'rational' and 'limited' ambition of establishing 'Socialism in one land' supplemented by a system of buffer states around the USSR. Hitler's political movement enjoyed a mass following and exercised terror against those identified as 'outsiders' and opponents of the regime; Stalin's party lacked a popular consensus and its terror knew fewer limits (Diner, 1995, p. 57; Dukes and Hiden, 1979, p. 69; Kershaw, 1996b, pp. 217–21).

There is scope for taking a broader approach towards what it is to be 'revolutionary' than the one implicit in Marxism. The concept was first recognised in ancient Egypt where it denoted dynastic conflict between the followers of Set and Horus. In classical Greece, it implied either a palace revolt or the rise of a new aristocratic élite (Calvert, 1970, pp. 16 and 30). According to Aristotle, men revolted either to achieve equality or else to assert superiority over others (Johnson, 1966, p. 4). By and large, in the ancient world 'revolution' identified neither a fundamental breach in history nor a deep-seated alteration in the foundations of state or society. It meant only a change in the identity of those fulfilling well-established political and social roles.

Intriguingly the actual term 'revolution' derives from astronomy and initially implied a cyclical, preordained course to human events (Greene, 1974, p. 7; Arendt, 1963, p. 35). In England it was first used in connection with the events of 1660. In

1649 the hereditary king Charles I was executed and thereafter a Commonwealth was established; but in 1660 the monarchy was restored in the shape of Charles II (Calvert, 1970, p. 69). Here was the idea of events coming full-circle and a natural order being reasserted. Not until the late eighteenth century, in connection with the American and French revolutions, did people begin to believe they could change the God-given order of things and remould society in line with their own ideas and through their own actions (Arendt, 1963, p. 40).

Today it is easy to find any number of competing definitions of 'revolution'. According to the *Oxford English Dictionary*, it is political action aiming at 'a complete overthrow of the established government in any country or state by those who were previously subject to it: a forcible substitution of a new ruler or form of government' (Close, 1985, p. 1). Along similar lines, Peter Calvert sees it as the use of deliberate and orchestrated force which is 'not regarded as legal in the strict sense . . . for the purpose of promoting political change' (Calvert, 1970, pp. 15 and 97). For David Close it is a cataclysmic, violent change of the basis of a government's legitimation, such that an old system is destroyed and a new one is created in its place (Close, 1985, pp. 2–3). Thomas Greene's definition both extends what has been said already and introduces a new element.

Document 1.9 Definition of Revolution

It is the almost unanimous opinion of writers on the subject that 'revolution' also means an alteration in the personnel, structure, supporting myth, and functions of government by methods which are not sanctioned by prevailing constitutional norms. These methods almost invariably involve violence or threat of violence against political elites, citizens, or both. And it is the opinion of a majority of scholars that 'revolution' means a relatively abrupt and significant change in the distribution of wealth and social status.

Source: Thomas H. Greene, Comparative Revolutionary Movements, *1974, p. 8*

Revolution becomes more than just political change, it involves social processes too. Trimberger identifies it as the destruction of 'the economic and political power of the dominant social group of the old regime' (in Kimmel, 1990, p. 4). Hagopian understands it as a crisis in a traditional system of social stratification (for example, class, status or power) which generates a violent attempt either to abolish or to reconstruct the ailing system (in Kimmel, 1990, p. 7). More simply, Dunn says revolution is 'massive, violent and rapid social change' (in Kimmel, 1990, p. 5).

Does just any form of social or political change constitute a revolution? Hannah Arendt has argued that true revolution has to bring about 'liberation from oppression' and promote 'the constitution of freedom' (Arendt, 1963, p. 28). Crane Brinton has agreed that proper revolutions should be progressive. They have to do away with the 'worst abuses, the worst inefficiencies of the old regime'; they have to increase government efficiency (Brinton, 1952, pp. 252–3). In other words, revolutions should result in the modernisation of the world. In practice, however, this claim is particularly hard to substantiate. By any standards Russia certainly saw a revolution in 1917, but it is too simplistic to say that the resulting Soviet regime was much more libertarian, efficient and modern than what had gone before. Perhaps what really matters is that the revolutionaries of 1917 *believed* beyond doubt that they were acting to promote these goals.

According to modern thinking, then, in a revolution people seize the *initiative* in *extralegal* ways and, backed up by *violence* or the threat of it, bring about a fundamental change in the constitution of a society's *political power*. In so doing, they reformulate the basis of political *legitimation* and the *myths* surrounding it. Revolution also involves the rooting out of perceived *social ills* with the result that the foundations of the prevailing *social structure* are transformed. Revolutionary actions are carried out in the belief that they will *modernise*, or *improve*, the world.

Naturally a revolutionary is anyone who acts in the ways outlined in the previous paragraph. But there is more to such a person even than this. In his classic study, Crane Brinton caricatured the way conservative American commentators conceptualised the revolutionary. Typically he was seen as 'a seedy, wild-eyed, unshaven, loud-mouthed person, given to soapbox oratory and plotting against the government, ready for, and yet afraid of, violence' (Brinton, 1952, p. 98). The truth as shown by Brinton's empirical study, is less prosaic. Revolutionaries have tended to be in their 30s or 40s, and have come from a such a wide variety of social backgrounds that at times the author despaired of finding a single characteristic uniting them. He admitted, 'it takes almost as many kinds of men and women to make a revolution as to make a world' (Brinton, 1952, p. 127). If they had anything in common, Brinton believed it was a kind of idealism which has made revolutionaries seem 'dissolute, or dull, or cruel, or heartless' (Brinton, 1952, p. 114). They believed in the possibility of creating a better world and were motivated accordingly.

Document 1.10 The Revolutionary as Idealist

It does not seem altogether wise to single out any one type as the perfect revolutionist, but if you must have such a type, then you will do well to consider, not the embittered failure, not the envious upstart, not the bloodthirsty lunatic, but the idealist. Idealists, of course, are in our own times the cement of a stable, normal society. It is good for us all that there should be men of noble aspirations, men who have put behind them the dross of this world for the pure word, for the idea and the ideal as the noblest philosophers have known them. . . .

Indeed, one of the distinguishing marks of a revolution is this: that in revolutionary times the idealist at last gets a chance to try and realize his ideals. Revolutions are full of men who hold very high standards of human conduct, the kind of standards which have for several thousand years been described by some word or phrase which has the overtones that 'idealistic' has for us today. There is no need for us to worry over the metaphysical, nor even the semantic, implications of the term. We all know an idealist when we see one, and certainly when we hear one.

Source: C. Brinton, The Anatomy of Revolution, *1952, pp. 121–2*

Thomas Greene's characterisation of the revolutionary argues a different line: what matters is not what a revolutionary thinks, but what he does (Greene, 1974, p. 16). To be precise, Greene does not believe that revolutionary leaders make revolutions since they can neither create the basic sources of unrest which generate mass movements nor define the general direction in which these proceed (Greene, 1974, p. 26). He says a revolutionary can only exert a slight influence over a revolutionary process by highlighting issues which unite diverse dissatisfied groups. Rather than the creator of a fundamental social movement, the revolutionary leader is at most a motivator making use of dissatisfactions and tensions which exist already.

Document 1.11 The Revolutionary as Motivator

The successful revolutionary leader, by definition, is able to interpret these greater events and more general conditions into terms that have meaning for everyday life of rank-and-file citizens. He does not implant new ideas as much as he summarizes them in an especially coherent and appealing way; he simplifies complexity. While more objective conditions lay the basis for revolutionary action, it is the consciousness of the revolutionary leader (as Marx argued) that revolutionary action begins. He must then be able to communicate his own insights and understanding of events to others, convincing and converting them very much like the religious reformers of an earlier age. His interpretive role is especially important when the revolutionary movement seeks to mobilize illiterate peasants, weighed down by traditions of oppression but unaware of the revolutionary options available to them and suspicious of all forms of collective organization.

Source: Thomas H. Greene, Comparative Revolutionary Movements, *1974, p. 27*

The more complex the ideology of the revolutionary leader, the more important becomes his personality in binding together his following. Typically the revolutionary is audacious, self-confident and optimistic. He is emboldened by the conviction that 'righteousness, justice and history are on his side' (Greene, 1974, p. 2). He sees the world in 'black and white' terms and is prepared either to love or hate whatever he encounters (Greene, 1974, p. 56). He is dedicated to motivating people to lend him their support.

Rajai's work offers additional psychological insights into 'persons who risk their lives by playing a *prominent, active and continuing role* throughout the revolutionary process' (Rajai, 1979, p. 13). They are said to suffer from an Oedipal complex. While children, they experienced conflicts over authority with their fathers which remained unresolved in later life. The inner turmoil entailed by the Oedipal syndrome was carried over into the political arena such that rebellion of son against father became rebellion of man against state (Rajai, 1979, pp. 30–1). Godspeed has echoed the idea that revolutionaries may be mentally unbalanced. He described leaders of the Irish rebellion as 'mystic, dreamers, men exalted, but they were not completely sane' and continued to identify both the Bolsheviks and Mussolini as 'clearly psychopathic' (in Kimmel, 1990, p. 68). It is Rajai, however, who has described the revolutionary personality at greatest length.

Document 1.12 The Revolutionary Personality

The sense of vanity, egotism, or narcissism of revolutionary leaders has been noted by a number of scholars. This self-aggrandizement, in turn, may be ignited by feelings of persecution – real or imagined – and a desire for revenge.

Revolutionary leaders are typically driven by a sense of injustice and a corresponding mission to 'set things right'. This sense of injustice may result from personal experiences of humiliation or brutality at the hands of the incumbent regime or from witnessing acts of humiliation or brutality inflicted upon others. This particular syndrome is most pronounced in colonial contexts, where it coincides with the feelings of nationalism and the hatred of the outsider.

If they are to be convincing in their drive for justice, revolutionary leaders must adopt a posture of virtue and purity. As such, it is not surprising that many revolutionary leaders adopt a simple, spartan life style. They shun luxuries and comfort, stressing sacrifice and hard work instead.

In the attempt to right the wrongs they perceive, some revolutionary leaders begin as reformers: they try to bring about change by working within the system. Since the system is typically unresponsive, frustration and disillusionment set in. Rejecting the system, the reformers turn to revolutionary politics.

Relative deprivation and status inconsistency may serve as other sources of revolutionary motivation. Where there is a felt discrepancy between one's aspiration and one's achievement (relative deprivation), one may set out to redress the situation accordingly – whether by reformist or by revolutionary action. Similarly, where there is discrepancy between one's socioeconomic status and one's political power (status inconsistency), reformist or revolutionary politics may offer relief.

Some revolutionary leaders are driven by a compulsion to excel, to prove themselves, to overcompensate. This compulsion is most likely due to feelings of low self-esteem or inferiority complex. How this inferiority complex comes about is a question that requires treatment on a case by case basis.

There is little doubt that the Oedipal complex and its attendant consequences play key roles in the emergence of some revolutionary leaders. The displacement of an internal psychological drama onto the political realm provides a compelling motivation for some revolutionary leaders, but this too must be examined on an individual basis. . . .

Revolutionary leaders, we suggest, require a set of skills with which to approach their calling. In particular, they have the capacity to devise and propagate an appropriate ideology and to create the necessary organizational apparatus.

Revolutionary leaders denounce the established order by appealing to 'higher' norms and principles. They evoke, conjure, and assimilate onto themselves myths and values of a transcendent nature, and they communicate these values through rhetoric, symbolism, and imagery – all simplified for popular consumption, as appropriate.

Revolutionary leaders articulate an alternative vision of society embodying a utopian image or a grand myth – the Fatherland, the Golden Age, The Classless Society. The grand myth elicits emotional response and becomes a rallying cry for the masses.

Revolutionary leaders propose plans and programs designed to realize the alternative order. In other words, the mere delineation of a utopian vision is not enough; the new vision must be embodied in a plan of action promising success in the near future.

In doing all this, revolutionary leaders highlight grievances and injustices, undermine the legitimacy and morale of the ruling regime, mobilize the masses to the cause, and lend dignity to revolutionary action. They evoke reverence and devotion among a large following. They generate commitment and elicit sacrifice from a small group of dedicated cadres. They promote unity, solidarity, and cohesion in the revolutionary ranks.

To be most effective, the verbal skills of revolutionary elites must be complemented by an ability to fashion an appropriate revolutionary organization. In effect, revolutionary leaders translate ideology into action through the medium of organization. Ideology helps mobilize the masses; organization functions to tap their energies and channel them toward the realization of revolutionary objectives. . . .

Source: M. Rajai with K. Phillips, Leaders of Revolution, *1979, pp. 57–9*

As a final point here, revolutionaries have a substantial toughness of mind (Calvert, 1970, p. 102). This is exemplified by Che Guevara, a Marxist revolutionary from Latin America. A friend once defined what he saw as the real difference between himself and Che. Guevara could look at a soldier through a sniperscope of a rifle and pull the trigger. In so doing he believed he was helping reduce social injustice and was improving the position of future generations. When the friend looked through a sniperscope, he saw only a man with a wife and children (Anderson, 1997, p. 571). Revolutionaries have cold minds capable of making tough decisions without flinching (Anderson, 1997, pp. 636–7).

Revolutionaries, then, are idealists who hope for a better future and feel strongly the injustices they perceive in society around them. They have the capacity to motivate the masses and the ability to unite the same into a coherent following. They are bold and confident individuals who think about the world in 'black and white' ways, are ruthless and (perhaps not so surprisingly) have much about them which is, frankly, off-putting. They may be marked by some kind of psychological instability, perhaps an Oedipus complex.

Discussion has now generated a non-doctrinaire definition of revolution and a non-partisan characterisation of the revolutionary. If Adolf Hitler really was a revolutionary, his actions should contain the elements ascribed to the one and his personality should overlap with the components of the other. It falls to the following chapters of this book to reveal whether this was the case. Each of these chapters is a thematic investigation into an aspect of Hitler's career which is also integral to our overall assessment of him. As the table here makes plain, the one-word chapter titles could be replaced by a lengthy question referring to a theme under investigation.

Summary of chapters

Chapter	Theme relating to Hitler's possible revolutionary credentials
Ideologue	Were Hitler's aims revolutionary?
Agitator	Did Hitler pursue revolutionary means during the years of the Weimar Republic?
Dictator	Did he lead National Socialism as a revolutionary movement and the Third Reich as a revolutionary state?
Deceiver	Can there be such a thing as a revolutionary foreign policy and, if so, did Hitler implement one?
Warlord	Was the Second World War a revolutionary conflict?
Artist	How did Hitler's interest in art and architecture relate to the possibility of him being a revolutionary?
Mind	Did Hitler have a revolutionary personality, that is to say one afflicted by an Oedipal complex or some other form of disturbance?

Ideologue | **2**

Did Adolf Hitler have a revolutionary vision for Germany? For that matter, did he have any sort of clear programme for his country? Very many studies indeed argue that he had no body of thinking so well developed and coherent as to merit the name 'ideology'. They leave the impression that analysing the man's ideas-world is a waste of time. This line was represented by commentators even before Hitler came to power. J.K. Pollock was a political scientist who wrote about the Reichstag elections of 1930 for an American academic journal. He described Hitler's political party as follows.

Document 2.1 Blithering Nonsense

Its [the NSDAP's] campaign talk was the sheerest drivel. Never – even at home – have I heard such blithering nonsense. Its leaders talked of the 'Third Reich', a confused mystical conception, where there will be no capitalists, no trade unions, no exploitation, no Jews, no negroes. With the utmost violence at times, always with hot emotion, they pelted the poor, kindly German middle classes where they secured most of their support, with cheap and vulgar but entrancing words. And now that they have won such a great victory they are utterly bewildered as to what to do next. They demand, not the places in the government where the real work has to be done to improve conditions, but rather the ministry of the interior, which controls the police, and the war ministry. With these offices in their hands, Germany would be safe and no longer enslaved!

Source: J.K. Pollock, 'The German Reichstag Elections of 1930', pp. 993–4

German contemporaries voiced comparable opinions. Literary giant Thomas Mann characterised Nazi ideas as an *ad hoc* conglomeration that was intellectually confused (in Broszat, 1958, p. 55). Herman Rauschning, who met Hitler personally on a number of occasions between 1932 and 1934, said his movement had 'no fixed aims' (Rauschning, 1939a, p. 23).

Historians, Anglo-Saxon and German alike, have followed this tradition of thinking. Hugh Trevor-Roper famously denounced Nazi ideology as a 'vast system of bestial Nordic nonsense' (Trevor-Roper, 1947, p. 3). A. Mohler dismissed it as based on the most diverse and inconsistent positions (Mohler, 1950, p. 8). Fritz

Stern stigmatised it as 'this leap from despair to utopia across all existing reality'. He did not believe for a minute that the ideology should be taken at face value and treated within the framework of the 'history of ideas' (Stern, 1961, pp. xi and xiv). The psychology of the men creating the concepts was what mattered, not the intellectual content itself. Questioning both the originality and consistency of Nazi ideas, Hans Mommsen has denounced them as 'an eclectic conglomeration of völkisch concepts indistinguishable from the programmes of out-and-out nationalist organisations and parties of the imperialist period' (Mommsen, 1976, p. 152). There was nothing new, or of particular interest in the ideas: Nazism was not an ideological movement, but a 'political propaganda organization', 'a negative people's party' (Mommsen, 1976, p. 154). It opposed everything, but offered only images and slogans in return.

Perhaps the most sustained attack on Nazi ideology came from Martin Broszat. He agreed that Hitler's movement based itself less on rational argument than on emotional appeal. The ideas at stake did not matter so much in their own right as how they operated psychologically (Broszat, 1958, p. 60). Nazi ideology was not a proper analysis of the world, just a mass of commonly held disappointments jumbled together (Broszat, 1966, p. 32). It was typified by 'intellectual chaos', a 'frightening lack of foundation' and 'moral perversion' (Broszat, 1966, pp. 38 and 50). Hitler was not concerned with clarifying concepts and systematising thought, he was not interested in understanding the world and trying to improve upon it, he was only expressing 'the fanaticism of pure aggression' which was 'without content, believing only in its own irresistible momentum' (Broszat, 1966, p. 59). The attractiveness and skill with which Hitler presented his movement covered up its complete lack of intellectual foundation. If you ignored Hitler's anti-Semitic obsession, even his personal ideology became just a set of propaganda slogans (Broszat, 1966, p. 53).

Views such as these have been taken on board wholesale. Ian Kershaw has characterised Nazi doctrine as 'a paradoxical concoction of conservative and radical elements without any basis in the intellectual rigour of a rational philosophy, a cynical "catch-all" programme offering a rag-bag of contradictions in which it is hard to distinguish "idea" from "presentation of an idea"' (Kershaw, 1983, pp. 162–3). Attempts have been made to divest even Hitler's anti-Semitism of an ideological element. As Hannah Arendt has put it, to try to understand anti-Semitism is to challenge your sanity (Arendt, 1966, p. 3). In the words of Peter Merkl, it remains 'no more an idea or an ideology than a common obscenity is' (Merkl, 1985, p. 448).

These are the views of full-time, professional scholars: individuals with the luxury of time to chase and define ideas. They have been trained to do just this. When Hitler as a young man was rejected by the Academy of Art in Vienna (see Chapter 7), his entrée to the academic world was closed firmly. What is more, as a full-time politician he had plenty of pressing practical issues to deal with ahead of clarifying to a pedantic degree ideological thinking. So are the standards applied by historians as they dismember and vilify Hitler's ideas really applicable? In other words, Hitler's ideas were certainly unpleasant, unevenly developed, downright wrong-headed and perhaps even derivative, but the nicety of rigorous thinking was something he was neither equipped for nor had time to get bogged down in. If he knew the main direction in which his ideas were going, did much else matter?

In this connection it might be helpful to distinguish 'working definitions' of the words 'ideologist' and 'ideologue'. 'Ideologist' we might use to label someone interested in generating sustained, sophisticated, refined, coherent and original thought, which would include constant critical reference towards both the premises on which the thinking is founded and of the way ideas could be put into practice. 'Ideologue' might be applied to a person whose thought is much blunter, less well developed and characterised by much less clarity and coherence. It may be founded on principles which are largely accepted uncritically and, as a result, ends up as a systematisation of that which already exists rather than a product of purer originality. Given the choice, certainly Adolf Hitler was an 'ideologue' rather than an 'ideologist'. But with this said, we still want to know the substance of his thought.

From a relatively early time Adolf Hitler was exposed to the power of ideas. During the First World War he was impressed by the way British propaganda galvanised Allied troops. In early Summer 1919, he became active in the Bavarian army persuading German troops that Communism was wrong (see Chapter 3). Part of his training consisted in attending a course at Munich University. At this point he became acquainted with the *völkisch* (i.e. radical nationalist and racialist) thinker, Gottfried Feder, who was helping to organise the event. The lectures Hitler attended there included titles such as: 'Socialism in Theory and Practice', 'Russia and the Bolshevik Dictatorship', 'German History since the Reformation', 'Germany 1870–1900', 'The Meaning of the Armed Forces', 'The Connection between Domestic and Foreign Policy', 'Foreign Policy since the End of the War', 'Price Policy in the National Economy', 'The Forced Economy in Bread and Grain' and 'Bavaria and the Unity of the Reich' (Deuerlein, 1959, pp. 192–3). Many of these topics could have served as headings for the talks Hitler himself gave in the early 1920s. They must have made a massive impression on a man who unquestionably absorbed information like a sponge.

But at first sight the single most important characteristic of Hitler's thought is missing from the list. It forms the basis of the first political tract he ever produced. The following was written by Hitler while he was still in the army. On 10 September 1919, Hitler's superior officer, Captain Meyer, asked him to state his attitude towards Jewry in a letter. Six days later, Hitler complied.

Document 2.2 Rational Anti-Semitism?

If the threat with which Jewry faces our people has given rise to undeniable hostility on the part of a large section of our people, the cause of this hostility must not be sought in the clear recognition that Jewry as such is deliberately or unwittingly having a pernicious effect on our nation, but mostly in personal intercourse, in the poor impression the Jew makes as an individual. As a result antisemitism far too readily assumes a purely emotional character.

But this is not the correct response. Antisemitism as a political movement may not and cannot be moulded by emotional factors but only by recognition of facts. Now the facts are:

To begin with, the Jews are unquestionably a race, not a religious community. And the Jew himself never describes himself as a Jewish German, a Jewish Pole or a Jewish American, but always as a German, Polish or American Jew. Never has the Jew absorbed more from the alien people in whose midst he lives than their language. And no more than a German who is forced to use the French language in France, the Italian language in Italy, and the Chinese language in China, thereby becomes a Frenchman, an Italian, let alone a Chinaman, no more can we call a Jew who happens to live amongst us and who is therefore forced to use the German language, a German. And even the Mosaic faith, however great its importance for the preservation of that race, cannot be the sole criterion for deciding who is a Jew and who is not. There is hardly a race in the world whose members all belong to a single religion.

Through inbreeding for thousands of years, often in very small circles, the Jew has been able to preserve his race and his racial characteristics much more successfully than most of the numerous people among whom he lives. As a result we have living in our midst a non-German, alien race, unwilling and indeed unable to shed its racial characteristics, its particular feelings, thoughts and ambitions and nevertheless enjoying the same political rights as we ourselves do. And since even the Jew's feelings are limited to the material sphere, his thoughts and ambitions are bound to be so even more strongly. The dance round the golden calf becomes a ruthless struggle for all those goods that we feel deep down are not the highest and not the only ones worth striving for on this earth.

The work of an individual is no longer determined by his character, by the importance of his achievement for the community, but solely by the size of his fortune, his wealth. The greatness of the nation is no longer measured by the sum of its moral and spiritual resources, but only by its material goods.

All this results in that mental attitude and that quest for money and the power to protect it which allow the Jew to become so unscrupulous in his choice of means, so merciless in their use for his own ends. In autocratic states he cringes before the 'majesty' of the princes and misuses their favours to become a leech on their people.

In a democracy he vies for the favours of the masses, grovels before 'the majesty of the people', but only recognizes the majesty of money.

He saps the prince's character by Byzantine flattery; national pride and the strength of the nation by ridicule and shameless seduction to vice. His chosen weapon is public opinion as falsified by the press. His power is the power of the money he accumulates so easily and endlessly in the form of interest and with which he imposes a yoke upon the nation that is the more pernicious in that its glitter disguises its dire consequences. Everything that makes the people strive for greater things, be it religion, socialism or democracy, merely serves the Jew as a means to the satisfaction of his greed and thirst for power. The results of his works is racial tuberculosis of the nation.

And this has the following consequences: purely emotional antisemitism finds its final expression in the form of pogroms (sic !). Rational antisemitism, by contrast, must lead to a systematic and legal struggle against, and eradication of, what privileges the Jews enjoy over other foreigners living among us (Alien Laws). Its final objective, however, must be the total removal of all Jews from our midst. . . .

Yours truly,
Adolf Hitler.

Source: W. Maser, Hitler's Letters and Notes, *1974, pp. 213–16*

Anti-Semitism was the first ideological element which really took root in Adolf Hitler (Haffner, 1988, p. 81). The standard stereotypes of the Jews as materialistic and manipulative were present even at this early time. In later life Hitler's mind never called into question this basic position. If anything his hatred only became more severe. Where had the prejudice come from?

Hitler offers an explanation in the first volume of *Mein Kampf.*

Document 2.3 Black Caftan

Once, as I was strolling through the Inner City [of Vienna], I suddenly encountered an apparition in a black caftan and black hair locks. Is this a Jew? was my first thought.

For, to be sure, they had not looked like that in Linz. I observed the man furtively and cautiously, but the longer I stared at this foreign face, scrutinising feature for feature, the more my first question assumed a new form:

Is this a German?

As always in such cases, I now began to try to relieve my doubts by books. For a few hellers I bought the first anti-Semitic pamphlets of my life. Unfortunately, they all proceeded from the supposition that in principle the reader knew or even understood the Jewish question to a certain degree. Besides, the tone for the most part was such that doubts again arose in me, due in part to the dull and amazingly unscientific arguments favouring the thesis.

Source: A. Hitler, Mein Kampf, *1985 ed., p. 52*

In truth we have to be careful about accepting Hitler's own account. It is not so plausible that a lifelong, vitriolic prejudice sprang from a single event (see Chapter 8). However, the period Hitler spent in Vienna before the First World War did contribute to his racism.

Political life in the Austrian capital had been dominated by two politicians, Karl Lueger and Georg von Schönerer. The former was mayor of the city from 1895 until his death in 1910; the latter was head of the Pan-German Party. Both were outspokenly anti-Semitic (Davidson, 1977, pp. 11–12). These figures made an impact on young Adolf and both are praised in *Mein Kampf* (Hitler, 1985, pp. 51 and 90). As it says in document 2.3, it was also in Vienna that Hitler began reading all manner of German nationalist, racialist literature, the like of which had been available since the previous century. He skimmed through whatever he could find, absorbing thirstily the trashy pseudo-political magazines that were 'ten-a-penny' around the capital. *Der Scherer*, for example, was supported by Schönerer and called for the months of the year to be given Nordic names. It spewed forth anti-Semitic diatribes, pioneered the use of the swastika image and utilised terms (such as '*Volksgenossen*' – member of the people) which the Nazi party later took over (Davidson, 1977, pp. 12–13). Hitler's personal favourite 'penny dreadful' was the magazine published by Lanz von Liebenfels called *Ostara*. On one occasion he even visited its publishing offices in order to acquire the full set of its editions (Fest, 1973, p. 37). *Ostara* defined its mission as follows.

Document 2.4 Ostara

Ostara is the first and only periodical for the research into and welfare of heroic races and the rights of man. It actually wants to apply the results of racial science in order to secure the heroic noble race on the path of planned pure breeding and to secure the rights of man in the face of annihilation by socialist and feminist subversives.

Source: Reverse of cover of Ostara, *Vol. 29 (1908)*

Ostara's pages were full of mystical claptrap. Von Liebenfels's writings made copious references to a fantastic study called 'theozoology'. His world was populated by 'love pygmies' and monkey people. Sacrifices were made to the gods. Blond Aryans battled inferior 'races' of apes and hobgoblins. Von Liebenfels advocated that the superior Aryan racial type make special use of breeding colonies to boost its numbers in the face of the inferior rivals. In the pages of *Ostara* he worked out policies of sterilisation, forced labour and deportation to the forest of the apes, as well as systems to promote pogroms and population liquidations. There was 'hardly one of the evils of National Socialism that is not anticipated here' (Heiber, 1961, pp. 19–20). A fuller flavour is provided in the following extract.

Document 2.5 Lanz von Liebenfels

The time has come! The old brood of Sodom is degenerate and wretched in the Middle East and all round the Mediterranean. . . . Our bodies are scurfy despite all soaps, they are udumized, pagatized and baziatized [i.e. extremely corrupt]. The life of man has never been so miserable as today inspite of all technical achievements. Demonic beast-men oppress us from above, slaughtering without conscience millions of people in murderous wars waged for their own personal gain. Wild beast-men shake the pillars of culture from below. . . . Why do you seek a hell in the next world! Is not the hell in which we live and which burns inside us . . . sufficiently dreadful?

Source: Extract from Ostara *quoted in Nicholas Goodrick-Clarke,* The Occult Roots of Nazism, *1992, p. 96*

It was rapid reading to titillate and reinforce prejudice, not to challenge and deepen the mind. Young Adolf lost himself in this pseudo-religious, quasi-mystical, but definitely nonsensical 'porridge of ideas' (Sternburg, 1996, p. 52).

Anti-Semitism was not limited to pre-war Vienna. Hitler moved to Munich, the capital of Bavaria, in 1913 and returned there after the First World War. Hostility towards the Jews was deeply entrenched in the region, as the following police report taken from the later period shows well.

Document 2.6 Anti-Semitism in Bavaria, November 1919

The anti-Semitic movement is in the process of increasing everywhere, even in northern Bavaria. It is not limited to a relatively small circle of (reactionary) personalities who stand on the far right, as it says time and again in both types of social democratic press, but rather extends to all layers of the *Volk* and embraces members of all political parties including the radical left.

An authority such as the political police cannot pass over so extensive a movement without care. It has the obligation to investigate the causes of the movement without bias, to research its goals and to observe its course.

The most essential reasons for the anti-Jewish current running through the *Volk* lie very deep. They are rooted in the racial contrast (that is hardly ever to be bridged completely) which separates the Israelite clan from our *Volk*. The separation is still more [significant] in terms of their mental make-up in comparison to that of the members of the European nations than in terms of the external appearance of individuals. The contrast really has to result in a certain in-born mistrust among the indigenous population towards their co-citizens from a different ethnic background [*Stammesfremden*].

War and revolution (with their unpleasant accompanying characteristics in all areas of public and private life) have brought the essential contrast between races into the clear light of day. They have had the effect of awakening the natural mistrust already mentioned, which until then as a rule had been dormant. As a result, broad circles which formerly [either] had rejected or been indifferent in their behaviour towards the anti-Semitic movement have adopted an increasing aversion towards the Jews. There are two main issues which have favoured and elicited anti-Jewish opinion. In the economic area, there is the particularly striking percent of Jewish war profiteers, whose arrogant behaviour may make the percentage of Israelites in the less popular margins of the most modern upstarts seem higher than it really is. In the political sphere there is the undeniable fact that among the most dangerous and conscienceless leaders of the international communist movement there is a disproportionately high number of Jews. So on the one hand the category 'war profiteer' is virtually replaced with 'Jew'; on the other hand not infrequently you hear judgements like these: it can't be just chance that people like Trotski, Joffe, Radek in Russia, Bela Kun, Sgamuely, Rosa Luxemburg, but then Haase too and his prospective successor in the leadership of the USPD, Cohn, finally Levien, Leviné-Niessen, Toller, Mühsam, Klingelhöfer from the days of the Munich councils are all of Jewish descent. It is argued in vain by the Jewish and Jew-friendly side that there are non-Jewish war profiteers and black marketeers too. Such means of proof which appeal to thought are to no avail in the face of a movement which has mobilised the emotions, and it is to be observed more and more that even in the ranks of the left-radical parties increasingly there is rejection of the Jewish leaders, [and as a result you] begin to doubt other idealistic, altruistic motives.

Chiefly the following are proclaimed as goals of the [anti-Semitic] movement: 'ruthless action against the major usurers, black marketeers and profiteers; severe seizure of large-scale capital which is avoiding taxes; breaking the slavery of taxation; complete removal (by the creation of a law for foreigners) of the domination of elements foreign to the land and *Volk* from the government, from public and economic life, from the theatre, writing and science by the creation of a law for foreigners'.

Source: P. Longerich (ed.), Die Erste Republik, *1992, pp. 157–60*

After the war, radical nationalist posters and pamphlets were said to be every-where; anti-Semitic slogans commonly were daubed on walls and doors. A 'pogrom mentality' was abroad. In the light of the evidence, we can understand the roots of Hitler's first political tract so much the better. In Austria and southern Germany, during the early twentieth century, anti-Semitic nationalism was a popular idea whose time had come.

Hitler personally announced the programme of the German Workers' Party on 24 February 1920.

Document 2.7 Party Programme

1. We demand the union of all Germans into a Greater Germany by virtue of the right to national self-determination.
2. We demand equality of rights for the German *Volk* vis-a-vis the other nations, and the revocation of the peace treaties of Versailles and St Germain.
3. We demand land and soil (colonies) for the nourishment of our *Volk* and the settlement of our surplus population.

4. Only members of the *Volk* can be state citizens. A member of the *Volk* can only be someone with German blood, without consideration of religious belief. Consequently no Jew can be a member of the *Volk*.

5. Whoever is not a citizen of the state, should only be able to live in Germany as a guest and must live according to the laws for foreigners.

6. Only citizens of the state are eligible for the right to vote for the state leadership and legislation. So we demand that every public office, of whatever sort, may be held by state citizens alone.

   We oppose the corrupting parliamentary economy in which offices are held only according to party politics without consideration to character and capacities.

7. We demand that in the first place the state is obliged to look after the livelihood of its citizens. If it is not possible to feed the entire population of a state, then the members of foreign nations (people who are not state citizens) must be deported from the Reich.

8. All further non-German immigration is to be prevented. We demand that all non-Germans who have migrated to Germany since 2 August 1914 be compelled to leave the Reich at once.

9. All citizens of the state must have equal rights and duties.

10. The first duty of each citizen of the state must be to produce with mind or body. The activity of the individual may not conflict with the interests of the community, but must be carried out in the framework of the community and to the benefit of all.

    Therefore we demand:

11. The abolition of income without work and toil.

The breaking of interest slavery

12. In view of the phenomenal sacrifice of property and blood, which each war demands of the people, personal enrichment through war must be regarded as a crime against the *Volk*. We demand therefore the tireless confiscation of all war profits.

13. We demand the nationalisation of all firms (trusts) which have already acquired the status of corporations.

14. We demand profit sharing in all big businesses.

15. We demand a generous extension of old age welfare.

16. We demand the creation of a healthy middle class and its preservation, the immediate communalisation of big department stores and their leasing at cheap rates to small firms, the utmost consideration to all small firms as regards state contracts (also contracts from the states and parishes).

17. We demand land reform suitable to our national requirements, the passing of a law for the expropriation of land for common purposes without compensation. The abolition of land tax and the prevention of any kind of land speculation.

18. We demand the ruthless struggle against those who damage the common interest by their activity. Common criminals, usurers, profiteers etc. are to suffer the death penalty, without consideration of religion or race.
19. We demand the replacement of the Roman law which serves the materialistic world order by a German law of the common community.
20. In order to facilitate, for each capable and diligent German, their admission to higher education and so advancement to a position of leadership, the state has to bear the responsibility for an extension of our entire national educational system. . . .
21. The state must bear the responsibility for raising national health standards by protecting mothers and infants, by banning child labour, by promoting bodily strength through legislative obligations to do with gymnastics and sport, through the greatest support of all associations which support physical exercise for youths.
22. We demand the abolition of a mercenary army and its replacement with a people's army.
23. We demand a legislative fight against deliberate political lies and their being spread by the press. In order to facilitate the creation of German press, we demand that:

    a) all editors and co-workers on newspapers that appear in the German language, must be members of the *Volk* [*Volksgenossen*].
    b) non-German newspapers must be authorised expressly by the state. They may not be printed in the German language.
    c) each financial participation in German newspapers or their influencing by non-Germans is prohibited by law and we demand as a punishment for infringements the closure of such a newspaper, and also the exclusion from the Reich of the non-German involved in the affair.

    Newspapers which offend against the common good are to be banned. . . .
24. We demand the freedom of all religious confession in the state, in so far as it does not endanger its condition or offend the ethical and moral feeling of the Germanic race. . . .
25. For the implementation of all this programme, we demand the creation of a strong central power of the Reich. Absolute authority of the political central parliament over the entire Reich and its organisations in general.

Source: A. Tyrell (ed.), Der Führer befiehl . . . , 1969, *pp. 23–6*

The precise detail of Hitler's role in generating the programme is hard to pin down. Albrecht Tyrell believes he helped Anton Drexler draft it, and this is the view represented most recently by Ian Kershaw (Tyrell, 1975, p. 85; Kershaw, 1998, p. 144). As the main agitator of the party at this time, it is reasonable to assume he must have had a hand in arranging its message (Jäckel, 1981, p. 72). It is very hard indeed to imagine Hitler proclaiming something he had not helped produce and with which he was not in agreement.

Much about the document was outstandingly commonplace in the Bavaria of the time. In many respects it was 'an enumeration of the *petit bourgeois* grievances and desires of the post-war period' (Jäckel, 1981, p. 72). It owed something to the standard nationalist tract by Heinrich Class, *Wenn ich der Kaiser wäre* (*If I were the Emperor*) (Tyrell, 1975, p. 85). It was remarkably similar to a programme already proclaimed by a group based in the Nuremberg area – the German Socialist Party (Tyrell, 1975, pp. 77–82). Just like the German Workers' Party (*Deutsche Arbeiter Partei* – DAP), the German Socialist Party demanded the nationalisation of the land (DAP programme point 17), the replacement of Roman law by a common law (DAP point 19), nationalisation of the money system (DAP point 11), exclusion of Jews from public offices (DAP points 4, 5 and 6), national management of industry (roughly DAP points 13, 14 and 15), the union of all Germans in a single state (DAP point 1) and the protection of German workers in the face of foreign exploitation (DAP point 14). But one thing in the DAP's message was distinctive – and here we identify a lasting characteristic of Hitler's movement. It was stamped with a much greater radicalism than that of any other party of the day (Tyrell, 1975, p. 82).

Hitler made special use of anti-Semitism to radicalise his early politics. In the following extract, he tries to differentiate the characteristics of Jews and Germans in ways which were supposed to render his talk memorable. The date was 13 August 1920, the place was the great hall of the *Hofbräuhaus* in Munich.

Document 2.8 Pyramid-Builders

We see that here in the race there lie two big differences: the Aryan race means a moral view of labour and so that which we so often have in our mouths today: Socialism, communal thinking, common benefit before individual benefit – Jewry means an egotistic view of labour and so mammonism and materialism, the contradictory opposite of socialism. (Very true.) And in this characteristic which he [the Jew] cannot overcome, which lies in his blood, he himself recognises that in this characteristic lies the necessity for the Jews absolutely to have to appear destroyers of the state. He cannot be otherwise, whether he wants to or not. He is no longer capable of building his own state, because to do so requires more or less all of the time a great deal of common feeling. As a result he [the Jew] is only in a position to live as a parasite in other states. He lives as a race in other races, as a state in other states. And here we see quite precisely that race in and for itself does not have a state-forming effect if it does not possess quite definite properties, which must lie in the race, which must be in-born to it by reason of its blood, and that quite by contrast a race which does not possess these properties must have an effect that is race-destructive and state-destructive, even if an individual is good or evil.

We can trace this fate of Jewry from the greyest of primeval times.

It is not necessary that everything the Bible says is literally true, but by and large it gives a summary at least of the view of the history of Jewry as the Jews made it themselves and there we see that the Jew writes this work with good intentions. It does not seem monstrous to him that he describes how he set race against race through cunning and deception, that he was always expelled, but without being offended sought out someone else [to live among]. How he copulated and haggled, and (if it was a question of his ideals) how he was prepared even to sacrifice his own family. We know that not long ago a man, Sigmund Fraenkel, stood here [giving a talk]. The man wrote recently that it would be quite unjustified to accuse the Jew of a materialistic spirit, because one only has to look at the radiant inner family life of the Jew. This inner family life did not for one moment prevent their own original father Abraham coupling his own wife immediately to the Pharaoh of the Egyptians so that he could do business. (Amusement.) And it is the one and only original father of the tribe, just like the '*Herr Papa*', whom the sons have become like and they have never rejected these goings on, and whoever wants to be convinced about this [need only notice the following]: they still do not reject them today. Whoever was a soldier will remember that in Galicia or Poland he could see this Abraham standing on any railway station. (Applause and amusement.) Throughout the millennia the Jew has perfected this penetration and squeezing into other races, and we know exactly that always then, when he made somewhere his home for a longer time, the trace of collapse was apparent and that the nations in the end had nothing left when they freed themselves from their undesired guest or collapsed. We know that serious plagues came over the nations; ten came over the Egyptians – we are experiencing all of the plagues today in our own body – and finally the Egyptians lost patience. When the chronicler describes that without doubt the Jew was the patient one and finally left, this cannot have been right; for they had hardly left than at once they yearned for the flesh pots again. (Amusement.) In reality it seems not to have been so bad for them. But even if it was true that the Egyptians were compelled to employ them all in the construction of their pyramids, then it is exactly the same as if we recommended today that this race be allocated wage labour in our mines, quarries etc., and just as you do not see this race going to these places today of their own free will, we can assume that *they* saw it just as little *in* Egypt, that they built the pyramids of their own free will and *there* remained no alternative but to force them. What hundreds of thousands of others do *as the most natural thing, for the Jew* it is a chapter of anti-Jewish hatred and persecution of the Jews.

Source: H. Phelps, 'Hitler's "Grundlegende" Rede', pp. 406–7

Hitler was energising his theme with humour and hoping thereby to make people take notice of his message. Once again he said that true Germans work hard for the common good, while Jews shirk and think of themselves alone (see also document 2.2).

Of course anti-Semitism was more than just a rhetorical device for Adolf Hitler; it was a matter of genuine belief too. Nor did he believe the only problem lay in individual Jews being lazy, corrupt and overly ambitious. He believed *all* Jews had much more serious designs and explained as much in a speech given in Munich's *Bürgerbräu* on 31 May 1920. Hitler started from the position that Jews commanded large amounts of finance capital.

Document 2.9 World Conspiracy

The huge size of [Jewish] loan capital in the face of industrial capital always needs new space to spread out, absorb and develop. Destroyed states, subjugated peoples and shattered cultures indicate its path. For its intellectual defence Jewry uses the press and freemasonry and for its physical defence the international labour movement, the real leaders of which are and always were Jews. The Jew lives from robbery as a state within a state, as a nomad, and still represents the most nationalistic race. In Jewry, nationality and religion supplement each other mutually and are forging ahead to world domination. In Germany at first there was the court Jew [Hofjude], but (because it is so expedient for him) today there is the national Jew [Volksjude]. In both cases he represents the leech on the people and proceeds over corpses in business and politics. For the establishment of world domination he pursues: 1. the de-nationing of the peoples, 2. the confiscation of land and soil, 3. the annihilation of the independent middle class – communalisation! 4. the rooting out of the national intelligentsia (Russia!) 5. eternal security by making the *Volk* perfectly stupid in the press, art, literature, cinema etc, confusion of public opinion, destruction of the feeling of law, fight against religious convictions, promotion of sects etc, undermining of morals and ethics (the Jew as the child slaver [*Mädchenhändler*] of all times! Communalisation of the woman!); for him money is love and character! And 6. as his ultimate means serves class conflict: workers as a means to the end in the service of the Jew for the protection of international stock market and loan capital; destruction of the solidarity of the *Volk* and the promise of international solidarity. . . . There is no difference between an eastern and a western Jew, brave or evil, rich or poor, hero or shirker, – the fight is only valid for the Jewish race. It should not be said: proletarians of all lands, unite! but rather the call to arms says: anti-Semites of all lands unite! Peoples of Europe, make yourselves free!'

Source: H. Phelps, 'Hitlers "Grundlegende" Rede', p. 399

Certainly Hitler's style of thinking attributed paradoxical qualities to the Jews (for instance, they were capitalists using Bolshevism to weaken those they sought to exploit), but there is no doubt that from an early point he believed quite genuinely that Jewish people were involved in a concerted plan to take over and destroy whole nations. The belief was not unique. It had been peddled in a tract called *The*

Protocols of the Elders of Zion which was forged by the Russian secret police during the nineteenth century in an attempt to persuade the Tsar that Russian liberals were Jews. It was published in German in 1920 (Pipes, 1997, pp. 85 and 94; Cohn, 1967). Hitler believed the message of the Protocols until he died (Welch, 1998, p. 13). He applied the paradigm to theorise an ultimate Jewish conspiracy to take over the whole world. The belief had an important consequence. Logically the only response to a global assault had to have a global dimension itself. From the outset, Hitler's racism had the potential to become a most comprehensive phenomenon.

Hitler's early anti-Semitic pronouncements are important, but centre-stage to any discussion of his ideology has to be given to *Mein Kampf*. Before this, Hitler was just one voice (albeit a particularly strident one) contributing to the general tumult of anti-Semitism in southern Germany (Maser, 1974, p. 233). But the volume marked him out as something special. As he dictated his book, Hitler began to re-appraise his past attitudes. In an interview with a National Socialist journalist in June 1924, while he was actually in Landsberg prison (where he wrote *Mein Kampf*), Hitler explained how in the past he had been too lenient in his racism. Now he had to apply the harshest methods against 'the plague of the world' (i.e. the Jews) (Schwaab, 1992, p. 133). As he wrote, Hitler became increasingly inflexible in his views. Although in later years he actually dismissed the book as 'fantasies behind bars', in reality it unmasked the dreadful potential of his prejudice (Fest, 1973, pp. 203–4). The Jew became more than ever an image representing everything Hitler hated in the world.

The first volume of *Mein Kampf* was completed in 1924 and published the next year. The second volume was written in 1925 and published in December 1926. The tract sold 10,000 copies in 1925, 7,000 in 1926, 5,600 in 1927 and 3,015 in 1928 (Taylor, 1961, p. xiv). In it, Jewish people were de-humanised completely. They were described in terms of rotting flesh, pustulent sores and racial tuberculosis; they became spreaders of syphilis and carriers of the Black Death. Of his time in Vienna Hitler said, when you 'cut even cautiously' into an 'abscess, you found, like a maggot in a rotting body, often dazzled by the light – a kike!' (Hitler, 1985, pp. 52–3). In anti-Semitism, Hitler clearly experienced a most profound motive force. It promised nothing except the radical removal of Jews from any sphere of life over which he would ever have influence.

In *Mein Kampf*, Hitler fleshed out his vision of the Jewish world conspiracy. Being so exploitative and selfish, Jews were said to lack the capacity to build their own state. Consequently they infiltrated the states of others, took them over and used them as their own needs dictated. Hitler believed there was a definite historical process whereby states were subverted. When society had its first settlements, Jews were said to arrive as merchants. As the local economy grew, they played the part of middlemen, facilitating commerce and making a profit in the process. Gradually Jews began to acquire bigger and bigger amounts of capital until they monopolised society's main financial occupations; thereafter they pushed up their rates of profit to a usurious degree. Then they approached the government with flattering words, and managed to bring their influence to bear to lead astray the prince of any given state. The result was chaos, and the Jews had to be baptised to save themselves from popular recriminations. As society modernised, the Jews began to work at exerting their control through the stock market. The effect was to pauperise formerly affluent indigenous groups, such as civil servants, turning them into proletarians. At this point, the Jews approached the workers of a country, simulating sympathy with their position through the introduction of Marxist doctrine and trades unions. At the same time they corrupted a nation's art and culture. In so doing, they were preparing for a final revolution against the established order with the aim of installing a Jewish government. Hitler believed this had happened in Russia in 1917, and feared as much for Germany (Hitler, 1985, pp. 280 ff.).

It is worth pausing to emphasise that Hitler believed Marxism was a cornerstone of the Jewish world conspiracy. The following extract explains what he objected to. Marxism denied the individual and the race as basic social units. In so doing it laid open society to all manner of abuses.

Document 2.10 Marxism as Jewish Strategy

By presenting it as inseparably bound up with a number of socially just demands, he [the Jew] promotes its [Marxism's] spread and conversely the aversion of decent people to fulfil demands which, advanced in such form and company, seem from the outset unjust and impossible to fulfil. For under this cloak of purely social ideas truly diabolic purposes are hidden, yes, they are publicly proclaimed with the most insolent frankness. This theory represents an inseparable mixture of reason and human madness, but always in such a way that only the lunacy can become reality and never the reason. By the categorical rejection of the personality and hence of the nation and its racial content, it destroys the elementary foundations of all human culture which is dependent on just these factors. That is the true inner kernel of the Marxist philosophy in so far as this figment of a criminal brain can be designated as a 'philosophy'. With the shattering of the personality and the race, the essential obstacle is removed to the domination of the inferior being – and this is the Jew.

Source: A.Hitler, Mein Kampf, *1985 ed., p. 290*

In the place of 'the individual' and 'the race' Marxism established 'class'. Hitler automatically associated the concept with the Russian revolution. He argued that under the Tsars, Russia had been governed by an élite caste of Germanic origin. This had been liquidated by the Bolsheviks in October 1917. The uprising had been carried out by a proletarian class mobilised by Jewish *agents provocateurs*. The outcome was a puppet government led by the same people (see also document 2.16 for evidence about this point). In his early writings, therefore, Hitler espoused a consistent opposition towards the Soviet Union. As a state controlled by Jews, it was the antithesis of all that was good. There should be no question of entering into an alliance with it. Ultimately Communism and western civilisation could not coexist (Welch, 1998, p. 15).

Document 2.11 Beelzebub

[I]t is sheer lunacy to ally ourselves with a power whose master is the mortal enemy of our future. How can we expect to free our own people from the fetters of this poisonous embrace if we walk right into it? How shall we explain Bolshevism to the German worker as an accursed crime against humanity if we ally ourselves with the organisations of this spawn of hell, thus recognising it in the larger sense? By what right shall we condemn a member of the broad masses for his sympathy with an outlook if the very leaders of the state choose the representatives of this outlook for allies?

The fight against Jewish world Bolshevisation requires a clear attitude towards Soviet Russia. You cannot drive out the Devil with Beelzebub.

Source: A. Hitler, Mein Kampf, *1985 ed., p. 605*

Anti-Semitism was certainly the most powerful emotion in Adolf Hitler's life, but there was more to his race hatred than this alone. He had been brought up in the Habsburg Empire. It comprised a variety of different nationality groups. Citizens of the Empire were not just Germans and, of course Jews, but also (amongst others) Hungarians, Croats, Serbs and Poles. While living in Vienna, Adolf Hitler visited the parliament of this multi-national empire. What he experienced, as recorded in *Mein Kampf*, is interesting in two ways. First it shows that his racism at an early time extended to Slavic peoples as well. Secondly it shows a dislike for parliamentary democracy. In the following extract, Hitler discusses the conduct especially of Slavic members of the Austrian parliament.

Document 2.12 Parliamentarianism

The intellectual content of what these men [the Slavic parliamentary deputies] said was on a really depressing level, in so far as you could understand their babbling at all; for several of the gentlemen did not speak German, but their native Slavic languages or rather dialects. I now had occasion to hear with my own ears what previously I had known only from reading newspapers. A wild gesticulating mass screaming all at once in every different key, presided over by a good-natured old uncle who was striving in the sweat of his brow to revive the dignity of the House by violently ringing his bell and alternating gentle reproofs with grave admonitions.

I couldn't help laughing.

Source: A. Hitler, Mein Kampf, *1985 ed., p. 71*

Hitler came to apply his racism in all manner of situations. On one occasion he visited a natural history museum in Munich. He began thinking about the tribes which populated Europe in primeval times, especially how their lives and migratory patterns must have been affected by past climatic changes. He came up with a whole theory of prehistoric European history.

Document 2.13 Racial History

'What enormous migrations those must have been, carried out over centuries and millennia by those inhabitants of northern Europe and Asia – which probably also had a different geography than they do today. What battles must have taken place as tribes decided to spread out toward the south, when the increasing cold threatened them from the north. Such times also generally breed great leaders in among peoples, whose clairvoyant insights and presentiments occasionally far outdistance the course of events. Thus, I can imagine that an outstanding personality with great military power once invaded the extensive territory that is now Russia to turn it into a billet, as it were, for his tribes and people for centuries to come.

'I am not familiar enough with the history of the earliest – that is, actually, the prehistoric – period to be able to point to this or that to support such ideas. But the fact that up there in northern Russia and in Siberia the ruins of powerful cultural epochs still lie buried under forests and debris has been proved by various excavations of the past and by accidental finds. And northern peoples migrated and settled much further down, as far as the shores of the Black Sea – yes, even past the Caspian, to the place where later we find the realm of the Medes – as is proven by the blond types with blue eyes and white skin in White Russia, in the Ukraine, and even south of the Caucasus. One arm of this northern invasion that crept slowly toward the south clearly also pushed into England to introduce extensive democratic principles and may perhaps one day lead to socialist measures. Then the upper class will quickly be absorbed and removed.'

Source: H.A. Turner (ed.), Hitler – Memoirs of a Confidant, *1985, pp. 81–2*

It did not matter that there was minimal evidence to support the theory. Although Hitler always was interested in history, his understanding of the currents which operated in the past was structured around little more than racial phobia (Kroll, 1996, p. 330). As a result his historical thinking was generally 'banal, vapid and irredeemably inaccurate' (Lewin, 1984, p. 26). Based on the slightest of evidence, his mind went on flights of fancy, displaying prodigious abilities to build castles in the air and to take general racial convictions to their logical conclusion (Fest, 1973, p. 4).

A premise of racialism is that competition exists between peoples to see which is best adapted to a given environment. A corollary is that even within races there is competition to see which individuals are the best adapted, or 'fittest'. Otto Wagener was chief of staff of the storm troop auxiliaries and head of the *Reichsleitung* office in the Brown House for economic affairs. He was in close contact with Hitler between about 1929 and 1934. He wrote his recollections of meetings with Hitler while interned by the British immediately after the Second World War. On one occasion, he remembered presenting a set of ideas to Hitler as a possible way in which the principle of 'fitness' might be applied to develop a new theory of economic life. At stake, as Wagener explained and Hitler soon realised, was the restructuring of German businesses in a racially sound way. Even though the ideas were never realised in practice, the conversation underlines that Hitler just could not get away from his prejudices.

Document 2.14 Survival of the Fittest

'This idea', I began, 'would mean that not all the people who work in a business can acquire a claim to ownership of it, but only the best of them, the most productive. On the other hand, a business proprietor can, in the long run, keep his property only if he continually reacquires, as it were, his claim to it through skill and achievement.

'Thus there would be no socialization, but a permanent, gradual, continuous transfer of ownership of any business into the hands of the most capable, the best – under certain circumstances, into the hands of the one best man.

'This idea, which is without doubt completely novel, seems to me in fact workable. I even have the impression that it is fully congruent with the ideas I have been systematically developing for some time concerning the overall financial and capital structure. I would ask you to let me present those ideas to you at some other time. . . .

'The fundamental principle that conclusively emerges from the overall reasoning is that a business can belong only to someone who works in it. Until now, it has been possible for someone to own a business and to allow a manager or director to run it, while he himself spent his time in Berlin or Monte Carlo, living on the earnings of his business, which are sent to him once a month. If we carry out the idea of the transfer of property, we must see to it that such a case cannot occur.'

'Very good!' Hitler interrupted. 'That means the abolition of income without work or effort. . . . [i.e. a 'Jewish' characteristic]

. . . 'Wagener, what you have told us is full of so much that is new and original that I did not absorb all of it sufficiently to be able to take a clear position. Please, come to see me again tomorrow morning at eleven o'clock, and give me the same report again, if possible in the same words you used just now. . . .

'Prepare yourself . . . to discuss with us in detail, one after the other, all the problems you have only touched on today, until the picture is complete. If my feelings are right, today is the birth date of a completely new economic theory, which will be capable of explaining and resolving the enormous problems of the conversion to socialism.'

Source: H.A. Turner (ed.), Hitler – Memoirs of a Confidant, *1985, pp. 41–3*

It should be no surprise that Hitler wanted to redefine the whole purpose of the state. As he made explicit once again in the pages of *Mein Kampf*, he intended to create a structure to promote the welfare of the German race.

Document 2.15 Racial State

The folkish state must make up for what everyone else today has neglected in this field. *It must set race at the centre of all life. It must take care to keep it pure. It must declare the child to be the most precious treasure of the people. It must see to it that only the healthy beget children; but there is only one disgrace: despite one's own sickness and deficiencies, to bring children into the world, and one highest honour: to renounce doing so. And conversely it must be considered reprehensible: to withhold healthy children from the nation. Here the state must act as the guardian of a millennial future in the face of which the wishes and the selfishness of the individual must appear as nothing and submit. It must put the most modern medical means in the service of this knowledge. It must declare unfit for propagation all who are in any way visibly sick or who have inherited a disease and can therefore pass it on, and put this into actual practice. Conversely, it must take care that the fertility of the healthy woman is not limited by the financial irresponsibility of a state regime which turns the blessing of children into a curse for the parents. It must put an end to that lazy, nay criminal, indifference with which the social premises for a fecund family are treated today, and must instead feel itself to be the highest guardian of this most precious blessing of a people. Its concern belongs more to the child than to the adult.*

Those who are physically and mentally unhealthy and unworthy must not perpetuate their suffering in the body of their children. In this the folkish state must perform the most gigantic educational task.

Source: A. Hitler, Mein Kampf, *1985 ed., p. 367*

Racism permeated every corner of Hitler's brain, so naturally he developed a racially based foreign policy. This related the population of a state to the quantity and quality of the land available to it. The starting premise was that Germany was hopelessly overcrowded. Hitler believed the problem could be tackled in one of four ways: birth rates could be restricted artificially, unused land inside Germany could be colonised, new land could be found outside Germany for colonisation, or Germany could turn herself into a kind of business, exporting her goods in order to acquire food to maintain her excess people (Hitler, 1985, pp. 125–6). Hitler believed the third option was the most healthy biologically and advocated the following plan for foreign policy.

Document 2.16 *Lebensraum*

And so we National Socialists consciously draw a line beneath the foreign policy tendency of our pre-War period. We take up where we broke off six hundred years ago. We stop the endless German movement to the south and west, and turn our gaze towards the land in the east. At long last we break off the colonial and commercial policy of the pre-War period and shift to the soil policy of the future.

If we speak of soil in Europe today, we can primarily have in mind only *Russia* and her vassal border states.

Here Fate itself seems desirous of giving us a sign. By handing Russia to Bolshevism, it robbed the Russian nation of that intelligentsia which previously brought about and guaranteed its existence as a state. For the organisation of a Russian state formation was not the result of the political abilities of the Slavs in Russia, but only a wonderful example of the state-forming efficacy of the German element in an inferior race. Numerous mighty empires on earth have been created in this way. Lower nations led by Germanic organisers and overlords have more than once grown to be mighty state formations and have endured as long as the racial nucleus of the creative state race maintained itself. For centuries Russia drew nourishment from this Germanic nucleus of its upper leading strata. Today it can be regarded as almost totally exterminated and extinguished. It has been replaced by the Jew. Impossible as it is for the Russian by himself to shake off the yoke of the Jew by his own resources, it is equally impossible for the Jew to maintain the mighty empire forever. He himself is no element of organisation, but a ferment of decomposition. The Persian empire in the east is ripe for collapse. And the end of Jewish rule in Russia will also be the end of Russia as a state. We have been chosen by Fate as witness of a catastrophe which will be the mightiest confirmation of the soundness of folkish theory.

Our task, the mission of the National Socialist movement, is to bring our own people to such political insight that they will not see their goal for the future in the breath-taking sensation of a new Alexander's conquest, but in the industrious work of the German plough, to which the sword need only give soil.

Source: A. Hitler, Mein Kampf, *1985 ed., pp. 598–9*

The coherence of Hitler's thinking is startling. Expansion of Germany's land at the expense of Soviet Russia ties in perfectly with both his anti-Marxism and his anti-Semitism. It would kill two birds with one stone: a major source of racial and ideological 'infection' would be eradicated and the much-needed land for the Germans would become available.

Hitler continued this theme throughout the 1920s, discussing it notably in his *Second Book*. This was written in Summer 1928 during a stay on Obersalzberg and had a number of purposes (Kershaw, 1998, p. 291). It was a means to sharpening his own understanding of foreign policy themes, an explanation to the party faithful of his thinking in the area and an appeal to potential supporters who were attached to more traditional nationalist organisations. More immediately still, it was a guide to how the movement should react to fascist Italy's policy of Italianization in the German-speaking South Tyrol. In the event, Hitler decided not to publish the book and so it remained secret until after the Second World War when it was discovered by G.L. Weinberg and printed in 1961. The pages of the *Second Book*, which was first published in German under the title of *Secret Book*, contained a remarkable vision. It recommended that 500,000 sq km of land be taken from Russia's thinly settled western borders (Hitler, 1961, p. 74). Germany had been deprived of just 70,000 sq km of territory by the Treaty of Versailles (Weinberg, 1995, p. 35). With such a vast amount of territory captured, Hitler believed Germans would no longer have to work in poorly paid factory jobs. They would be free to take over a homestead and live as farmers (Hitler, 1961, p. 210). He foresaw Germans flocking east and argued that the purpose of the war effort in 1914 should have been for just such a type of eastward expansion in order to provide land for veterans of the campaign (Hitler, 1961, p. 78).

Hitler returned to these ideas in conversations which were attended by Herman Rauschning between 1932 and 1934. Rauschning (a Nazi party member from Danzig) made notes of what was said and published these in Britain in 1939 under the title *Hitler Speaks*. Although there has been a vigorous debate about the status of Rauschning's records, the balanced judgement is that they say nothing 'which is not consonant with what is otherwise known of Hitler's character and opinions' (Kershaw, 1993, pp. 109 and 127). One of the most startling of the recollections concerned Hitler's response to a series of lectures given by Walther Darré and his staff regarding the *Lebensraum* (or living space) to be acquired in eastern Europe.

Document 2.17 Hitler Speaks

'In the main I approve what has been said about our eastern, or "Eastern space" policy. Only one thing, my party comrades, you must always remember. We shall never be great statesmen unless we have a nucleus of might at the centre as hard and firm as steel. A nucleus of eighty to one hundred million colonising Germans! My first task will therefore be to create this nucleus which will not only make us invincible, but will assure to us once and for all time the decisive ascendancy over all the European nations. Once we have succeeded in this, we shall find everything else comparatively simple.

'Part of this nucleus is Austria. That goes without saying. But Bohemia and Moravia also belong to it, as well as the western regions of Poland as far as certain natural strategical frontiers. Moreover – and this you must not overlook – the Baltic States too, are part of it – those states which for centuries have had a thin upper crust of Germanhood. To-day in all these regions, alien races predominate. It will be our duty, if we wish to found our greater Reich for all time, to remove these races. There is no excuse for neglecting this. Our age provides us with the technical possibilities for

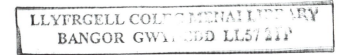

carrying through such transfers of population comparatively easily. Besides, the post-war period brought with it an internal migration of many millions of people, compared to which our enterprise will seem a trifle.

'The Bohemian–Moravian basin and the eastern districts bordering on Germany will be colonised with German peasants. The Czechs and the Bohemians we shall transfer to Siberia or the Volhynian regions, and we shall set up reserves for them in the new allied states. The Czechs must get out of Central Europe. As long as they remain, they will always be a centre of Hussite–Bolshevik disintegration. Only when we are able and willing to achieve this shall I be prepared to answer for the blood-sacrifice of another young German generation. But at this price I shall not hesitate for a moment to take the deaths of two or three million Germans on my conscience, fully aware of the heaviness of the sacrifice.

'In the Baltic countries', Hitler went on, 'the case is different. We shall easily Germanise the population. They are peoples who are racially closely related to us and would have been German long since, had not the prejudices and social arrogance of the German Baltic barons artificially prevented it. For the rest, frontier problems as such interest me very little. . . . I shall put an end, too, to the absurdly sentimental views about the South Tyrol. I have no intention of allowing this problem at any time to deflect me from the basic line of our policy, namely, an alliance with Italy. . . . Alsace and Lorraine are in a different class. We shall never give them up – not because Germans live there, but because we require these and other parts to round off our central regions in the west, just as we require Bohemia in the south and Posen, West Prussia, Silesia and the Baltic countries in the east and north.'

Hitler continued:

'Thus far there are no doubts. In the east and south-east I do not follow General Ludendorff nor anyone else; I follow only the iron law of our historical development. When Germany has rearmed, all these smaller states will offer us their alliance of their own accord. But we have no intention of manufacturing a peaceful Pan-Europe in miniature, with the good Uncle Germany in the centre, pleasantly shortening the time of his nephew's studies. We shall not breed our own usurpers. We must once and for all time create the politically and biologically eternally valid foundations of a German Europe. . . .

'There will be a *Herren*-class', he said, 'an historical class tempered by battle, and welded from the most varied elements. There will be a great hierarchy of party members. There will be a new middle class. And there will be the great mass of the anonymous, the serving collective, the eternally disenfranchised, no matter whether they were once members of the old *bourgeoisie*, the big land-owning class, the working-class or the artisans. Nor will their financial or previous social position be of the slightest importance. These preposterous differences will have been liquidated in a single revolutionary process. But beneath them there will still be the class of the subject alien races; we need not hesitate to call them the modern slave class. And over all of these will stand the new high aristocracy, the most deserving and the most responsible *Führer-personalities.*'

Source: H. Rauschning, Hitler Speaks, *1939, pp. 40–7*

Elements of this thinking were not entirely novel. During the time of the *Kaiserreich* several voices had spoken up for the winning of colonial territory. Theodor Schiemann had believed Germans were 'forced by our geographical situation, by poor soil, . . . by the amazing increase in our population, . . . to spread and to gain for us and for our sons' (in Röhl and Sombart, 1982, p. 149). During the First World War German troops occupied vast tracts of eastern territory, from the Baltic to the Black Sea (Reid, 1998, p. 101; Taube *et al.*, 1995, pp. 83–4). At the time, voices spoke out in favour of colonisation. General Erich von Ludendorff (mentioned in the last document) commented in 1915 of Poland that 'Here we shall win breeding ground for the men needed for further battles in the East'. In December 1917 he advocated the 'Annexation of Lithuania and the Courland, including Riga and the islands, as we need more land for the people's nourishment' (Binion, 1975, p. 86). He wanted to annex a strip of Polish territory in western Poland, expel its Polish population and settle it with Germans (Macartney and Palmer, 1962, p. 78). Likewise he wanted to settle ethnic Germans in territories located on the Crimean peninsula in the Ukraine (Kamenetsky, 1994, p. 97). To recognise this heritage is important, but Hitler's ideas about the acquisition of living space for his German people moved on from their origins. They were of a completely different order. Whether you want to talk about the scale of the lands to be annexed, or his plans for deporting whole Slavic populations (the last document mentions Czechs and Bohemians), his goals outstripped all established traditional, bourgeois parameters (Hitler, 1961, pp. 87–8). His ideas were on the verge of science fiction.

Hitler did adapt what he said to the needs of different times and audiences. He toned down his overt anti-Semitism in the key electoral period which lasted from the late 1920s until he won power, even though the basic structures of his speeches remained largely the same as ever (Binion, 1975, p. 96). On 27 January 1932, he addressed Germany's leading industrialists in Düsseldorf. It was a fine opportunity for him to win their support at a vital time. Hitler spoke for over two hours and received both a standing ovation and financial backing. What sort of arguments did he apply?

Document 2.18 To the Industrialists

Today we are confronted with a world situation which is only comprehensible to the white race if one recognizes as indispensable the marriage between the concept of domination in political will and the concept of domination (*Herrensinn*) in economic activity, a miraculous consensus which left its mark on the whole of the past century and in the consequences of which the white peoples have, in part, undergone a remarkable development: instead of expanding in a territorial sense, instead of exporting human beings, they have exported goods, have built up a worldwide economic system which manifests itself most characteristically in the fact that – given that there are different standards of living on this earth – Europe, and most recently, America as well, have gigantic central world factories in Europe, and the rest of the world has huge markets and sources of raw materials.

The white race, however, is capable of maintaining its position, practically speaking, only as long as discrepancies between the standards of living throughout the world remain. If today you were to give so-called export markets the same standard of living we have, you would witness that the privileged position of the white race, which is manifested not only in the political power of the nation, but also in the economic situation of the individual, can no longer be maintained. . . .

We shall, in any event, witness the following development: Bolshevism will – if today's way of thinking in Europe and America remain as it is – slowly spread throughout Asia. Whether it takes thirty or fifty years is of no consequence at all, considering it is a question of Weltanschauungen [ideologies]. Christianity did not begin to assert itself throughout the whole of southern Europe until 300 years after Christ, and 700 years later it had taken hold of northern Europe as well. Weltanschauungen of this funda-mental nature can manifest their unrestricted capacity for conquest even five hundred years later if they are not broken in the beginning by the natural instinct of self-preservation of other peoples. But even if this process continues for only thirty, forty or fifty years and our frame of mind remains unchanged, then, Gentlemen, one will not be able to say: what does that have to do with our economy?

Source: M. Domarus, Hitler. Speeches and Proclamations, *1990, pp. 96–9*

Obvious race hatred was absent here. After all, Hitler was talking to north German businessmen as a prospective Chancellor, not to Bavarian peasants as a beer hall agitator. But still the honesty of the speech was overwhelming and it was clearly couched in racist terms. Why weren't the bankers and businessmen scared to death of this man? (Davidson, 1977, p. 373).

Hajo Holborn was right that Hitler had 'an unkempt and primitive mind that lacked the power of discrimination but excelled in reducing simple ideas to even simpler terms while believing thereby to have achieved a higher wisdom' (Holborn, 1952, pp. 542 ff.). His thinking in itself was not so original. It drew on many common ideological currents which existed in Austria, Bavaria and wider conservative circles in Germany during the late nineteenth and early twentieth centuries. This is an important point in itself (see Chapter 9, thesis 3), but equally striking is the consistency of Hitler's arguments and the persistence with which he applied racism to every area of life. He developed racial interpretations of the morality of labour, political systems, history, economics, the state and foreign policy. As a result we have to treat with great care the words of historians who would 'down-play' the importance of ideas to Hitler. They should not be minimised in importance, but incorporated fully into an understanding of what made him 'tick' (Breitling, 1971, p. 9).

Although Hitler's vision was derivative, obviously it cast him as a revolutionary (as defined in Chapter 1). He was so decisively at odds with what existed in the world, that in effect he had declared war against its basic premises (Eitner, 1994, p. 91). For reasons associated with racism, he despised the *dominant structures of political power* in Austria and Germany, that is to say parliamentarianism and the democratic (non-racial) state. He wanted both state and economy redefined in such a way that they would be *legitimated* by nothing other than his racial *myth*. His anti-Semitism defined a perceived '*social ill*' (i.e. Germany's Jews) which he was determined to deal with one way or another. His stigmatisation of 'the Jew' as the embodiment of everything evil and *unjust* in the world certainly displayed a mind attuned to '*black and white' ways of thinking.* For ideological reasons, he wanted to establish a new order of foreign policy that would *overturn the international political order*, capture massive tracts of central Europe and Russia, and expel population groups wholesale. This implied the *transformation of the continent's social structure.* More than this, whether he spoke in beer halls or to industrialists, he was always careful to express himself in such a way that would *motivate people* to seek common cause with him.

On the basis of what he said and wrote, Hitler was clearly an *idealist* and in later years he would baffle everyone by pursuing exactly the ends he had outlined long ago (Ensor, 1939, pp. 30–1). There would be hardly any conflict between 'Hitler the ideologue' and 'Hitler the politician'. This reality has consequences for the way we must interpret the life of Adolf Hitler (see Chapter 9, thesis 1). His vision may have been based on irreducible prejudice rather than objective scholarly thought, but it was perfectly serious and clear to all with eyes to see.

3 | Agitator

Did Adolf Hitler pursue his ideas with revolutionary means during the years of the Weimar Republic? The answer must begin by explaining why Hitler chose a career in politics anyway. His time in Pasewalk hospital during the final stages of the First World War played a part (Eitner, 1994, p. 45). To a patriot lying blinded by mustard gas, to a man who had fought four long years for his adopted country, November 1918 was a singular trauma. German sailors rebelled, the General Staff capitulated, the Kaiser abdicated, across the nation traditional political order fragmented in favour of Soviet-style workers' and soldiers' councils. In *Mein Kampf* Hitler wrote that during these days 'my own fate became known to me' (Hitler, 1985, p. 187). Gerald Fleming says that this period 'gave him his true raison d'être' (Fleming, 1986, p. 15). It set Hitler on a trajectory which led in unswerving fashion to his subsequent career. The truth of the matter was probably not quite so simple. Hitler's transition from soldier to politician was actually a gradual one.

Upon being discharged from hospital, Hitler found himself in an unenviable position. With both parents dead and having lived in hostels for 'down and outs' during the years before 1914 (see Chapter 8), Hitler now faced the prospect of becoming 'singularly homeless' (Flood, 1989, p. 39). Twice decorated for valour (he received the Iron Cross Second Class in late 1914 and the Iron Cross First Class in Summer 1918), he had the prospect of a civilian future which promised little more than a return to his pre-war days: life in a spartan home for single men painting cheap watercolours (Maser, 1973, pp. 78–83 and 88). The forthcoming demobilisation of the army can only have caused Hitler deep uncertainty and foreboding (Eitner, 1994, p. 46).

In March 1919 Hitler returned to barracks in Munich. The city was wracked by the most intense political turmoil. Bavaria's Independent Socialist leader, Kurt Eisner, had been assassinated on the city's streets only weeks before by Count Arco-Valley, a German nationalist from Austria. Thereafter the city descended into near civil war. On 7 April 1919 Bavaria was declared a Soviet Republic and rumours began to spread that Communist troops were ready to march from Russia and Hungary to shore up Socialism there. Lenin sent the Red revolutionaries telegrams of support. He urged them to consolidate their rule through terror (Davidson, 1977, pp. 119–21; Flood, 1989, p. 48). When bands of anti-Communist troops (made up of right-wing, nationalist veterans of the First World War, some with swastikas painted on their helmets) under Captain Ehrhardt approached the city, the 'Reds' executed a number of radical nationalist hostages held in the Luitpold *Gymnasium* (Flood, 1989, p. 55). Munich was a political hothouse in which anything was possible. Hitler soon had the point illustrated to him personally. For the most part he was serving at a military camp near Traunstein, guarding Russian and French prisoners of war who were awaiting release. Alternatively, he received RM 3 per day counting gas masks at a military store (Flood, 1989, p. 50). Despite such a low profile, Hitler came into conflict with Communism and to the attention of Red sympathisers. The following document is based on an interview with a man who had been friendly with Hitler in Munich. It shows that politics had become a matter of life and death that just could not be ignored.

Document 3.1 Pistol Point

'Then one day armoured cars were to be seen racing through the streets distributing leaflets in favour of the Hoffman [sic] administration. [Johannes Hoffmann was authorised by the Bavarian Landtag to re-establish law and order in the state.] . . . Those who opposed such propaganda were at once shot down by machine guns. Next came armoured cars advertising the Red regime in the same manner, with placards demanding the fall of Hoffman. Those who failed to comply with this new coercion were also at once shot down by more machine guns. Hardly had both sets of armoured cars disappeared than a force of Spartakists [supporters of the Soviet system], three thousand strong, marched on the principal railway station which was already held by Hoffman's troops. Firing broke out and the Spartakists gave back, only to rally, and bombard the place in their turn for over half an hour. The station was captured and its defenders all shot, to a man. This seemed to break the back of the resistance to the "Red" regime for the moment. New strikes were immediately organised.

'Hitler and I looked on at all this with the uttermost repugnance, as you can well suppose. Hitler had already come up against the Communists, for disobeying some of their orders [i.e. in the army]. They already had an eye on him. It seemed better, they thought, to get him out of the way.

'One morning, very early, three Red Guards entered the barracks and sought him out in his room. He was already up and dressed. As they tramped up the stairs Hitler guessed what was afoot, so grasped his revolver and prepared for the encounter. They banged on the door which immediately opened to them:

'"If you don't instantly clear out", cried Hitler, brandishing his weapon, "I'll serve you as we served mutineers at the Front."

'The Reds turned instantly, and tramped downstairs again. The threat had been all too real to face an instant longer.'

Source: Heinz A. Heinz, Germany's Hitler, *1934, pp. 105–6*

By the start of May 1919 anti-Soviet forces loyal to Hoffmann had gained the upper hand in Munich (Craig, 1981, pp. 410–11). Investigations were set up in the army to weed out soldiers who had sympathised with the Communists. The initiative gave Hitler an opportunity to become active in politics. He participated in a commission of inquiry investigating his regiment. His testimony ensured that ten people were executed in the purge that followed (Heiber, 1961, p. 39; Flood, 1989, p. 57). His diligence in denouncing Communists impressed his military superiors, and within a few weeks Hitler was enrolled to become an 'education officer' for the 1st Bavarian Rifle Regiment. In the first instance, the aim was to prepare speakers for the 'political education' of German troops returning from the war, in other words to bolster nationalist sentiment among soldiers who might have become 'infected' by left-wing sympathies during the turmoil of the preceding months. In May and June 1919 Hitler attended an educational course at Munich University. In so doing he was accorded the status of a *V-Mann* – *Vertauens-Mann*, a kind of low-level political agent who had the job not only of giving political talks, but also of acquiring political information secretly.

By accepting the role of *V-Mann*, Hitler had become a sort of agitator on behalf of the German army. The role came naturally to him. The following document is the recollection of Munich historian Karl Alexander von Müller who lectured to the *V-Männer* during their initial course at Munich University.

Document 3.2 Pale, Thin Face

After the end of my speech and the lively discussion which followed it, I bumped into a small group in the emptying room which held me up. It seemed completely absorbed by the man in the middle who was speaking to it irresistibly in a strange guttural voice and with growing passion: I had the strange feeling that their excitement was his work and that at the same time it was encouraging him more and more. I saw a pale, thin face beneath an unmilitary hank of hair, with a close cropped moustache and striking large light blue eyes which shone with a fanatic coldness. After the next lecture I waited to see if he would register to speak in the discussion session, but, just like the last time, he did not. 'Do you know that you have an oratorical natural tenor among your students?' I asked my old school friend [who was running the lecture course] after the hour was up. . . . 'Where is he sitting then?' I pointed out the place. 'Well', he said, 'that is Hitler from the List Regiment. You, Hitler, come over here!' And the person he had called came obediently up onto the podium, with awkward movements, as if, I felt, in a kind of defiant embarrassment.

Source: E. Deuerlein, Der Aufstieg der NSDAP, *1974, p. 197*

During July and August 1919 Hitler lectured troops at Lechfeld camp on topics such as 'The Conditions of Peace and Reconstruction' and 'Social and Economic-Political Slogans' (Deuerlein, 1959, pp. 179–80, 199–200; Davidson,

1977, pp. 123–5). The military section compiled reports of how soldiers reacted. One, dated 24 August, said Hitler's 'emotional speeches' met with 'approval' because they drew on examples from real life. His lectures were 'effective and easy to understand'. They brought people into an 'almost enthusiastic frame of mind'. Hitler was a 'born popular speaker' whose 'fanaticism' and 'popular behaviour' compelled 'the listeners absolutely to take notice and to agree' (Deuerlein, 1959, p. 200). Hitler had found he could excel at the art of persuasion.

Nor was the army's role in shaping Hitler's future over yet. The *Deutsche Arbeiter Partei* (DAP or German Workers' Party) was backed by Munich's most important radical nationalist and anti-Semitic circles. It owed its existence to two men who had been active in local right-wing politics for some time. During the later stages of the war, Anton Drexler had tried to shore up patriotism among Bavarian workers (Hatheway, 1994, p. 449). His initiative brought him into contact with Karl Harrer. He was a member of the Thule Society, a shady nationalist–racialist group which had some of its members killed among the Luitpold hostages. The two men decided to pool their efforts and to form the DAP (Hatheway, 1994, pp. 455–7). The organisation held its first public meeting on 5 January 1919 (Fest, 1973, pp. 115–18). As part of his job as a *V-Mann*, Hitler was ordered to infiltrate the group and report on a meeting held on 12 September 1919. He heard Gottfried Feder lecture about capitalism and Jewry. In many respects the evening was a waste of time. Hitler had already heard Feder give the exact same lecture during the course at Munich University and only about twenty people were present. When the party chairman, Anton Drexler, handed over a political pamphlet to Hitler, it made no impression on him. The most significant thing about the encounter was that a few days later Hitler received from Drexler a postcard informing him that he had been allocated membership of the DAP. This came completely out of the blue since Hitler had never requested the 'honour' (Heiber, 1961, pp. 40–1). Nevertheless on 3 October 1919 Hitler asked his superior officer, Captain Mayer, that he be allowed to join the party. On 16 October he was one of 111 people to attend a meeting at the *Hofbrauhauskeller* (a beer hall in Munich), at which Dr Erich Kühn, editor of the radical nationalist journal *Deutschlands Erneuerung* (*Germany's Renewal*), spoke about the Jewish Question. Hitler spoke too. A reporter from the *Munich Observer* reported that he 'used inflammatory words' and incited those present against especially the Jewish press (Flood, 1989, p. 74). Three days later, and notwithstanding Drexler's prior offer, Hitler wrote requesting membership of the party.

What had brought Hitler to this position? Was he trying to work his way deeper into the group, the better to inform on its activities? Had he taken a decision based on personal political principles that he had much in common with these people? Was he starting to think that a career in politics would suit his talents once he was demobilised? Any (or all) of these issues could have played a part. Whatever his precise motive, Hitler worked hard to change the small secretive organisation, which he considered too much like a cosy tea club, into something grander (Orlow, 1969, pp. 17–19). On 13 November 1919 he spoke in public again. This time 129 people were present at the *Eberlbräukeller* (another beer hall in Munich) and, on Hitler's say-so, they had each been charged 50 pf entrance fee. Hitler held the floor for an hour and a half. He denounced Jews and Red revolutionaries. When heckling began, some of his fellow soldiers removed the culprits. At the end, according to a police observer, Hitler received tumultuous applause (Flood, 1989, p. 77). Now 30 years of age, Hitler had found his vocation. On 1 April 1920 he resigned from the army, rented a cheap room with hardly any furniture, and embarked on a full-time career as a speaker and recruiter (*Werbeobmann*) for the movement. By this time the DAP had changed its name, partly at Hitler's instigation, to the *Nationalsozialistische Deutsche Arbeiter Partei* (NSDAP or National Socialist German Workers' Party) (Knopp, 1995, p. 38). The new title was supposed to broaden its basis of popular appeal.

On 14 August 1920 the Socialist-inclined *Munich Post* described Hitler as 'the smartest agitator who is plying his mischief in Munich at the moment'. It was a label Hitler accepted. In conversation with Munich publisher Max Maurenbrecher in May 1921 he described himself as 'the agitator who understands how to gather the masses together' (*Deutsche Zeitung*, 10 November 1923, evening edition). His activism was always intense and he appeared at 31 of 46 meetings held by the party that year, including venues far beyond Munich, namely in Rosenheim, Stuttgart, Vienna, Berlin, Nuremberg, Würzburg, and even the town where he was born, Braunau (Knopp, 1995, p. 38). So what was it like to witness a Hitler speech during this period? One of the most sustained descriptions comes from Hitler's personal friend and financial backer, Ernst 'Putzi' Hanfstaengl. In the early days he donated RM 30,000 to the movement. During the 1950s he wrote his memoirs which include the following account of an adventure in a Munich pub full of people wearing Bavarian costume.

Document 3.3 Waiter

I looked round the hall and could see no one in the audience or on the platform whom I knew. 'Where is Hitler?' I asked a middle-aged journalist next to me.

'See those three over there? The short man is Max Amann, the one with the spectacles is Anton Drexler and the other is Hitler.'

In his heavy boots, dark suit and leather waistcoat, semi-stiff white collar and odd little moustache, he really did not look very impressive – like a waiter in a railway station. However, when Drexler introduced him to a roar of applause, Hitler straightened up and walked past the press table with a swift, controlled step the unmistakable soldier in mufti.

The atmosphere in the hall was electric. Apparently this was his first major public appearance after serving a short prison sentence for breaking up a meeting addressed by a Bavarian separatist called Ballerstedt, so he had to be reasonably careful of what he said lest the police should arrest him again as a disturber of the peace. Perhaps this is what gave such a brilliant quality to his speech, which for innuendo and irony I have never heard matched, even by him. No one who judges his capacity as a speaker from the performances of his later years can have any true insight into his gifts. As time went on he became drunk with his own oratory and his voice lost its former character through the intervention of microphone and loudspeaker. In his early years he had a command of voice, phrase and affect which has never been equalled and on this evening he was at his best.

I cannot have been more than eight feet away and watched him carefully. For the first ten minutes he stood at attention, while he gave a very well argued résumé of the historical events of the previous three or four years. In a quiet, reserved voice, he drew a picture of what had happened in Germany since November, 1918: the collapse of the monarchy and the surrender at Versailles; the founding of the Republic on the ignominy of war guilt; the fallacy of international Marxism and pacifism; the eternal class-war leitmotiv and the resulting hopeless stalemate between employers and employees, between nationalists and Socialists.

There was almost a note of Viennese coffeehouse conversation in the grace of some of his phrases and the sly malice of his insinuations. There was no doubt of his Austrian origin. Although he spoke most of the time in a good high German accent, occasional words would give him away. I remember him pronouncing the first syllable of the word 'Europe' (Europa) or 'European' (europaische) in the Latin fashion, *ayoo*, which is typical of Vienna, instead of the North German *oy*, and there were other examples difficult to render into English. As he felt the audience becoming increasingly interested in what he had to say, he gently moved his left foot to one side, like a soldier standing at ease, and started to use his hands and arms in gestures, of which he had an expressive and extensive repertoire. There was none of the barking and braying he later developed and he had an ingenious, mocking humour which was telling without being offensive.

He scored his points all round the compass. First he would criticise the Kaiser as a weakling and then he rounded on the Weimar Republicans for conforming with the victors' demands, which were stripping Germany of everything but the graves of her war dead. There was a strong note of appeal to the ex-servicemen in his audience. He compared the separatist movement and the religious exclusiveness of the Bavarian Catholics with the comradeship of the front line soldier who never asked a wounded comrade his religion before he sprang to help him. He dwelt at length on patriotism and national pride and quoted approvingly the role of Kemal Ataturk of Turkey and the example of Mussolini, who had marched on Rome three weeks earlier.

He stormed at war profiteers and I remember his getting a roar of applause when he criticised them for spending valuable foreign currency on importing oranges from Italy, when gathering inflation was facing half the population with starvation. He attacked the Jews, not so much on a racial basis, as on an accusation of black marketeering and waxing fat on the misery round them, a charge which it was only too easy to make stick. Then he thundered at the Communists and Socialists for designing the destruction of German traditions. All these enemies of the people, he declared, would one day be beseitigt – literally 'removed' or 'done away with'. It was a perfectly proper word to use in the circumstances, and I read no sinister connotation into it. I even doubt whether it had the meaning in Hitler's mind that it later acquired, but then that was to be a long story.

Source: E. Hanfstaengl, Unheard Witness, *1957, pp. 34–7*

Hitler magnified common resentments until those present gave themselves over to his distortion of reality. What it felt like to be a member of the audience falling under Hitler's spell is described in the memoirs of one-time Nazi, Kurt Ludecke. The document was written closer to the event than the Hanfstaengl extract.

Document 3.4 Convert

Critically I studied this slight, pale man, his brown hair parted on one side and fallen again and again over his sweaty brow. Threatening and beseechingly, with small, pleading hands and flaming, steel-blue eyes, he had the look of a fanatic.

Presently my critical faculty was swept away. Leaning from the tribune as if he were trying to impel his inner self into the consciousness of all these thousands, he was holding the masses, and me with them, under a hypnotic spell by the sheer force of his conviction. . . .

It was clear that Hitler was feeling the exaltation of the emotional response now surging up toward him from his thousands of hearers. His voice rising to passionate climaxes, he finished his speech with an anthem of hate against the 'Novemberlings' and a pledge of undying love for the Fatherland. 'Germany must be free!' was his final defiant slogan. Then two last words were like the sting of a lash:

'Deutschland Erwache!'

Awake, Germany! There was thunderous applause. Then the masses took a solemn oath 'to save Germany in Bavaria from Bolshevism'.

I do not know how to describe the emotions that swept over me as I heard this man. His words were like a scourge. Later when he spoke of the disgrace of Germany, I felt ready to spring on any enemy. His appeal to German manhood was like a call to arms, the gospel he preached a sacred truth. He seemed another Luther. I forgot everything but the man; then, glancing round, I saw that his magnetism was holding these thousands as one.

Of course I was ripe for this experience. I was a man of thirty-two, weary of disgust and disillusionment, a wanderer seeking a cause; a patriot without a channel for his patriotism, a yearner after the heroic without a hero. The intense will of the man, the passion of his sincerity seemed to flow from him into me. I experienced an exhortation that could be likened only to religious conversion.

I felt sure that no one who had heard Hitler that afternoon could doubt that he was the man of destiny, the vitalising force in the future of Germany. The masses who had streamed into the Koenigsplatz with a stern sense of national humiliation seemed to be going forth renewed.

The bands struck up, the thousands began to move away. I knew my search was ended I found myself my leader and my cause.

Source: Kurt G.W. Ludecke, I Knew Hitler, *1938, pp. 22–3*

The event was like a revivalist meeting. Despite what Hanfstaengl said (document 3.3), this power to impress with a tremendous force of deep emotion was a quality which Hitler never lost. The three photographs of document 3.5 show just some of the myriad of expressions through which the face of even the older man passed as he transported himself, and his audience, on the charging roller-coaster of a public speech.

Document 3.5 Public Speech of an Older Hitler

Source: The Wiener Library, London

Hitler's talks were not so much about the fine points of political analysis: they did not define academically rigorous categories; they conveyed and demanded full-blooded devotion (Heuss in Carr, 1978, p. 12). They were a means to unchaining a popular political force. Undoubtedly Hitler did have a genuine talent for finding and exploiting fellow feeling with his audiences. As one-time senior party member Otto Strasser put it, he responded 'to the vibrations of the human heart with the delicacy of a seismograph' (Langer, 1973, p. 205). The spoken word became '*the* instrument of Hitler and his party' (Heiber, 1961, p. 67).

Of course, not everyone was impressed. The sharp-eyed author Heinrich Mann criticised Hitler's 'uneducated voice' with the 'pronunciation of a backwoodsman' which was 'slow but threatening' (in Knopp, 1995, p. 33). His talks could be perceived as vulgar, cynical and frequently dirty, his choice of words coarse (Knopp, 1995, p. 46). He could be dogmatic and repetitive. He lacked the fine turn of phrase necessary to coin epigrams likely to outlast his life (Schramm, 1972, p. 21). The basic structure of his talks seldom varied and the style of presentation followed a strict cycle. He would begin in slow, halting fashion. His tempo would increase as he felt more and more members of the audience offering him their support; at the end, when maximum support had been achieved, he would be shouting (Price, 1937, pp. 39–40). The net effect, as far as Kurt Ludecke's English girlfriend was concerned, rendered Hitler absurd. She was not even won over by a personal introduction (Ludecke, 1938, pp. 70–1). Something as trivial as his dress sense could alienate people. Kitted out in a poorly fitting blue suit, Edward Mowrer likened him to a 'travelling salesman for a clothing firm' (Mowrer, 1938, pp. 193–4). Dorothy Thompson called him the 'very prototype of the little man' (Thompson, 1934, pp. 12–14). Initially Field Marshal Paul von Hindenburg believed the best Hitler could aspire to being was a Post Master General (Heiber, 1961, p. 84).

But Hitler worked hard at his chosen profession. His presentations were never just 'off the cuff' (Knopp, 1995, pp. 41 and 45). He drafted out themes personally and in detail beforehand so that he spoke not from a complete text but from one-word notes. This encouraged maximum rapport between himself and the audience.

He spent time in front of a mirror practising gestures which were to accompany his words, as well as the modulations of voice he could use for given passages of text. By deliberate choice he dashed away at the end of meetings, rather than stay to chat, in order to encourage a sense of mystique. At times he even carried a revolver and dog whip – the latter of which he wielded during talks to emphasise points (Cross, 1973, pp. 58–9). No one had ever held party rallies like Hitler did; no one mastered an audience like him (Knopp, 1995, pp. 34–6). For all his failings, Hitler had simply the best show in town. Crowds poured in to witness it.

Hitler used techniques to encourage a sense of audience participation. There was deliberate stage management here. Sometimes his followers began chanting immediately before he began to talk. But take the next document, a police report of the meeting of 24 February 1920 at which Hitler proclaimed the basic programme of the German Workers' Party. The text combines anti-Semitism and anti-Bolshevism, but look at the way the points are made.

Document 3.6 Audience Participation

New offices are being created [by the government], but nothing is being done [to help the German workers who are experiencing hard times]. Time and again the workers are told they should go to Russia. Wouldn't it be more expedient if the eastern Jews stayed there if there is so much work? (Enthusiastic applause.) You can only wonder what the work must be like if even these are migrating. (Applause.) Get rid of those who are to blame, the Jews, then we will clean ourselves up! (Enthusiastic applause!) – Fines are no punishment for those guilty of usury and extortion. (Corporal punishment! String them up!) We will protect our fellow men in the face of this bloody crew! (String them up!) Without doubt we are good theoreticians, but not practitioners. We must learn that our existence is bound up with the entirety of the *Volk*. Our *Volk* always hopes for solidarity. (Applause!) The international workers should tell themselves this: whoever depends on someone else, he is left behind. (Storming applause!) You enjoy yourself and dance, in order to forget our suffering. It is not by chance that new pleasures are found time and again. They even want to break our nerve culturally. (Applause!)

Source: H. Phelps, 'Hitler als Parteiredner im Jahre 1920', pp. 294–5

With the speech at its climax, every expression was a unit designed to elicit a cheer. Applause became a kind of punctuation. The overall effect was of an event in which the audience participated itself. The listeners were offering solutions to identified problems – usurers and extortioners should be strung up or flogged. Speaker and audience played off each other to create a common experience and bond. The whole hall was unified.

The way to deal with hecklers was well planned beforehand. This was especially important because they could often make up a sizeable part of the crowd. The following extract involves the recollections of a former Storm Trooper. Hitler had set up the paramilitary *Sturm Abteilungen* (or SA) on 3 August 1921, not long after gaining decisive personal power in the NSDAP (Fest, 1973, p. 141). Their purpose was especially to preserve order during the party's meetings. The next document shows how in one instance in 1922 they were put to use.

Document 3.7 Scrag Him

'Well, as I was saying, we got to Tölz. It wasn't to be a big affair, only a small meeting in a little inn. Anyhow the room was full when we arrived so that things could start straight away. I took a place near where the Führer was to stand and speak. He turned round to me, and said softly, "Look out Comrade, it's pretty sultry in here. If anyone starts a racket you scrag him by the collar, and you – to my mate – shove him along behind. Get the door open, slick, and chuck him out. Only don't start unless I give you the tip."

'We didn't have long to wait. A heckler soon bobbed up. My mate and I exchanged looks but Hitler put up with the yelling and the nuisance for a bit. When the fellow showed no sign of shutting up, he at last signalled with his hand to me. In a trice we'd nabbed the chap and run him to the door. A good one on the backside sent him flying down the steps. . . . We didn't have to repeat the lesson, Hitler finished what he had to say to the good folks of Tölz without further interruption.'

Source: Heinz A. Heinz, Germany's Hitler, *1934, pp. 149–50*

This was the context in which Hitler functioned. He believed he was using the Communists' own violent tactics against themselves (Fest, 1973, p. 143). The result was the militarisation of politics. Meetings in beer halls took on all the characteristics of battlefields across which troops had to be marshalled. Women would be positioned near the front of the podium to keep hecklers away. The 'opposition' would collect beer mugs under their tables for use as 'ammunition' (Heinz, 1934, pp. 136–8). It was a world of threat and counter-threat.

The most high-profile operation for the SA came in October 1922 when Hitler and his most loyal supporters travelled to Coburg to hold a meeting. Upon arrival at the town's station, the visit developed into a military campaign. It came as close as civilian life could to recapturing the '*Fronterlebnis*' (the experience of fighting at the Front).

Document 3.8 Coburg / Koburg

There was a deputation of the big-wigs in Koburg [sic] awaiting us at the station, all very solemn and proper in frock coats and top hats. But they got the shock of their lives, I can tell you, when they saw what sort of 'accompaniment' Herr Hitler had brought along. I was close up to them, there on the platform, and heard what they said to him.

We must earnestly beg you to control your following! The city of Koburg explicitly forbids these men to march through the streets in rank and file with flags flying. It would be highly provocative of disorder.

Our Leader was a bit astonished at this and asked for explanations. What sort of trouble, then, did they expect? They said there's been a bit of a misunderstanding in the City over the organisation of the festival and its promoters had had to give a strict guarantee that nothing would be done in the least likely to provoke the Communists.

Hitler received this with undisguised scorn. What kind of 'patriotic' day did they suppose could be held if the Communists were to have it all their own way! 'Good Lord!' he said, 'aren't we in Bavaria? Haven't we the right to move about as we like?'

Whereupon he turned sharply round, much to the discomfiture of the deputation, and gave us the word to move off.

We of the 3rd Company [of the SA] marched two by two into the town on both sides of the band, and sure enough soon encountered storms of abuse from the crowds on route. Hitler led and we followed. At the fire station they were ready to turn the hoses on to us, but just didn't – at the critical moment. Stones, however, began to fly around. Then things got hotter. The Reds set upon us with iron rods and cudgels. That was going a bit too far. Hitler swung round, flourished his walking-stick (that was the signal), and we flung ourselves upon our assailants. We were unarmed save for our fists, but we put up so good a fight that within fifteen minutes not a Red was left to be seen. So we arrived finally at the place in the centre of the city where the meeting was to be held.

When it was over we formed up to betake ourselves to the Schützenhalle, a big hall on the outskirts of Koburg where we were to spend the night. On the way the former racket got up again. Hitler decided once and for all to lay this Red menace here, and gave us the word of command. We counter-attacked for all we knew. It was jolly hard work, I can tell you! They rained tiles on us from the roof and windows and tore up the cobble stones for missiles. I got a thundering blow on the head which had to be attended to before I could carry on. I only found out afterwards how serious the wound was.

We reached the Schützenhalle and dossed down, without undressing, on a thin spreading of straw. Hitler turned in amongst us, on the floor like the rest. But first he set the watches, and arranged for patrols. He came in quite the old soldier over this, anxious to provide against possible surprise.

I was detailed, with another man, for patrol work. Our watch began at 2 a.m. We cast around a bit at some distance from the hall and found ourselves creeping through a spinney in its neighbourhood. We caught a glitter – made cautiously in that direction. Detected two of the enemy with their party-masks off. One of them had a revolver in his belt, the other carried hand-grenades.

'So they'd try that dirty trick', I thought, and rage seized me at the thought of that whole barnful of sleeping men being suddenly blown sky-high into the night. At a concerted signal my comrade and I flung ourselves upon the pair, and for the next few seconds there was a beserker struggle in the underbush. We got them under, and unarmed them. We tied them up good and tight and went through their pockets. There were a few 'egg bombs' to be sequestered in the latter. Then we marched them into quarters. I could hardly stand, myself; the blood was pouring from the wound in my head, and blinding my eyes. I turned the precious pair over to Hitler and showed him the bombs.

He looked ugly at that, but made no further sign. Quietly he ordered the captives to be taken to a room at the back, beckoned to a hefty couple of our chaps, furnished them with a stout stick apiece, and signed to them to get busy within. Some time afterwards the two would-be bomb throwers were seen to leave our camp, very much sadder and very much wiser men. It is to be doubted if they'll forget the whalloping and basting they got that night to the last day of their lives.

On the Sunday morning we all took an oath of fidelity to the Cause, and then marched off to have a look at the Castle Koburg.

Source: Heinz A. Heinz, Germany's Hitler, *1934, pp. 151 ff.*

Hitler's agitation reached a crescendo in 1923. It began on 1 May. Before dawn, thousands of right-wingers gathered around Munich armed with weapons procured from the army to disrupt left-wing demonstrations (Carr, 1978, p. 17). They were stopped by the Reich authorities. By Autumn 1923 rumours were rife that Munich's nationalists were preparing a coup. Germany's political context made a dramatic step appear likely. That January the French had occupied the Ruhr in protest against a shortfall in reparations payments. Over the summer, French-backed separatist demonstrations occurred in some of the cities under French edict. Inflation became rife. There was an attempt by right-wing paramilitaries to march on Berlin (Davidson, 1977, p. 192). Left-wing regional governments had been established in Thuringia and Saxony. In October, Communists rose up in Hamburg (Flood, 1989, p. 450). Tensions existed between the national government in Berlin and the regional government in Munich. After printing scurrilous stories about the Reich Minister of Defence, von Seeckt, alleging his wife was Jewish, Berlin demanded the closure of the National Observer (*Völkischer Beobachter* – the NSDAP's paper). The Commissioner to Bavaria, von Kahr, refused to order any such step. At the same time, Hitler's followers began staging war games.

It was a chaotic time in which anything seemed possible. Hitler decided to mobilise his forces for the night of 10–11 November 1923 with the aim of marching on the government in Munich and then on to Berlin (Davidson, 1977, p. 197). When Commissioner Kahr called a meeting in the *Bürgerbräukeller* for 8 November, Hitler and his entourage feared they would be upstaged. While Kahr was in the middle of a rambling speech denouncing Marxism, Hitler and a handful of followers burst in. Jumping onto the podium, he fired a shot at the ceiling and announced that the building was surrounded by 600 heavily armed men. He said the national revolution was under way. In due course Field Marshal Ludendorff, a German hero from the First World War and the darling of the nation's radical right, turned up wearing full dress uniform in order to lend support to Hitler.

This was the logical culmination of Hitler's beer hall politics. It was also the action of a man who believed passionately in the German nation and wanted to hold it together at all costs. It was a step his audiences expected him to take.

A press release published the next day announced that the Bavarian government had been replaced (Conze, 1983, p. 41). On 9 November, Hitler and 3,000 followers gathered outside Munich's city centre ready to march and prove the reports correct. It is easy to be humorous about the failure of a putsch that saw Hitler scrambling around on a road trying to avoid shots from Bavarian militiamen. As one historian puts it, despite shooting by the police, Erich von Ludendorff marched upright straight through the cordon 'which speaks more for his courage than his reason' (Heiber, 1961, p. 64). With the weight of the Reich and the Bavarian state against them, Hitler and his cohorts never stood a chance. But too much humour is misplaced, as the following extract from the memories of *Polizeioberleutnant* Michael Freiherr von Godin makes plain.

Document 3.9 Beer Hall Putsch

On 9 November 1923 Reinforcement Station Middle 2 was mobilised at about 12.30 in the afternoon in Theatre Street . . . to defend against a troop of Hitler supporters marching from the direction of Wine Street. Reinforcement Station Middle 2 had just marched up to the line when a terrible din and screaming began in Residenz Street. At the same time, a few police officers from the direction of the Feldherrnhalle-Theatin Church waved for reinforcements for Residenz Street. With this I hurried with my troop back into Theatin Street around the Feldherrnhalle and recognised that the counter-attack by the Hitler troops, which were armed with all kinds of military equipment, had succeeded brilliantly in penetrating the positions in the Residenz Street. I arrived with the command: 'Second Station Reinforcement, march, march!' for a counter-attack against the successful breakthrough by the Hitler troops. At the breach made by the opponents, we were met with fixed bayonets, weapons with their safety catches off and drawn pistols. Individual members of my people were grabbed and pistols with the safety catches off were pointed at their chests. My people worked with rifle butts and rubber truncheons. For my defence, in order not to have to make use of my pistol prematurely, personally I had taken a carbine. I parried two bayonets pointed at me with it and knocked over those concerned with a carbine held out diagonally. Suddenly a Hitlerite, who stood one step diagonally to the left of me, loosed off a pistol shot at my head. The shot went past my head and killed an officer of my Station Reinforcement who was standing behind me. It was later established that it was junior officer Hollweg

Nikolaus. For a split second my Station Reinforcement was paralysed. Even before it was possible for me to give an order, my people shot back, which gave the appearance of a salvo. At the same time the Hitlerites began to fire and for the space of 20 to 25 seconds there was a firefight good and proper. We were showered by the Hitler troops with heavy fire from the Preysing Palace and from the Rottenhöfer Café. The Demelmeyer unit from Middle 5 took up the firefight against these opponents. At the very moment shots were loosed off by Station Reinforcement Middle 2, five men from the same group jumped up to the Feldherrnhalle and returned fire against Hitlerite guards who were firing from a kneeling position behind the lions at the chapel door of the Residenz. After a timespan of thirty seconds at most, the Hitlerites turned to disorderly flight.

Source: E. Deuerlein, Der Aufsteig der NSDAP, *1974, pp. 198–9*

Just as Hitler's supporters had been determined in facing the Reds of Coburg, on 9 November 1923 they were determined in the face of the Bavarian police. This time, however, they were hopelessly outgunned and as a result were put to flight. A Baltic German called Scheubner-Richter, marching at Hitler's shoulder, was shot dead (Taube *et al.*, 1995, p. 92). Altogether 16 Nazis and policemen lost their lives that day (Welch, 1998, p. 17). This had been a determined effort by true believers willing to risk the ultimate sacrifice in the quest for practical political power through direct action.

In due course the authorities found Hitler hiding in the attic of a well-wisher. Already imprisoned for 4 weeks in 1922 for inciting political violence, Hitler's attempted insurrection made another term a certainty. All that was left for him was to use the trial before the Bavarian court, which began on 24 February 1924, to the best effect for his movement. In the full glare of national publicity (events surrounding the beer hall putsch were reported in newspapers across Germany), Hitler played a glorious role (Asmuss, 1994, chapter 6). His final statement to the court is one of his few speeches which resonates even today. Appealing to a higher authority, capturing the moral high ground through his ringing prose, he dared the judges to question him.

Document 3.10 Court of History

The army we have created grows ever more quickly from day to day, from hour to hour. In these very days I have the proud hope that one day the time will come that these unruly crowds will grow into battalions, the battalions into regiments, the regiments into divisions; that the old cockades will be picked up out of the dirt, the old flags will be waved again, and then the reconciliation will come before God's eternal and ultimate court, before which we are prepared to appear. Then from our bones and from our graves will be heard the voice of the court that alone is called on to sit in judgement over us. For not you, my dear gentlemen, will pronounce judgement over us, it will be done by the eternal court of history which will speak out on the accusation that is levelled against us. I recognise the judgement that you [judges here] will reach. But that court will not ask us whether we have committed high treason. That court will judge us, will judge the Quarter-master General of the old army [i.e. Ludendorff], the officers and soldiers who, as Germans, wanted the best for their *Volk* and Fatherland, who wanted to fight and die. You may pronounce us guilty a thousand times over, but the goddess of the eternal court of history will, with a laugh, tear up the motion of the state prosecutor and the judgement of the court, because she acquits us.

Source: Der Hitler Prozeß vor dem Volksgericht in München, *1973, p. 91*

For his attempt to overthrow the Bavarian and Reich governments, Hitler received a sentence of five years' imprisonment (with the possibility of parole after 6 months) and a fine of RM 200. The punishment was far from harsh.

Between April and December 1924 Hitler was confined to Landsberg prison along with several other captured Nazis, including future deputy leader of the party, Rudolf Hess. Conditions were not actually so bad in this 'cross between a spa hotel and a barracks' (Heiber, 1961, p. 54). Wooden partitions were erected to give the prisoners privacy. They were allowed to mix to such an extent that Hitler dictated *Mein Kampf* while there, and received visitors freely. Party insignia were hung from the walls and other Nazis stood to attention before dinner when Hitler entered the hall and took his seat. Perhaps helped by the singularly mild rules of the institution, Hitler was regarded by the warders as a model prisoner (Fest, 1973, p. 224). Upon Hitler's release in December 1924, the prison governor said that if anyone could save Germany, it would be this man (Heinz, 1934, p. 224).

While still in prison, Hitler once commented that instead 'of working to achieve power by an armed coup' he and his fellow party members would now 'have to hold our noses and enter the Reichstag against the Catholic and Marxist deputies' – even if 'out voting them takes longer than out-shooting them' (Fest, 1973, p. 228). Hitler decided to compromise his earlier principles and began to gear up his party to participation in the electoral process. At the party conference held in Bamberg in 1926, Hitler set about reunifying a party left fragmented by his time in prison. He organised personal meetings with senior party members from around the country. At the party congress in Weimar, in July 1926, the party emerged as a 'unified, disciplined political organisation with clearly established lines of authority' (Orlow, 1969, p. 74). A whole series of reforms followed. A proper chain of command was established, subordinating local party leaders (*Kreisleiter*) to their regional superiors (*Gauleiter*), and the regional party leaders to Munich headquarters. Regional party boundaries (*Gau* boundaries) were redrawn to correspond to actual electoral boundaries. Even the party headquarters was regenerated. Under the leadership of Gregor Strasser, the *Reichsleitung* (Reich leadership) was built up as a kind of 'shadow cabinet'. It had departments dealing with German domestic politics, legal affairs, foreign affairs, economics, labour and so on. It was staffed by a team of technocrats able to produce memoranda about the sort of policies which might be pursued in a National Socialist Germany. In other words, under Hitler's renewed leadership, the party began to look a bit like a modern political machine.

As of 1928, the self-presentation of Hitler changed according to the needs of national popularity. So effective was the 'marketing' of the man and his message that Ian Kershaw has spoken of the creation of a 'Hitler Myth' (Kershaw, 1987, 1994) An image was built up which offered a benevolent kind of hope to almost everyone. From 1929 onwards, Hitler took particular pains to appeal to small-town, middle-class voters and their neuroses. Play was made on economic fears and the dangers of Communism. Hitler took steps to disassociate himself from the more radical, socialist-inclined pressure groups within his party. When, in 1929, the party congress was held in the heartland of its more left-wing (relatively speaking) followers, the Ruhr, Hitler did not attend (Orlow, 1969, p. 152). By contrast, he was happy to allow more mainstream middle-class organisations to be established in the party. In 1928 the Fighting Association for German Culture (*Kampfbund für deutsche Kultur*) was set up as a cultural-cum-intellectual organisation to pull professional people, such as school and university teachers, towards the party (Steinweis, 1991, p. 406). In the same year the Association of National Socialist German Jurists was set up with a comparable aim in mind (Jarausch, 1985, p. 391). Similar organisations were established to attract civil servants and doctors.

The new strategy was ripe for the times. In May 1928 the party received only 2.6% of the national vote in the Reichstag elections and so received only 12 seats (the figures in 1924 had been 3% and 14). But the drive to capture middle-class interest was accompanied by the Wall Street crash of October 1929. It was a time when the bourgeoisie, like everyone else, began to feel under threat (Jarausch, 1990b). As a result of Hitler's political reorientation and crisis, the Reichstag election of September 1930 saw support for the NSDAP rise to 18.3% and the number of seats to 107. A breakthrough had been achieved.

Had Hitler and his movement put their revolutionary origins behind them once and for all? Was this now a respectable leader heading a respectable party deploying respectable arguments to rally respectable voters? Actually this was only one side of a dual-track approach. Hitler had to look this way. After the failure of 1923, the strategy was a last resort rather than a first choice. In truth, Hitler despised the German bourgeois middle classes deeply and told Richard Breitlin, a journalist from the *Leipziger Neusten Nachrichten*, as much in May 1931 (Calic, 1968, pp. 22 ff.). Respectability was something only grafted onto the man and his movement. It was not the main stem of National Socialism. Munich's police department understood the true character of Hitler at an early point. Before his release from prison in 1924, it reported as follows.

Document 3.11 Permanent Danger

Numerous acts of violence committed by his followers . . . must be ascribed entirely to his influence. With his energy, he will undoubtedly be the instigator of serious fresh disturbances and constitute a permanent danger to the security of the state. The moment he is released . . . Hitler will resume his ruthless struggle against the government and will not be afraid to break the law.

Source: Quoted in C. Cross, Adolf Hitler, *1973, p. 102*

Two weeks after his release, Hitler visited Bavarian Minister President Held and persuaded him of his peaceful intent. The party had been banned in the wake of the putsch, but now Held lifted all bans on the NSDAP and on Hitler being allowed to speak in public. He waited until 27 February 1925 for his first puplic appearance (i.e. not including closed party meetings), and then decided to make it in Munich's biggest beer hall. People queued for two hours to get a seat; 3,000 gained admittance, a further 2,000 were turned away. As Hitler got into his stride he soon began to threaten violence against Jews and Marxists. He promised that either 'the enemy passes over our bodies or we pass over theirs'. He announced his hope that should he fail to win power at his next attempt, then the swastika flag could be draped across his body. He incited the crowd to violence and as a result was banned from speaking publicly in Bavaria for two years (Cross, 1973, pp. 108–9; Tyrell, 1969, p. 97). Most other German states followed suit. Bans of two years' duration came in Baden, Saxony, Hamburg and Lübeck. Bans of three years were imposed in Prussia and Anhalt (Tyrell, 1969, pp. 107–8). If Hitler stopped sounding radical in the years immediately after his release from prison, the characteristic was helped by the German authorities' doing much to ensure this was so.

What is more, Hitler's first choice for a new strategy upon release was not actually to begin to curry the support of Germany's most respectable classes. He was still playing with the possibility of direct action. As late as 1927 Hitler's commitment to the electoral process was lukewarm. He had issued no specific orders about what form participation should take. These only began to emerge in November 1927. Before this point he was considering an 'urban plan'. The aim was to develop more than twenty cities into heartlands for the movement based neither on paramilitary nor electoral strength, but rather on the establishment of successful party organisations. These were to become so strong that, should the need arise, Hitler and his followers could strangle the cities and catapult themselves to power. The urban plan implied the need to attract city workers away from Communism and Socialism, and towards National Socialism. The following leaflet was circulated around the industrial centre of Karlsruhe in May 1927. It reflects the needs of the time. National Socialist racial doctrine was applied to argue that workers should not be worried so much about 'capitalist' as 'Jewish' exploitation.

Document 3.12 Marxism is Madness

Creative Workers! Social Democrats! Communists!
    Almost seventy years of struggle and sacrifice. And what are the results?

The bank Jews stash away massive profits. The department store capitalists live the high-life without creating anything.

You slave and suffer! Why?

Because Marxism is madness. Your leaders are liars and traitors. We can show you the way to bread and freedom.

The miner and National Socialist, Comrade Kaufmann, will speak on the theme: 'The proletariat – the bodyguard of the bank-Jews'. (Members of the SPD [German Socialist Party] and KPD [German Communist Party] who produce membership cards may come into the meeting free of charge.)

Source: S. Taylor, Prelude to Genocide, *1985, p. 49*

Hitler toyed with the urban strategy until its shortcomings became all too clear. National Socialist organisation in large towns and cities was often chaotic and feud-ridden. The party found it hard to compete with the well-established Communist and Socialist organisations which proliferated there. Wholesale violence with the Reds led to bans which hindered the very purpose of the plan. As a result, Hitler allowed the urban plan to lapse.

The quintessence of Hitler's deception of respectability became manifest during the trial of the Ulm officers which took place in September 1930. The episode showed that he remained as much of a revolutionary agitator as ever. It was one of the most important political events in the life of the Weimar Republic and a 'milestone' in the development of the party (Bucher, 1967, p. 1; Broszat, 1987, p. 23). At stake was much more than the actions of the three junior army officers who were accused of treason on account of setting up National Socialist cells within the army. Eventually the three received sentences of 18 months' imprisonment. But in the midst of weighty accusations, Hitler took the stand. His testimony, made once again in the full glare of the national press, rambled across the history of his party. Its main thrust was as follows.

Document 3.13 Hitler at Ulm

a) Hitler: . . . But I may assure you: if our movement is victorious in its legal battle, then a German supreme court will come and the sins of November 1918 will be found out, and then heads will roll.

The last part of Hitler's comments was accompanied by a lively shout of 'Bravo' from the audience, which the chairman immediately reprimanded.

Chairman: I will not tolerate such talk, we are not in either a theatre or a political meeting where you can shout 'Bravo' and hiss. Rather we are in a court of law, with all earnestness to seek out justice. . . .

b) Hitler: . . . What is more, I have not created an instrument in order to implement a violent revolution. I have organised nothing to implement it. Our party is not the mouthpiece of a German revolutionary movement. The propaganda which we practise, is a mental/spiritual revolutionising of the

German *Volk*, a transformation to a new ideology, which at the very least is as gigantic as the transformation to Marxist thinking or the transformation from feudal state to a democratic–parliamentary system. The NSDAP wants a perfectly new ideas world, to construct a completely new state. It cannot occur to me for one second to fight against a state with a consolidated army and a police force. Violence is not necessary for our movement.

Source: P. Bucher, Der Reichswehrprozess, *1967, pp. 260–1, 266–7*

This was a clever performance meant to satisfy the needs of both the court and his followers. In purely formal terms Hitler emphasised time and again constitutional intent (as in document 3.13, quotation 'b'). The chairman of the court accepted the comments. He found there was no proof of genuine revolutionary purpose on Hitler's part at this time. Hitler hoped that the view appealed to the respectable middle-class individuals being drawn to the party's new organisations. But the more radical, longer-established wing of the party would have taken heart too. Clearly Hitler's commitment to legality was paper-thin (as shown in document 3.13, quotation 'a'). He was seeking to win power within the framework of the law, only to overthrow the state as it existed at the time and institute a dreadful day of reckoning against his opponents. Hitler used the Ulm trial to deride the Weimar system.

His taunting took a remarkable turn when the so-called 'Boxheim' documents were handed over to the Frankfurt police in November 1931 by a one-time National Socialist supporter who had defected from the party's ranks. Although Hitler personally was not involved in this débâcle, it emphasises further the true character of the movement. The documents had been drafted over the previous summer by National Socialist activist Werner Best and were agreed by leading figures in the Hesse division of the party in a meeting held at the 'Boxheimerhof' near Worms. The documents were written as if a Communist insurrection had been staged and it was left to the National Socialist organisation to restore order and govern the land. In other words, the documents laid down the basis for a Germany in which National Socialism came to power through force (Herbert, 1996, p. 112).

Document 3.14 Boxheim

Draft of the first announcement of our leadership after the dissolution of the prior supreme state authorities [i.e. the Weimar authorities] and after the supersession of the commune [i.e. a hypothetical Communist administration] in favour of an area suitable for a uniform administration.

Citizens!

The previous bearers of state power in the Reich and Land have been dissolved by the events of recent days (weeks). By this actual alteration – as in Nov. 1918 – a new legal condition has been created. At the moment power stands with the. . . . (SA, territorial army, or some other formation) alone. As

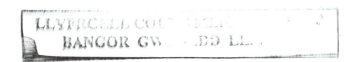

a result, our leadership has the right and the duty to seize the power of state which has been abandoned and to exercise it for the salvation of the *Volk*. It does this in the name of the German nation, before whose future alone it is responsible for the fulfilment of its tasks and for the choice of its means.

The unheard of danger demands extraordinary measures, in order in the first place to save the naked life of the *Volk*. The first task is the creation of public security and the organisation of food supplies for the *Volk*. Only the severest discipline of the population and the rigorous application of armed force allows the solution of these tasks to appear possible.

As commander of the . . . (SA, territorial army or any other force), in . . . (Starkenburg, Rheinhessen, Oberhessen) I issue the following order to the whole population of the land:

1. any order of the . . . (SA, territorial army or any other force), issued by whatever rank of member, is to be carried out immediately. Resistance will be met basically with the death penalty. Summary courts can impose other penalties by the presentation of special circumstances;
2. every gun is to be handed over to the . . . (SA, territorial army or any other force) within 24 hours. Whoever is found in possession of a gun, after the expiry of the period, will be shot on the spot as an enemy of the . . . (SA, territorial army or any other force) and of the German *Volk*;
3. every official, employee and worker in the service of public authorities or public transport organisations must resume his post at once. Resistance and sabotage will be punished with the death penalty.

    In the place of the supreme offices of state (ministries) appears the leadership of the . . . (SA, territorial army or any other force) represented by me.
4. the emergency orders issued by the leadership of the . . . (SA, territorial army or any other force) hold the force of law for everyone on the day of their publication on posters. Offences against these emergency orders will be punished above and beyond the penalties they stipulate with death in especially severe cases.
5. in so far as they are not contradicted by the emergency orders issued by the leadership of the . . . (SA, territorial army or any other force) or the individual orders of the . . . (SA, territorial army or any other force), all the other laws which exist remain in force and are to be followed by the population in every respect.

Source: Das Parlament, *3, 11 (1953) p. 2*

With a clear statement of totalitarian control for the community, and the proliferation of death penalties for offences large and small, the document was as radical as any likely be agreed by leading regional members of a party which had over 100 seats in the national parliament. An investigation by the Republic's police lasted for almost a year, but in the end no court case was brought. Once again, however, the commitment of the National Socialist movement to legality showed itself highly superficial. Hitler never held this affair against Werner Best, who later rose through the ranks of the SS to become one of Heinrich Himmler's leading acolytes.

Hitler played an agitatory role in the Potempa affair of 1932. The year marked the climax of his political struggle. There were 15 electoral campaigns across the nation. On 13 March the inconclusive first round of the presidential election saw Hitler receive 11.3 million votes and Hindenburg 18.6 million. The second round followed in April. Hitler received 13.4 million votes but Hindenburg won with 19 million. In the Reichstag elections, the party received 37.3% (230 seats) of the vote in July. It slipped back a little to 33.1% (196 seats) in November. Hitler's personal workload during this year was legendary. His use of an aircraft during June and July to take him from meeting to meeting meant his campaign became dubbed the 'Freedom Flight over Germany'. (For an additional insight regarding Hitler's energy, see Chapter 9, thesis 4.)

The party faithful were highly active too. By 20 July 1932 the year had seen 500 clashes between Nazis and left-wingers in Prussia alone; 99 were left dead and 1,125 wounded (Fest, 1973, pp. 338–9). Competing paramilitaries battled for control of the streets. President Hindenburg tried to take decisive action. On 9 August 1932 he introduced a law providing the death penalty for politically motivated manslaughter. On the night of 9–10 August, in the town of Potempa in Silesia, five drunken SA men burst into the home of a Communist, Konrad Pietzuch (who was an ethnic Pole), and kicked him to death in front of his family. The trial of the five was held later that month in Beuthen. When they were found guilty and sentenced to death, local National Socialists went on the rampage, smashing up Jewish shops (Bessel, 1977, p. 252). More remarkable, given the horrendous nature of the crime and the political sensitivity of the period, was Hitler's reaction. He sent an open telegram to the five.

Document 3.15 Monstrous

My comrades! As a result of this monstrous blood judgement [*Bluturteils*] I feel myself bound to you with unlimited loyalty. From this moment on your freedom is a question of our honour. The fight against a government under which this was possible is our duty!

Source: M. Hirsch, D. Majer and J. Meinck, Recht, Verwaltung und Justiz, 1984, p. 77

He went out of his way to publicise his support for the convicted murderers. On 29 August 1932 in Berlin Hitler addressed the National Socialist deputies in the Reichstag. He said it was incomprehensible that five National Socialists could go to the guillotine for the sake of a Polish insurgent. Whoever fought for Germany had rights, whoever fought against the country had none (Domarus, 1990, p. 161).

He published a special article in the National Observer which argued along similar lines (Hirsch et al., 1984, p. 77). Hitler could not have been clearer in his support for violent, terroristic action.

Agitatory élan was so much a part of Hitler's make-up that he carried it into the negotiations he was holding at this time with President von Hindenburg. As head of the largest party in the Reichstag, Hitler was exploring the possibility of establishing a government in association with other parties. On 21 November 1932, just weeks before he was actually made Reich Chancellor, Hitler wrote to the Reich President as follows.

Document 3.16 Waging a Fight

Dear Reich President,

From press reports and the declaration by Secretary of State Meissner I have learned of Your Excellency's intention to ask me officially to start negotiations with other parties even before the formation of a new Presidential Government. This request seems to me so important that, for the sake of Your Excellency's name and authority, no less than the urgent salvation of the German people, I feel that I must set down my views on the matter in writing.

For the past thirteen years I have been waging a fight against the parliamentary system. I consider it an obstacle to political decision-making and also the expression of the national will. Thanks to unflagging propaganda by myself and my collaborators, this conviction is now shared by millions of Germans, who have welcomed Your Excellency's decision to do justice to this new awareness and to appoint a new national leadership. But if this leadership is not to end in catastrophe then it must have a constitutional basis and become the true spokesman of the nation in a relatively short time. It must therefore have an inner, vital contact with a capable section of the German nation, and must make it its business to increase its numbers until it eventually extends to the whole nation. If this is not done, the result will be a dictatorship based on and protected by bayonets alone. It is bound to collapse for internal reasons or else during the first attack from abroad. The result can only be Bolshevism. Hence foreseeing the failure of the von Papen government after the experience of its first six weeks I said on 13 August that it was only by entrusting the National Socialist Movement with this mission that the task could be performed satisfactorily.

For reasons into which I need not enter here, Your Excellency saw fit to reject my proposal.

[Hitler goes on to say he would consider leading a government based on a Presidential Cabinet with the same authority as the previous comparable governments.]

Source: W. Maser, Hitler's Letters and Notes, *1974, p. 176*

Hitler was quite open in his demand for considerable governmental authority to create an alternative type of political system (i.e. not parliamentary democracy) which would bind together the whole of the German people. Understandably, Hindenburg was unnerved and sent a reply to Hitler refusing to hand power to him (Michalka and Niedhart, 1980, p. 340). As late as 27 January 1933 Hindenburg commented, 'You cannot for one moment, gentlemen, imagine that I intend to appoint that Austrian corporal Reich Chancellor' (Davidson, 1977, p. 357). But with the Communists having gained 96 Reichstag seats in the November elections, Hindenburg and the traditional conservatives around him were desperate men.

So did Hitler employ revolutionary means against the Weimar Republic? In terms of the definition presented in Chapter 1, the answer is unequivocal: he did. Always a skilled orator who knew how to *motivate a following*, Hitler was swift to grasp the political *initiative* and pursued *violent, illegal* action which in 1923 culminated in a direct attack on the state. As a result he was consigned to prison. Upon release, he changed to political methods which, although nominally legal and respectable, still gloried in both the threat and the application of *violence* against his enemies. Even now elements among his supporters showed evidence of sustained revolutionary zeal, both in the nature of their plans to seize political power (see document 3.14) and in their assaults on political opponents. Always *bold* and *confident*, Hitler remained locked in a remorseless and fundamental struggle with the Weimar system (as he explained unequivocally in document 3.16). It is simply remarkable that he behaved as he did and still managed to capture almost 40% of the votes cast in the free national elections of so sophisticated a country.

4 | Dictator

Document 4.1 Hitler at the Olympic Stadium, 1938

© Planet News
Source: The Wiener Library, London

Document 4.2 Hitler after the Fall of France, 1940

© Associated Press
Source: The Wiener Library, London

Did Adolf Hitler lead National Socialism as a revolutionary movement and the Third Reich as a revolutionary state? In fact, what kind of a dictator was he? The question sounds strange because his name is synonymous with dictatorship in twentieth-century Europe; but we have to beware of this very familiarity. It is easy to find impressive and compelling images drawn from the years of the Third Reich (1933–45) which show Hitler receiving the adulation of teeming crowds at vast open-air gatherings and parades (see documents 4.1 and 4.2). Hitler commanded substantial, genuine and enthusiastic support among the German people. But we must be careful not to let propaganda images overpower and limit our thinking even today. Certainly Hitler was the most powerful dictator of his day. Unrestrained by institutional rules, he led a modern industrial state in which his concept of 'order' was maintained by a thoroughly professional police force (Mommsen, 1991, p. 163; Browder, 1996, p. 11). But he did not fit the popular stereotype of the dictator. He did not operate a simple system of 'command and obey'. His style was something more flexible and could prove all the more effective for it. At a first meeting he did not necessarily strike you as the material to become an effective dictator. Here is the record of an interview with Hitler at the Brown House (party headquarters) in about 1930. The man who wrote it came to hold quite a senior post in the NSDAP.

Document 4.3 Meeting 'the Old Man'

When I was demoted [in the civil service] in Oppeln, Heinz Hüttmann (the deputy Gauleiter) explained immediately that I had to 'speak to the old man personally'. The smart businessman with the philanthropic heart had known the party for a long time and understood that this sort of thing could only be dealt with properly at the top and that any sort of reticence would only bring disappointment. And so straight away he took me by car to 'the capital city of the movement' for an introduction. The determined man pressed Hess [i.e. Rudolf Hess, Hitler's deputy] without any formalities, and argued with him, that he absolutely had to see 'the chief', and after three days he managed it.

The Brown House at that time was a pompous villa kitted out in a not unpleasant way in something approaching imperial style; but it was quite useless for the purpose it was meant to serve. It did not have the right office rooms. Hitler's work room was on the first floor, in the corner. The entrance led through a little room in which Hess worked. I don't know if this word 'worked' is actually suitable here. The first impression which I . . . had was of boundless disorder. Letters, newspapers, magazines, everything lay strewn around the room. . . .

Hitler stood up behind his writing desk when we entered his work room. At that time he wore a blue suit which looked as though a bad tailor had made it. The room was clean and tidy, but looked like a cold and bare hotel room, that is to say without soul. You saw at once that no work was ever done in this work room. On the left, a bronze bust of Mussolini stood on a pedestal.

He greeted me with a normal handshake. Only later did he appropriate the well-known pose of looking the person he was greeting sharply in the eye and holding his hand for half a minute. We sat down opposite Hitler and 'Huli', as was his nickname, laid out what he wanted. 'Herr Hitler' – at the time he was generally addressed in this way, because only the SA said 'My Führer' as a 'military' style of speaking – might like to speak in Upper Silesia one time. Hitler declined, since the large rooms which he needed were lacking. In the course of a few minutes, Hitler became heated at the sound of his own words and sprang up. Naturally I got up too, only Huli stayed sitting in all calm. 'Don't you see', he said later, 'you've got to let the old man rage about in peace, since you're not allowed to lose your cool at all. That's all there is to it. Afterwards he calms down again.' This tough Westphalian presumably had the only correct diplomacy in dealing with people. My case was presented by him, I said I only wanted to see what I could do to help in Munich. Hitler nodded and then we were dismissed.

A great deal was said about Hitler's big blue, impressive eyes with which he saw right to the heart of things. There was already a section of the groupies who were hypnotised by him and could not do enough to praise the incredibly great personal impact which Hitler made on people. I never had a similar impression.

At once I noticed that Hitler was notable in the Brown House by his absence. He ignored his colleagues and advisers completely and let them do whatever they wanted. He was only there to talk by chance about anything substantial, and only then about what interested him or about what he wanted to discuss. Already he had a special circle around him which was in no way identical with the office holders in the party.

Source: H. Nicolai, Mein Kampf ums Recht. *Manuscript in the Institute for Contemporary History, Munich*

The bad suit, the indifferent handshake, no sign of work going on, the nonsensical storming around the room, the lack of interest in the formal structure of the organisation – these were not the obvious characteristics of successful dictatorial leadership. Even when he had become Reich Chancellor, Hitler still created odd, ambiguous impressions. His methods could be so inexact that followers were left unclear about what he expected. Orders could be obtained in the most bizarre ways. Sometimes people just noted down chance comments. On one occasion Hitler was driving through Munich when he saw an unsightly pile of rubble in front of St Matthew's Church. He told his escort that he wanted 'that heap of stones' removed. He was misunderstood, and the church was demolished at once (Heiber, 1961, p. 113)!

If Hitler did not always possess the obvious attributes of a dictator, how did he come to be one? Most biographies gloss over questions like this (Eitner, 1994, p. 52). At an early age, he may well have led groups of neighbourhood tearaways in games of 'cowboys and indians', but Hitler was not a born leader. During the First

World War, he rose no higher than the rank of corporal. He did not possess a leadership drive pushing him ever onwards towards power for its own sake (Tyrell, 1975, p. 11). Just as his entry to politics grew out of a process rather than a single decision, so did his assumption of the role of dictator. What is more, it was a process he did not control entirely himself.

Understanding Hitler's transition to becoming a political leader is complicated by at least two points. On the one hand, a leader can only lead, if his followers agree to this. When in July 1921 Hitler assumed dictatorial control of the NSDAP, it was with the agreement of a special party congress which sanctioned the move by 553 votes to 1 (Orlow, 1969, p. 30). What is more, the idea of running the party according to a well-developed 'leadership principle' did not really originate with Hitler. It marked the conclusion of a process agreed by the party as a whole. This began when the Bamberg congress confirmed Hitler's political pre-eminence in 1926 and was underscored at the party meeting held in Nuremberg in 1929 (Kershaw, 1998, p. 278). In this light, Hitler's role of dictator owed as much to the expectations of his followers as to his own ambitions (Tyrell, 1969, p. 216). On the other hand, Hitler underwent a learning process about how to exercise political power. Once again referring to events of Summer 1921, Hitler had long been wrangling with the party's old leaders over the possibility of merging the NSDAP with other radical right-wing organisations in Bavaria (Kershaw, 1998, p. 163). His initial response to confrontation was to bring in new members, loyal to himself, to improve his position in the movement. A crunch came that July, when Hitler actually left the party. He agreed to return only when plans for amalgamation were shelved and he was promised increased organisational efficiency. The party faithful gave him a massive vote of confidence and made him head of a new, slim-lined action committee (Orlow, 1969, pp. 29–30). In other words, Hitler took an important step towards becoming a dictator within the NSDAP not because he always wanted the role in itself, but because he, like the party congress, saw it as the best way to respond to the most pressing problems of the day facing the party. Hitler stumbled along the path to becoming a dictator as he tried to get his own way; he did not have a concerted career plan determining this route. What is more, Hitler learned from his experiences. The acquisition of power was clearly a good way of responding to dangerous and complicated political situations (Zitelmann, 1993, p. 117). He was getting the idea that dictatorship could be an effective political strategy.

When did Hitler begin to think of himself as a dictator not just for his party, but for the entire German nation? As early as March 1920, Countess Marie Gabrielle d'Allemont described him as 'a man appointed by God', 'the Messiah' (Eitner, 1994, pp. 52–3). But this date is far too early. At the start of his political career Hitler referred to himself as a 'drummer' preparing the way for a greater man to follow. In May 1921 he said he was not the future leader of Germany, only a man working on his behalf (*Deutsche Zeitung*, 10 November 1923, evening edition). Speaking in Bamberg in October 1923, he called on God to send someone to save Germany. On the evening of the beer hall putsch, he nominated General von Ludendorff as national leader, an opinion he repeated during the subsequent trial. He told the court that he himself should be in charge of just national propaganda (Eitner, 1994, p. 54). Only while in prison after the putsch did he 'cross the river Jordan' and begin to think of himself as a national leader. Between February and December 1924, as he worked on *Mein Kampf*, he came to understand his own fate as inextricably bound up with that of Germany. He saw himself less as a 'John the Baptist' prophesying the political saviour, than that saviour himself (Eitner, 1994, pp. 52, 56 and 57).

So only a good four or five years into his career, did Hitler begin to think of himself as having the potential to become a top-rank national political figure. Even well after this point, he still gave out contradictory signals. As late as 1929–30 there was barely a leadership cult around Germany's future Führer (Eitner, 1994, p. 52). During the final years of the Weimar Republic Hitler even said, 'I am not the Messiah. He will come after me' (Turner, 1985b, p. 172). It was not until he was on the very verge of national power, in 1932, that once and for all he finally stopped thinking of himself as a 'drummer' for someone else (Zitelmann, 1993, p. 120). Hitler's passage to considering himself a national figurehead was only very gradual indeed.

It was as if Hitler was a reluctant, almost an accidental, leader. Some characterisations of his management style fit well with the idea. He has been called a 'weak dictator', that is to say someone whose scope for decision-making was critically limited by the confines of both the organisations and personalities surrounding him (see Kershaw, 1993, chapter 4). This is how Hermann Rauschning, who attended meetings with Hitler several times, saw things.

Document 4.4 No Dictator

Hitler was no dictator. Nor was he merely carried like a cork to the surface. He always marched with the big battalions. Over and over again in conversation he declared that we must always choose the weaker for opponent and the stronger for ally. It might sound a commonplace, he would say, but it was the essential rule for all political activity. One thing, especially, Hitler never did – he never ran counter to the opinion of his *Gauleiter* [regional party bosses], his district commissioners. Each one of these men was in his power, but together they held him in theirs; and accordingly, whenever differences arose, he so steered his course as to carry the overwhelming majority of them with him. The secret of his leadership lay in knowing in advance what course the majority of his *Gauleiter* would decide on, and in being the first to declare for that course. Thus he was always in the right, and the opposition was put in the wrong. These *Gauleiter* watched jealously over their prerogatives, they admitted no new members into their ranks. They resisted with robust unanimity every attempt to set limits to their rights of sovereignty. Hitler was at all times dependent on them – and not on them alone.

He was no dictator. He allowed himself to be guided by the forces at his back, often against his better judgement. It was the sum of these forces that at all times kept him to the fore. But the result was that his policy continually developed along wholly different lines to those which he had envisaged. He maintained his position of supremacy, but he had lost his freedom of decision.

Source: H. Rauschning, Hitler Speaks, *1939, pp. 214–15*

The document reminds us that even Hitler was aware of practical pressures when he made political decisions. But is this chapter giving us an adequate image of the man in his political milieu? For all the confusion over decision-making, despite the lengthy route he took to becoming a political Messiah, and notwithstanding possible limits on his scope for action, what else was there to Adolf Hitler?

Hitler had an astute and cynical understanding of how organisations can work. During the Weimar period, he once explained how he 'chose' people for different party offices.

Document 4.5 Associates

I have my own way of choosing my associates. I do not like to appoint someone to a position simply because I want him there or because I think he is suited to it. Rather, I give him a chance to busy himself in the general area. If he succeeds, I see that for myself and I hear about it from others. Then he will automatically like the position he is called upon to fill. If he is not successful, someone else – someone who is more productive – will run rings around him just as automatically.

Source: H.A. Turner (ed.), Hitler – Memoirs of a Confidant, *1985, pp. 4–5*

As Hitler also put it, people 'must be allowed friction with one another; friction produces warmth, and warmth is energy' (Fest, 1973, p. 420). Individuals were deliberately placed in positions of conflict and allowed to fight over a given policy area. The one who won would be the best man for the job. The notion corresponded well to his racialist way of thinking in which the 'fittest', best-adapted individual prevailed over all others.

It is not hard to find examples of Hitler's Machiavellian tactics. In 1929 Otto Wagener, an economist working in the Brown House, spoke to Pfeffer von Salomon about his attempt to create a nationwide organisation of Storm Troopers. Local party chiefs did not like the invasion of their power this implied. Why was the initiative being pursued, and what on earth did Hitler think he could gain from it?

Document 4.6 The Use of Pfeffer von Salomon

'If each Gau [party region] had its own deputy, there's no doubt that over a period of time the Gauleiter [regional party boss] would swallow him, or the

Gauleiter would keep digging away at him, until he was assigned the deputy most to his liking. As things are, three or four Gauleiter are at each others' throats because of my deputies. And since Gauleiter can never agree, I always claim the upper hand.'

'I'm moving to get the impression', I interrupted, 'that you are engaged in a permanent feud with the Gauleiter. Isn't that impractical?'

'It's not very practical. But there's no help for it. Look – every one of the Gauleiter is a little Hitler. Some really are, some just think they are.

'After all, the movement did not originate in Munich solely and alone. There was someone in the Ruhr district who gathered honourable men around him; another established an organisation in Baden while Hitler was still confined to his fortress prison; a rump party remained in existence in Munich after 1923; and so on.

'But Hitler was the magnet, unequivocally the strongest among all little Nicolais [i.e. petty dictators]. And just as, when the Christian Church began, the Bishop of Rome was readily recognised by the others as foremost – the papa, the pope – so Adolf Hitler gradually became recognised as the head of the movement. Nevertheless, each Gauleiter had his personal pride and his own sense of direction.

'That left the SA [Storm Troops] as the sole unifying force. They don't like it, it's true, because at the outset each had his own SA. But Hitler understood that the final dependence of the Gauleiter on him could be achieved only by creating an SA with a central command. Hitler never speaks about this part of it, because actually he cheated the Gauleiter. Using the justification, with which you are familiar, of the necessity of a unified command – in itself perfectly right and valid – he took the SA from the grasp of the Gauleiter, simultaneously subordinating the Gauleiter to himself. A federation turned into a centralised organisation. In time we may get to the point where Hitler can even dismiss a Gauleiter if he doesn't suit him. That was not possible before the SA was combined into one unit under a centralised region. I'm the guinea pig chosen to perform the thankless task. And it is your job to bolster and secure my work by creating the staff of the SA supreme command. That is why you, too, are to some degree vulnerable to the hostility of the Gauleiter.' . . .

'You are coming to learn one of Hitler's special tactics, which you may interpret for yourself. He wishes to bring the Gauleiter to heel. He has no choice. The movement can be strong only if it is tightly unified. But what he wants – and he's absolutely right – is not to burden himself and his relationship with these Gauleiter with the means necessary to the end. And so, as I said, he uses the SA. He gives the Gauleiter free rein to assault me, so that the struggle that should be played out between him and the Gauleiter takes place between them and me. I think it quite possible that he carries this somewhat devious game to the point where he even gives some encouragement to one or other Gauleiter, making me seem more and more of a scapegoat. And one day – I'll take an oath on it, Wagener – he'll drop me with the greatest aplomb, sacrificing me to the fury of that mob, after which he can confront the Gauleiter as the great man of justice while they, following this sacrifice, willingly bow to the yoke of his leadership, which has been secured.'

'Pfeffer', I exclaimed, are you serious or are you joking?'

'I'm very serious. That's politics – a sour tune. But you have to look at the whole picture. The various little groups had to be unified. The party needs firm leadership. And this is what Hitler has achieved.'

Source: H.A. Turner (ed.), Hitler – Memoirs of a Confidant, *1985, pp. 10–11*

At a later date Otto Wagener found himself discussing Pfeffer von Salomon with Hitler. The latter admitted the SA chief was soon to be sacrificed on some pretext or other, and that he personally planned to take over the leadership of the SA intact (Turner, 1985b, p. 29). It has been said that Hitler never manipulated deliberately the rivalries which developed under his command (Mommsen, 1991, p. 171). This evidence shows quite a different picture. Hitler had both the skill and inclination to be a puppet master. He learned to control the way subordinate organisations worked and took the most draconian decisions when circumstances dictated. It may be correct that he was in search of 'a kind of political servo-mechanism, which would protect him' (Lewin, 1984, p. 60). That is to say, with everyone's energies dissipated in mutual strife, no one was able to place Hitler's primacy under threat. But clearly the structural chaos allowed Hitler to enter the arena, make a popular sacrifice, and retire with an enhanced reputation, not to mention an improved degree of control over his organisation. As a way of doing business, it had much to commend it.

Hitler could manipulate organisations; he could manipulate individuals too. The following example is drawn from the war years and is related by one of Hitler's secretaries.

Document 4.7 Forster's Change of Mind

He [Forster – a Nazi leader from eastern Germany whose land was being threatened by the Russian advance] told me that 1,100 Russian tanks were standing before Danzig, which the Wehrmacht opposed with just 4 Tiger tanks, and what is more that not one of those had the necessary fuel. Forster had decided not to hold back on his view and to lay the whole terrible reality of the situation before Hitler.

Aware of the position, I pressed Forster really to tell the whole truth and to make Hitler come to a clear decision. Forster answered me: 'Of that you can be sure, I will tell him everything, even the danger that he has put me in.'

How great was my surprise when, after his conversation with Hitler, he returned completely changed. 'The Führer has promised me new divisions for Danzig', he said.

To my sceptical laugh he said, 'Admittedly I don't know where he will get them. But he has explained to me that he will save Danzig and that there is no doubt about it.'

I was truly disappointed by Forster's words. This man, who I had heard proclaiming in my office so aggressively only shortly beforehand that he would tell Hitler the truth, believed in the empty words with which he had let himself be fobbed off. Without doubt it was Hitler's disastrous power of suggestion which had been at work on him.

I could relate innumerable examples of thoroughly rational and reasonable people who let themselves literally be duped by Hitler.

Source: A. Zoller, Hitler Privat, *1949, pp. 30–1*

An example of how exactly Hitler got people on his side may be shown in a section of memoirs written by Leni Riefenstahl who became a major film-maker in the Third Reich. The only difficulty in using her evidence is that it has to be assumed accurate and not a distortion of reality which is attempting to show her relationship to National Socialism in as favourable a light as possible. We have to be prepared to believe she participated in Hitler's Germany with reluctance rather than enthusiasm. This film-maker visited Hitler at the Reich Chancellery in August 1933. She says she entered the room determined not to undertake any project on behalf of National Socialism. But the meeting went as follows.

Document 4.8 Persuading Leni Riefenstahl

'I invited you here today in order to find out how far you've got with your preparations for the film on the Party rally, and whether you're getting enough support from the Ministry of Propaganda.'

I stared at him [Hitler] in amazement – what was he talking about? Surprised at my reaction, he said: 'Didn't the Propaganda Ministry inform you that I want you to make a film about the Party rally in Nuremberg?'

I shook my head and Hitler was clearly perplexed. 'You know nothing about it?' he asked angrily. 'Why, that's impossible. Brückner transmitted my request to Dr Goebbels weeks ago. Haven't you been notified?' Once again I had to say no and Hitler grew even more upset. He summoned Brückner and angrily asked him, 'Didn't you pass my request on to the doctor? Why wasn't Fräulein Riefenstahl informed?' As he spoke he clenched his fists, glaring with anger. Before his terrified aide could reply, Hitler jeered, 'I can imagine how the gentlemen at the Propaganda Ministry must envy this gifted young artist. They can't stand the fact that such an honour has been awarded to a woman – and, indeed, an artist who isn't even a member of the party.' Neither Brückner nor I dared to respond. 'It's outrageous of them to boycott my request', Hitler ranted. He snapped at Brückner to telephone Dr Goebbels and tell him to order the people in his cinema department to support me and my work in Nuremberg in every possible way.

I myself was by now very agitated, and I interrupted Hitler. 'My Führer, I cannot accept this – I have never seen a Party rally, I know nothing about what goes on there, and I have no experience in making documentaries. It would be better if such films were made by Party members who know the material and are happy to be given such assignments.' I talked to Hitler almost beseechingly, and slowly he relaxed and calmed down.

Looking at me, he said, 'Fräulein Riefenstahl, don't let me down. You would only have to take a few days off. I am convinced that you alone have the artistic ability to turn real-life events into more than ordinary newsreel footage – certainly the officials at the cinema department of the Propaganda Ministry do not.' I stood before him, eyes lowered, as he went on urging me more and more insistently. 'The party rally will begin in three days. Naturally you won't be able to make a really great film this year. But you can go to Nuremberg in order to gain some experience and try to film whatever can be filmed without preparations.' He took a few steps, then resumed. 'My wishes were probably never communicated to the doctor. I will personally ask him to support you.'

My God, I thought, if Hitler knew how impossible any collaboration would be between Goebbels and myself. But I had no desire to tell him about his Minister's escapades. Besides, I felt less and less able to contradict him. I simply lacked the courage. As Hitler took leave of me, his last words were: 'Hold your head up high, everything will work out. You will receive further information before the day is over.' Hitler had not understood how unhappy this project would make me. My most passionate desire was to work as an actress.

Source: L. Riefenstahl, The Sieve of Time, *1992, pp. 143–4*

The example, if honest, implies Hitler was well able to manipulate people into just the position he wanted. He was well able to persuade people according to his desires and to get what he wanted out of them.

Hitler was effective at dealing with the currents and tensions which proliferated among his subordinates and throughout the organisations they staffed. There was plenty of substance to his techniques of dictatorship and he cannot be written off as a 'weak dictator'. Moving through arcane and contrived means, he was certainly chaotic, but nonetheless could provide an effective mastery of the political forces around him. Most important of all, he succeeded in establishing an organisational system populated by dedicated workers, none of whom (with the exception of Ernst Röhm – see below) would contemplate seriously acting against his wishes (Knopp, 1998, p. 7).

Hitler became Reich Chancellor of Germany on a bitterly cold 30 January 1933. The event was marked by the high drama of impressive torch-lit processions in the national capital that very evening (Maschmann, 1964, pp. 10–12; Housden, 1997, pp. 70–1). These events need to be kept in their proper perspective. Reich President Hindenburg and those around him were highly suspicious of Hitler's movement and so that day the NSDAP received only three Reich cabinet offices: Hitler became Chancellor, Wilhelm Frick Interior Minister and Hermann Göring Minister without Porfolio. All the other Reich posts, including the Ministries of Foreign Affairs, Defence, Justice, Agriculture, Labour, Economics and Finance, remained in the hands of traditional conservative political figures. It was planned by the established élites surrounding the President that true power in the government would not reside with Hitler, but with the Deputy Chancellor, Franz von Papen, who really held the confidence of von Hindenburg (Michalka, 1996, p. 11). It was hoped that the whole mass of traditional conservatism would neutralise Hitler. Any remaining signs of radicalism on Hitler's part would (it was also hoped) be squashed under the weight of new responsibilities and the requirements of office. This is why von Papen commented to the Reich President of Hitler, when the negotiations establishing the government were completed, 'We've hired him!'

The foreign press in Germany did not regard the new cabinet as a revolutionary break with the past (Craig, 1981, p. 240). These journalists were not so surprised by the collapse of the previous government under General von Schleicher. After all, in its 13 years of life, the Weimar Republic had seen 20 governments come and go. The country had been ruled since March 1930 by a series of presidential cabinets (under Reich Chancellors Brüning, von Papen and lastly von Schleicher) which lacked widespread parliamentary approval. Why should this change have been any more important than any of the others (Knopp, 1995, p. 173)? When the Socialist Hubertus von Löwenstein asked on this day, 'Comrades, have you understood that the Second World War has begun today?', he was ahead of his time (Knopp, 1995, p. 175).

Still, something was happening. Hitler may not have toppled the German establishment in one go, but this was predictable. Fundamentally modern, industrial states, such as that which existed in Germany in the 1930s, provide a whole array of functions (from administration to transport, from welfare to law and order) needed by the population in general. Given at least a minimal degree of competence on its part, and notwithstanding even the degree of crisis faced in Germany in the wake of the Wall Street crash, it is hard to see a decisive popular momentum developing for the state's complete, radical overthrow. In modern states, revolutions are most likely to proceed through collusion with the established élites (Löwenthal, 1981, pp. 256–7). In this connection, when Hitler's traditional conservative partners in government became allied with him, they knew they were taking a dreadful risk (see also p. 65). The day after Hitler became Chancellor, cabinet member Alfred Hugenberg was reputed to have said, 'I've just committed the greatest stupidity of my life; I have allied myself with the greatest demagogue in world history' (Jones, 1992, p. 63). Over the next few months, Hitler managed gradually to exclude traditional conservatives like Hugenberg from the corridors of power (Jones, 1992, p. 78). He had no intention of allowing these people to regain the ascendancy (Welch, 1998, p. 35). Viewed properly, 30 January 1933 was a decisive first step taken by Hitler in gaining control of the nation. In due course it was supplemented by a whole series of further initiatives.

Mid-morning on the day of the seizure of power, Hitler left the Kaiserhof Hotel for talks with the Reich President in the Reich Chancellery. He returned two hours later with tears in his eyes. Goebbels recorded in his diary: 'It is almost like a dream. We are all speechless with emotion' (Knopp, 1995, p. 174). A tremendously exciting experiment was starting across the nation. As one committed Nazi put it: 'It was an incredibly creative and exciting period. . . . People of my age (i.e. relatively young) were given unprecedented opportunities, and we came to feel there was nothing we couldn't achieve' (Sereny, 1995, p. 182). Albert Speer became Hitler's architect, and during the war he was appointed Reich Minister for Armaments. He considered himself an unemotional man, but still he believed that in the Third Reich there developed an irresistible atmosphere which was hard to avoid (Sereny, 1995, p. 116). A person was simply sucked into a vortex of enthusiasm which swirled around Hitler's regime. He was fired with loyalty for the new government. The following extract was written in the private diary of Hans Frank in 1937, by which time he was Reich Minister without Portfolio. He records the highly emotional impact a trip to a musical concert had on him when the Führer was present.

Document 4.9 Festival Concert

This evening I was with Lasch at the great festival concert in support of the German *Volk*'s Winter Aid Project to hear Furtwängler conduct the Freischutz Overtures. These sounds caused the years of my own existence to pass me by in unspeakable emotion – this magical web of my fate strung together from point to point. . . . And with the arousing sounds I trembled before youth, might, hope, thankfulness. The Führer sat there in the box with his most loyal followers, the soldier and the speaker – with Göring and Goebbels. Whatever other celebrities in Berlin were there too. Sparkling and in a mood to celebrate, the leadership of the Reich was present. The representatives of all lands, the bearers of names which the whole world knows. And I was amongst them as a Minister of the Reich – the youngest – the music bore me up. Eternal Germany: now you are alive again. Wonderful Reich: now you are saved. Undying *Volk*: now may you remain happy! The Führer was beaming all over his face. And I was silent . . . and lost in a dream: that he became us. . . . Oh God: how fortunate you have made us, to allow this unique man, the greatest in world history, to be called ours! Generations will come and envy us to have been your contemporaries. And what's more I was allowed to do my part for this man, I may call myself a colleague.

Source: N. Frank, Der Vater, *1993, pp. 42–3*

It was an exciting time to be in politics and later the same night Frank confided to his diary, 'I belong to the Führer and his wonderful movement'. In more sinister fashion he added, we 'are in truth God's tool for the annihilation of the bad powers of the earth. We struggle in God's name against the Jews and their Bolshevism. God protect us!' (in Frank, 1993, pp. 43–4).

So what was the first project of Hitler's dictatorship? Many of his early actions were designed to remove Socialism from society. (Cross-reference the aim with document 2.10.) For example, he took over May Day, the traditional left-wing holiday. This was done by passing a law on 10 April 1933 which defined 1 May as a 'holiday of national labour' (*Reichsgesetzblatt*, 1933, p. 191). Celebrations became propaganda for the NSDAP. The following extract is drawn from the memoirs of the French Ambassador to Berlin. It describes a major May Day gathering at the Tempelhof Field.

Document 4.10 May Day

At dusk the streets of Berlin were packed with wide columns of men headed for the rally, marching behind banners, with fife and drum units and regimental bands in attendance.

Stands had been set up at one end of the field for the guests of the government, among them the diplomatic corps, compulsory spectators, bidden to be awed into respect and admiration. A forest of glittering banners provided a background for the spectacle: a grandstand, bristling with microphones, cut forward like a prow looming over a sea of human heads. Downstage, Reichswehr units stood at attention with one million civilians assembled behind them; the policing of this stupendous rally was effected by SA and SS troopers. The Nazi leaders appeared in turn as the crowd cheered. Then came Bavarian peasants, miners and fishermen from other parts of Germany, all in professional garb, then delegates from Austria and the Saar and Danzig, the last being guests of honour of the Reich. An atmosphere of good humor and general glee pervaded the assembly, there was never the slightest indication of constraint. . . .

At eight o'clock the crowds backed up as Hitler made his appearance, standing in his car, his arm outstretched, his face stern and drawn. A protracted clamor of powerful acclaim greeted his passage. Night was now fallen; floodlights were turned on, set at spacious gaps, their gentle bluish light allowing for dark interjacent spaces. The perspective of this human sea stretched out to infinity, moving and palpitant, extraordinary when at once sighted in the light and divined in the darkness.

After some introductory remarks by Goebbels, Hitler took the stand. All floodlights were turned off save such as might envelop the Führer in so dazzling a nimbus that he seemed to be looming upon that magical prow over the human tide below. The crowd lapsed into a religious silence as Hitler prepared to speak.

Source: A. François-Poncet, The Fateful Years, *1949, pp. 67f.*

The aim of this pageant at worst was to portray Hitler as an immovable force that could not be resisted; at best it was to persuade established left-wingers he deserved their support. National Socialist labour leader Robert Ley attempted the same ends rather differently when he spoke to a crowd of workers on 2 May 1933.

Document 4.11 Your Friend

Already after three months of National Socialist government it has been proved to you: Adolf Hitler is your friend! Adolf Hitler is struggling for your freedom! Adolf Hitler gives you bread! Today we are entering into the second phase of the National Socialist revolution. You will say, what else do you want, after all you have absolute power. Certainly we have power, but we do not have the whole *Volk*. You, workers, we do not have you 100%. . . . You should be freed from the last Marxist chains so that you will find your way to your *Volk*.

For we know: there is no German *Volk* without the German worker. And above all we must prevent your enemy, Marxism, and its satellites being able to fall on your backs again.

Source: Lauber and Rothstein, Der 1.Mai, 1983, pp. 70–1

Events were not solely peaceful. The day after May Day, armed SA men took over and closed down by force trades union headquarters around the country. This was just the tip of an iceberg. The year 1933 saw a profound National Socialist assault on Marxism (Knopp, 1995, p. 176).

Once he was Reich Chancellor, Hitler did little to mislead about his intentions in this respect. When he spoke in secret to the commanders of the armed forces as early as 3 February 1933, he emphasised the need to eradicate Marxism 'root and branch'. He vilified the Left in public too, as the following extracts show.

Document 4.12 Public Anti-Socialism/Anti-Marxism/Anti-Bolshevism

a) Hitler at the Sportpalast, 10 February 1933
'Marxism means the tearing in pieces of the nation, and thus the weakening of the whole people. Marxism means the reduction to misery of this people and is thus treachery to the very class which it regards as its support and to which it promises a better future. And just as treachery to the working classes is the result of Bolshevism, similarly Marxism means treachery to the German peasants and to the masses in their millions of equally poverty-stricken members of the bourgeoisie and the craftsmen.

'Marxism is . . . an attack on the foundations of our community-life and thus an attack upon the bases of our life as a whole.'

b) Hitler at the Congress of the German Labour Front on 10 May 1933
'I regard it as my task before posterity to destroy Marxism, and that is not an empty phrase but a solemn oath which I shall perform as long as I live. . . . This is for us no fight which can be finished by compromise. We see in

Marxism the enemy of the people which we shall root out and destroy without mercy.'

Source: N.H. Baynes (ed.), The Speeches of Adolf Hitler, Vol. 1, 1942, pp. 665–8

This anti-Socialism was quite genuine on Hitler's part. One of his secretaries relates the way he used to plan out his speeches.

Document 4.13 Speech Writing

At first he dictated in a quiet voice. When, however, his thoughts began to flow, then the rhythm of the sentences began to flow one after the other in rapid succession. Then without a pause one sentence rushed after the other, with emphasis given by his steps alone [he was pacing about] which became quicker all of the time. The tempo was uneven and his voice rose and fell. Hitler dictated his speeches exactly as he gave them in front of his audience, with the same passionate outbreaks of temper. Now and again he swallowed down Cola-Dallmann tablets.

Hitler really did experience his speeches. If he wanted to give his passion free rein, then he stopped walking about and fixed his view at an unreal point on the floor, as if he received a special kind of solace from there. As soon as he came to speak about Bolshevism, his voice cracked, and a hefty rush of blood made his face go red. Then he declaimed with such violence that his voice could be heard in the most distant rooms and through double doors. After such times I was always asked by employees outside why the chief had been in such a bad temper.

Source: A. Zoller, Hitler Privat, 1949, p. 17

Hitler prepared well the application of the full weight of the state against Germany's Socialists and Communists. On 22 February 1933 Göring appointed 50,000 SA and SS men auxiliary police. Then, on the night of 27 February, a deranged Dutch Communist called van der Lubbe was caught trying to burn down the Reichstag. The government took this as evidence of a decisive Communist threat. During the night, Göring ordered the arrest of Communist officials, banned the Communist press and issued a 14-day ban on Socialist publications (Broszat, 1981, p. 71). The very next day, Hitler issued the famous 'Reichstag Fire Decree' (Ordinance for the Protection of *Volk* and State). Using emergency article 48 of the Weimar constitution, he suspended the personal liberties of the German population (*Reichsgesetzblatt*, 1933, p. 141). The detention of left-wingers began. In a mood of intimidation, on 5 March 1933 Germany held her last national election for twelve years. The US Ambassador in Berlin called the event 'a farce' and Hitler's party received 43.9% of the vote (Knopp, 1995, p. 186). Anti-left-wing actions continued. The longer they ran, the more the 'political' troops of the SA and SS were merged with the established professional police. By 15 March 1933, 7,784

Communists had been arrested in Prussia alone (Broszat, 1981, p. 72). By the end of April, the figure was 25,000 (Broszat, 1981, p. 79).

The newly elected parliament met in the Kroll opera house on 23 March 1933. The Communist deputies were terrorised into non-appearance. All other parties, except the German Socialist Party, by this time were prepared to support the government. Hitler could now muster the two-thirds majority required to alter the German constitution. This he did by passing the Enabling Act (Law for the Rectification of Crisis in the *Volk* and Reich). With this statute, parliament was no longer required to agree the measures which were to become legislation. In effect, Hitler could dispense law whenever and however he wanted. It was hardly a surprise when he simply decreed the dissolution of the German Socialist Party on 22 June 1933. The other political parties dissolved themselves in June and July of the same year. The supremacy of the NSDAP was confirmed on 14 July when Hitler decreed that no other political parties could be established. Stage by stage 'the political institutions and processes of liberal democracy were obliterated' (Neocleous, 1997, p. 56). As if endorsing the changes, people flocked to Hitler's party. NSDAP membership increased from 850,000 in January to 2.5 million in May 1933.

By Autumn 1933 Hitler faced no organised political opposition. His word quite literally was law. The death of President von Hindenburg in August 1934 strengthened his position further. He unified in his own person the posts of Reich Chancellor and Reich President. Now he truly was the Führer, with hardly a countervailing power to hold him in check. On 'the surface, Hitler's supremacy appeared absolute' (Mommsen, 1991, p. 178).

When significant opposition began to threaten, ironically it came from within Hitler's own movement. The SA (Storm Troops – *Sturm Abteilungen*) were renowned as the home of social–radical Nazis. These men wanted a particularly rapid and far-reaching restructuring of society and its wealth. They had dedicated themselves for years to fight on behalf of the movement, but felt forgotten once National Socialism took power. Choice jobs in the administration of the state, when they were distributed at all, tended to go to relatively new adherents to the party who often came from professional backgrounds. Dissatisfaction led the head of the SA, Captain Ernst Röhm, a long-standing friend of Hitler, to denounce the government in a newspaper article written in June 1933 (Michalka, 1996, pp. 40–2). Towards the start of 1934, especially unhappy about the lack of reform in the ranks of the German army, he became more outspoken still.

Document 4.14 Anti-Hitler

'Adolf is a swine', he swore. 'He will give us all away. He only associates with reactionaries now. His old friends aren't good enough for him. Getting matey with the East Prussian generals. They're his cronies now.'

He was jealous and hurt.

'Adolf is turning into a gentleman. He's got himself a tail-coat now!' he mocked.

He drank a glass of water and grew calmer.

'Adolf knows exactly what I want. I've told him often enough. Not a second edition of the old imperial army. Are we revolutionaries or aren't we? Allons, enfants de la patrie! If we are, then something new must arise out of our élan, like the mass armies of the French Revolution. If we're not, then we'll go to the dogs. We've got to produce something new, don't you see? A new discipline. A new principle of organization. The generals are a lot of old fogeys. They never had a new idea.'

'Adolf has learnt from me. Everything he knows about military matters, I've taught him. War is something more than armed clashes. You won't make a revolutionary army out of the old Prussia NCOs. But Adolf is and remains a civilian, an "artist", an idler. "Don't bother me", that's all he thinks. What he wants is to sit on the hilltop and pretend he's God. And the rest of us have to sit around doing nothing.'

He filled his glass, with wine this time, and went on:

'They expect me to hang about with a lot of old pensioners, a herd of sheep. I'm the nucleus of the new army, don't you see that? Don't you understand that what's coming must be new, fresh and unused? The basis must be revolutionary. You can't inflate it afterwards. You only get the opportunity once to make something new and big that will help us lift the world off its hinges. But Hitler puts me off with fair words. He wants to let things run their course. He expects a miracle. Just like Adolf! . . . '

Source: H. Rauschning, Hitler Speaks, *1939, pp. 154–5*

The chief of the SA was the only senior Nazi who expressed anti-Hitler views in public. He was the Führer's only threat (Fest, 1973, p. 476). By March 1934 Röhm was demanding that several thousand SA men be taken in the army at once. Within a few months, during early Summer 1934, reports began circulating around government circles that Röhm was planning an armed revolt. At this point Hitler decided his first priority was to stabilise his rule and consolidate the gains the Nazi state had achieved so far. Unlike Röhm he was not dedicated to doing absolutely everything at once. Just as he had compromised and entered government with traditional conservative politicians, now he decided to build on the foundations of co-operation which existed with the traditional élites who ran Germany's armed forces. These people had already proved amenable to the National Socialist project. By the middle of 1933 they had understood that revolutionary changes were taking place, but had raised not a single objection to the liquidation of democracy and parliamentarianism. In November 1933, recognising that a debt was owed for this passivity, Hitler took time to applaud the unity of purpose he identified between the leaders of his movement and the chiefs of the armed forces (Graml, 1997, p. 368). By Summer 1934 the Führer was ready to choose between Röhm and the Wehrmacht. The following extract is taken from the memoirs of Helmut Nicolai, a senior civil servant in the Reich Interior Ministry.

Document 4.15 Possible Coup?

When I returned, the devil was abroad again in Berlin. You heard almost nothing apart from assaults by SA people. I had ordered that the Minister [Reich Interior Minister Frick] would be supplied with regular reports about the political situation by the middle administrative posts. This was done and in several you really could see that it was the SA which was restless. Other reports said very little; you could see that the authorities no longer dared to report anything unfavourable to Berlin about the Party or the SA. . . .

Then came wild rumours about Röhm. He was supposed to have said that order had to be created in Berlin and that Frick should be strung up or beaten. Then came a report from Upper Bavaria from the border near Salzburg. The SA was in possession of weapons and hand grenades had been exploded. From Pomerania came the news that with some form of transport or other the SA there had got weapons from Stettin harbour, that is to say thousands of weapons. Other individual reports fed together, from which it was to be concluded that the SA suddenly was supplying every post possible with weapons. . . .

On the same day as I was with him, a memorandum written by me was sent to the Führer and Reich Chancellor in which report was made of illegal arming by individual parts of the SA and request was made for orders about what should be done. . . . Three, six, ten, fourteen days went by and nothing happened. Things stayed as they were, they did not become worse, but neither did they get better. . . .

On that morning [of 30 June 1934] my secretary [in the Reich Interior Ministry, Berlin] met me with a worried expression. News had just come by telephone that Schragmüller had been imprisoned. . . . The door opened and there appeared a journalist from the National Observer who I knew superficially. He was very worked up and asked my advice. What was going on, surely I had to know. He was, incidentally, an SA leader, and suddenly all of the SA leaders in Berlin had been arrested by the SS. He did not know what it all meant and so had personal worries. My counter-question as to whether the SA or even he himself had done something wrong, he answered with a straightforward no. Therefore, I said, he really had nothing to worry about – but still he should buy a train ticket to Potsdam or Grunewald and go walking there and wait quietly until the affair had worked itself out. . . .

The telephone rang and the Minister [i.e. Reich Interior Minister Frick] asked me to see him. Erbe was there already and we sat down opposite Frick. He was rather paler than usual and stuttered somewhat with embarrassment. 'I only wanted to tell you – the Führer has had Röhm shot – in Munich – I don't know exactly – perhaps it is something to do with his inclination [Röhm was homosexual] and . . . [name illegible] has been shot too – and Heims and. . . . '

Erbe stood up horrified. The telephone went. 'I have just heard that Ministerial Director Klausen was shot in his office, and two Ministerial Advisers to von Papen – one knows nothing at all about it. . . . '

Erbe turned around and covered his face with his hands, I can still hear today how he said 'Oh God'. I was terrified through and through.

'Yes, I wanted to tell you – I don't know any more about what is happening . . . the Führer is so often lacking in self-control . . . ' [said Frick].

Source: H. Nicolai, Mein Kampf ums Recht. *Manuscript in the Institute of Contemporary History, Munich*

The strike against Röhm was completely ruthless. There were 'no trials, no weighing of evidence, no verdicts; there was nothing but an atavistic slaughter' (Fest, 1973, p. 466). Lasting from 30 June 1934 to 2 July the purge shows how incorrect it can be to view Hitler as just a careless leader tightly confined in the political options open to him. On this occasion Hitler showed how elastic the boundaries to his action could be when he chose to make them so. Murders were carried out wherever victims happened to be found. Thirty people, including Röhm himself, were killed at Stadelheim prison in Munich alone. Some former leading conservative political figures, such as former Reich Chancellor General von Schleicher, were eliminated as well.

On 3 July 1934 the Reich Ministers passed a single sentence law justifying what had happened. The measures had been taken to 'suppress treasonable activities' and were 'in emergency defence of the State' (Höhne, 1969, p. 118). On 17 July Hitler addressed the Reichstag. He said that Röhm and his cohorts had wanted to continue the National Socialist revolution, but that 'for us, revolution is no permanent condition'. On the basis that 'mutinous divisions have in all periods been recalled to order by decimation', and acting as 'the supreme judge of the German *Volk*', he had given 'the command to burn out the ulcers of our domestic well-poisoning . . . right down to the raw flesh'. Hitler stated that just 77 people had been killed. The actual number ran into the hundreds (Michalka, 1996, p. 41; Baynes, 1942, pp. 301, 321–2). In public Hitler showed not the slightest remorse for having killed a man who had once been a close personal friend. If there was any justice, it came only in Hitler's mind. After the murder of Röhm, apparently he found it particularly hard to sleep. He could do so only in snatches and woke up frequently with nightmares. To complete the picture, it is worth noting that after the Röhm putsch, no senior military figures denounced what had happened, not even the murder of von Schleicher. Without the logistical support of the armed forces, the action would have been quite impossible (Graml, 1997, pp. 368–9).

As a dictator, Hitler was his own man. He manipulated organisations and individuals effectively. He used the state to take decisive action against Socialists, Communists and anyone else who got in his way. He contrived to apply murderous violence against dissenters in the ranks of his own party. But he also gave his own particular political content to the state being forged. Unique to any modern industrial nation, Hitler founded the Third Reich on anti-Semitic racism.

A facet of Hitler's anti-Semitism was discovered by the same film-maker who was persuaded so skilfully to work on his behalf (document 4.8). Talking with the Führer in the Reich Chancellery, on one occasion Leni Riefenstahl tried to raise the Jewish Question. His replied curtly that it was not a matter he could discuss with her (Riefenstahl, 1992, p. 137). At another time in 1934, a big black limousine picked her up for a meeting in the less formal surroundings of the Berghof (Hitler's mountain retreat). They went for a walk on the mountain slopes and discussed Paris, French history, the landscape and the Church. Then came the following.

Document 4.16 Not Open to Discussion

I felt perplexed, for it was impossible to talk to him about the things that were most on my mind, for instance, his anti-Semitism. Whenever I knew I was to see him I resolved beforehand to raise the subject, and I prepared my questions accordingly. But the moment I broached the topic Hitler cut me off, saying he hadn't invited me here to talk about things that were not open to discussion.

'I know you, and I know how obstinate you are', he said, 'as obstinate as I can be. But there are certain things about which we will never see eye to eye. Believe me', he said, relenting a little, 'I do not reach my decisions lightly. Before making up my mind I do a lot of soul searching. I spend days and nights thinking of nothing else. I test the very foundations of my beliefs', he said, 'I review them with the most critical eyes and consider all the arguments against them. I keep attacking my own convictions until I am certain that black is black and white is white.'

I ventured to object. 'But what if you are mistaken?'

'I believe I am not mistaken. One has to be convinced of the rightness of one's own principles. Otherwise one can achieve nothing of value.'

'Do you believe in God?' I asked, gazing at him directly. Hitler looked at me in surprise, then smiled and said: 'Yes – I believe in a divine power, not in the dogmas of the Church, although I consider them necessary. I believe in God and in a divine destiny.' He turned away then and, folding his hands, gazed into the distance. 'And when the time is ripe, a new Messiah will come – he doesn't have to be a Christian, but he will found a new religion that will change the world.'

'Only if he loves all human beings' I said, 'and not just the Germans.'

I don't know whether Hitler had taken my point. In any case, he didn't say another word to me and we walked slowly back to the Berghof, where he said goodbye rather distantly, and had me driven back to my hotel in Berchtesgaden.

Source: L. Riefenstahl, The Sieve of Time, *1992, p. 211*

Hitler was a secretive, brooding man who hid his anti-Semitic core from anyone he felt might challenge it. There was something equally neurotic and paranoid at stake here. This side of Hitler undermines further still the stereotype of him as a careless ruler. It is common knowledge that only initially did he arrive at his desk in the Reich Chancellery by 10 a.m. More usually he got there by about noon and then decided to take an early lunch (Heiber, 1961, p. 112). At most, it is said, he gave two or three hours' consideration per day to running the country. As much as possible, he preferred to be out of Berlin, spending his afternoons walking the hills above Berchtesgaden (Remme, 1997). Consequently the image threatens to emerge of Hitler failing to give real thought to political choices. He is in danger of becoming someone defined as only capable of making snap decisions during mealtime conversations. But just because he did not sit at a desk all day does not mean he failed to consider deeply what he identified as his most pressing problems. After all, Röhm was despatched with a chilling efficiency that spoke of careful forethought. The Jewish Question needs to be understood in a similar light. Hitler never wrote innumerable memoranda outlining his ideas about how to proceed on the matter, but this does not mean he failed to *think* about things. Given the all-consuming nature of his prejudice (see especially Chapter 2), the overall direction that policy would take was obvious. While Hitler paced the Bavarian slopes, most likely he spent a lot of time brooding over how best to proceed against his nation's Jews.

Very soon after coming to power, Hitler began to implement anti-Semitic discrimination. The Law for the Restoration of a Professional Civil Service was issued on 7 April 1933. It retired state employees who were not of Aryan descent (*Reichsgesetzblatt*, 1933, p. 175). This was just a start. At the Reich party meeting of September 1935 Hitler made two laws without precedent in twentieth-century Europe. In a moment of high drama he defined the place of Jews in German society. Admittedly he decided upon this course of action only days before his closing speech, and certainly the laws were drafted by civil servants brought to Nuremberg from Berlin at the very last minute, but their basic content could have been predicted by anyone who had read *Mein Kampf.*

Document 4.17 Reich Citizenship Law

Reich Citizenship Law.

15 September 1935

The Reichstag has unanimously decided the following law, which is herewith proclaimed:

Section 1

1) A member of the state is anyone who belongs to the protective association of the German Reich and who, as a result, has special obligations to it.
2) The membership of the state is acquired according to the prescriptions of the law of Reich and State membership.

Section 2

1) A Reich citizen is only a member of the state who is of German or related blood, who proves by his conduct that he is willing and suitable to serve the German *Volk* and Reich faithfully.
2) The right of being a Reich citizen is acquired through the granting of a Reich citizenship certificate.
3) The Reich citizen is the sole bearer of full political rights according to the stipulation of the law.

Section 3

The Reich Interior Minister, in association with the Deputy Führer, will issue the legal and administrative prescriptions necessary for the implementation and supplementation of the law.
Nuremberg, 15 September 1935
on the Reich Party Day of Freedom
Führer and Reich Chancellor
Adolf Hitler
Reich Interior Minister
Frick

Source: Reichsgesetzblatt, *Vol. 1, 1935, p. 1146*

Document 4.18 German Blood and Honour

Law for the Protection of German Blood and of German Honour
15 September 1935
In the realisation of the fact that the purity of German blood is a prerequisite for the continued existence of the German *Volk*, and enthused by the inflexible will to secure the German nation for the whole future, the Reichstag has unanimously decided the following law, which herewith is proclaimed.

Section 1

1) Marriages between Jews and members of the German state or of any type of related blood are banned. Marriages which are concluded all the same are rendered void, even if they are concluded abroad in circumvention of this law.
2) Only the state prosecutor can undertake annulment proceedings.

Section 2

Sexual intercourse outside of wedlock is banned between Jews and members of the German state or of a related blood.

Section 3

Jews may not employ in the household female members of the German state, or of related blood, who are aged less than 45 years of age.

Section 4

1) Jews are banned from flying the Reich or national flag and from displaying the Reich colours.
2) On the other hand they are allowed to display the Jewish colours. The power of the state guarantees the right to do this.

Section 5

1) Whoever offends against section 1 of this ban, will be punished with imprisonment with hard labour.
2) A man who violates the second section of this ban will be punished with imprisonment with or without hard labour.
3) Whoever contravenes sections 3 or 4 will be imprisoned for up to a year and fined, or will be punished with one or other of these penalties. . . .

Nuremberg, 15 September 1935
on the Reich Party Day of Freedom
Führer and Reich Chancellor
Adolf Hitler
Reich Interior Minister
Frick
Reich Justice Minister
Dr Gürtner
Deputy to the Führer
R.Hess

Source: Reichsgesetzblatt, *Vol.1, 1935, pp. 1146–7*

In the Reich Citizenship Law, Hitler defined who could be a German citizen; in the Law for the Protection of German Blood and Honour, he banned marriage and sex between Germans and Jews. These were the infamous 'Nuremberg Laws'. They were supposed to preserve and enhance the superiority of the German race by 'preventing cross-breeding' (Quine, 1996, p. 111). Even if their implementation did not actually affect as many people as it might have done (due to exemptions being made on the grounds of individuals having special economic or military importance), still their principles implied a restructuring of society based on racial grounds (Steiner and von Cornberg, 1998, p. 187).

A period of relative calm in terms of anti-Semitic initiatives followed. True, as 1938 developed, more and more Jewish businesses were being taken over by Germans. In early November, however, stimulated by a rabble-rousing speech given by Josef Goebbels at a conference celebrating the anniversary of the beer hall putsch, a wave of semi-organised anti-Semitic violence broke out across the nation. It was backed by an SA organisation which had renewed itself after the purge of 1934 and stood ready as an 'extra-legal and extra-ordinary weapon of the party' (Campbell, 1993, p. 665). Thousands of Jewish shops were ransacked, synagogues were burned and Jewish people were abused physically. This was the so-called 'Crystal Night' pogrom. At first, Hitler was quiet in their wake (Graml, 1992, p. 13). Then on 30 January 1939 he made a public speech which contained one of his most famous and violent anti-Semitic statements ever.

Document 4.19 The Prophet

The world has sufficient space for settlements but we must once and for all get rid of the opinion that the Jewish race was only created by God for the purpose of being in a certain percentage as parasites living on the body and the productive work of other nations. The Jewish race will have to adapt itself to sound constructive activity as other nations do, or sooner or later it will succumb to a crisis of an inconceivable magnitude.

One thing I should like to say on this day which may be memorable for others as well as for us Germans: in the course of my life I have very often been a prophet, and have usually been ridiculed for it. During that time of my struggle for power it was in the first instance the Jewish race which only received my prophecies with laughter when I said that I would one day take over the leadership of the state, and with it that of the whole nation, and that I would then among many other things settle the Jewish problem. Their laughter was uproarious, but I think that for some time now they have been laughing on the other side of their face. Today I will once more be a prophet: if the international Jewish financiers in and outside Europe should succeed in plunging the nations once more into a world war, then the result will not be the bolshevization of the earth, and thus the victory of Jewry, but the annihilation of the Jewish race in Europe!

. . . The nations are no longer willing to die on the battle-field so that this unstable international race may profiteer from a war or satisfy its Old Testament vengeance. The Jewish watch word 'Workers of the world unite' will be conquered by a higher realisation, namely 'Workers of all classes and of all nations, recognize your common enemy!'

Source: N.H. Baynes (ed.), The Speeches of Adolf Hitler, Vol. 1, *1942, p. 741*

This was vintage Hitler. The dictator was revealing his true essence as a committed racist. The tone fitted perfectly with the early beer hall speeches and the prison writings. It corresponded completely to the brooding paranoia he had shown Leni Riefenstahl. In the last analysis, and most important of all, Hitler was a racial dictator and his career has to be understood accordingly (see Chapter 9, thesis 2).

So did Adolf Hitler lead his party and state as a revolutionary (for definition of 'revolutionary', see Chapter 1)? By transforming a multi-party democracy into a single party structure he brought about a fundamental *change in the nature of political power* in Germany. His attack on Socialism and Communism constituted a major effort to root out a perceived *social ill*. His offensive against the Jews was an attempt to do the same, but also represented a change to the nation's *social structure*: it was a step on the way to the creation of a racial state. Whether through the internment of Socialists, pogroms against Jews or a purge of the SA he sponsored political violence that, according to all reasonable standards, can only be termed *illegal*. Through his style of leadership, he managed effectively (if cynically) to *motivate followers* to do his bidding and, once Reich Chancellor, sponsored a major effort to *mobilise the nation* behind him.

Of course, there is a case for saying he was not a revolutionary in every sense. His first taste of national political power was in a cabinet shared with traditional conservative politicians and he parted company from Röhm over the aim of bringing about the early Nazification of the armed forces. But these points should not be emphasised to excess. It is worth repeating that in a modern industrial state, to be successful a revolutionary needs, on a temporary basis, to work with the established élites in the state (Löwenthal, 1981, pp. 256–7). This is how Hitler assessed his situation. In January 1933 and again in June 1934 he compromised his revolutionary instincts in the short term to ensure he would be in a position to bring about changes in the long term (for some further discussion of the future role of the army in the Third Reich, see Chapter 6). There should be no serious doubt that Hitler was a revolutionary political leader.

5 | Deceiver

Can there be such a thing as a revolutionary foreign policy, and if so did Adolf Hitler implement one when he was Reich Chancellor? In this connection it is most striking that Hitler was no cosmopolitan. By 1933, his knowledge of life beyond the German-speaking lands was limited to a soldier's experiences in France. Even after the seizure of power, he rarely travelled abroad. But limited horizons never stopped him pronouncing on life further afield.

Document 5.1 The Russian

In the eyes of the Russian, the principal support of civilisation is vodka. His ideal consists in never doing anything but the indispensable. . . .

It is doubtful whether anything at all can be done in Russia without the help of the Orthodox priest. It's the priest who has been able to reconcile the Russian to the fatal necessity of work – by promising him more happiness in another world.

The Russian will never make up his mind to work except under compulsion from outside, for he is incapable of organising himself. And if, despite everything, he is apt to have organisation thrust upon him, that is thanks to the drop of Aryan blood in his veins. It's only because of this drop that the Russian people has created something and possesses an organised state.

It takes energy to rule Russia. The corollary is that, the tougher the country's regime, the more appropriate it is that equity and justice should be practised there. The horse that is not kept constantly under control forgets in the wink of an eye the rudiments of training that have been inculcated into it. In the same way, with the Russian, there is an instinctive force that invariably leads him back to the state of nature. People sometimes quote the case of the horse that escaped from a ranch in America, and by some ten years later had formed huge herds of wild horses. It is so easy for an animal to go back to its origins! For the Russian, the return to the state of nature is a return to primitive forms of life. The family exists, the female looks after her children, like the female of the hare, with all the feelings of a mother. But the Russian doesn't want anything more. His reaction against the constraint of the organised State . . . is brutal and savage, like all feminine reactions. When he collapses and should yield, the Russian bursts into lamentations. This will to return to the state of nature is exhibited in his revolutions. For the Russian, the typical form of revolution is nihilism.

Source: Entry of 5 July 1941. H.R.Trevor-Roper (ed.), Hitler's Secret Conversations. 1941–1944, *1961, pp. 33–4*

When Hitler dealt with his nation's foreign policy, he thought in terms of the well-established clichés that had abounded among Germany's nationalists since before at least 1914 (Schramm, 1972, p. 52). This point requires due attention (see Chapter 9, thesis 3) and the contrast with the foreign policy exponents of the Weimar period could not have been greater. The likes of Walther Rathenau and Gustav Stresemann had been outward-looking, sophisticated thinkers. While no German Foreign Minister could ever have settled for (especially) the loss of the Polish Corridor separating East Prussia from the rest of Germany as stipulated by the Treaty of Versailles, men like Rathenau and Stresemann believed their country had the best chance of improving her position through the achievement of understanding based on the fulfilment of international obligations (Funke, 1996, p. 138). They saw Germany's future inside, rather than outside, the League of Nations and worked consistently to make Germany respected in conventional terms (Hofer, 1989, p. 171). The approach bore some fruit. In September 1926 Germany was allowed to join the League of Nations, in January 1927 the Interallied Military Commission was withdrawn from Germany, in June 1930 allied troops were withdrawn from the Rhineland and in December 1932 the western powers agreed in principle that Germany should be allowed equality in terms of armaments (Schöllgen, 1995, p. 49).

Although Hitler was at heart a very different kind of person from Rathenau and Stresemann (basically he was a provincial bigot), like them he was desperately interested in foreign policy. He spent considerable time thinking about it and his early speeches often dealt with the Treaties of Brest-Litovsk and Versailles (Hiden, 1996, p. 216; Jarman, 1955, p. 204; Jäckel, 1986, p. 147). He knew well and despised the provisions of the latter: for example, the territorial redefinition of Germany, the demilitarisation of the Rhineland, the ban on her unification with Austria and the strict limitations on her military power. His ideology as explained in *Mein Kampf* and subsequent programmatic pronouncements had an explicit expansionist foreign policy angle (see documents 2.16 and 2.17). With all this said, Hitler's initial dabblings in the international arena *on the surface at least* had something in common with the way policy had developed since 1918 (Funke, 1996, p. 137). To the Reichstag, on 17 May 1933, he peddled a message of which Stresemann and Rathenau might have approved.

Document 5.2 Peace, 17 May 1933

'Speaking deliberately as a German National Socialist, I desire to declare in the name of the National Government, and of the whole movement of national regeneration, that we in this new Germany are filled with deep understanding for the same feelings and opinions and for the rightful claims to life of the other nations. The present generation of this new Germany, which, so far, has only known in its life the poverty, misery, and distress of its own people, has suffered too deeply from the madness of our time to be able to contemplate treating others in the same way.

'Our boundless love for and loyalty to our own national traditions makes us respect the national claims of others, makes us desire from the bottom of our hearts to live with them in peace and friendship.

'We therefore have no use for the idea of Germanization. The mentality of the past century which made people believe that they could make Germans out of Poles and Frenchmen is completely foreign to us; the more so as we are passionately opposed to any attempt on the part of others to alienate us from our German tradition. We look at the European nations objectively. The French, the Poles, &c., are our neighbours, and we know that through no possible development of history can this reality be altered.

'It would have been better for the world if in Germany's case these realities had been appreciated in the Treaty of Versailles. For the object of a really lasting treaty should be not to cause new wounds and keep old ones open, but to close wounds and heal them. A thoughtful treatment of European problems at that time could certainly have found a settlement in the east which would have met both the reasonable claims of Poland and the natural rights of Germany. The Treaty of Versailles did not provide this solution. Nevertheless no German Government will of its own accord break an agreement which cannot be removed without being replaced by a better one. . . .

'On behalf of the German people and the German Government, I have to make the following statement: Germany has disarmed. She has complied with all obligations imposed upon her in the Peace Treaty to an extent far beyond the limits of equity and reason. Her army consists of 100,000 men [as stipulated at Versailles]. The strength and the character of her police are internationally regulated. . . .

'Nevertheless Germany is at any time willing to undertake further obligations in regard to international security, if all the other nations are ready on their side to do the same, and if this security is also to benefit Germany. Germany would also be perfectly ready to disband her entire military establishment and destroy the smallest amount of arms remaining to her, if the neighbouring countries will do the same thing with equal thoroughness. But if these countries are not willing to carry out the disarmament measures to which they are also bound by the Treaty of Versailles, Germany must at least maintain her demand for equality.'

Source: N.H. Baynes, The Speeches of Adolf Hitler. Vol. 2, *1942, pp. 1046–7 and 1052–3*

Respect for other nations, a desire for peace with neighbouring states, regard for international treaties, support for disarmament and, at most, a statement of a desire for equality in armaments – there was little sinister here. Two years later, on 21 May 1935, Hitler repeated the exercise in reasonableness. He dismissed war as a tool of policy. He said it could only bring about 'petty adjustments of national frontiers' which were 'of no consequence in comparison with the sacrifices made' by nations at war. Because of its 'fundamental convictions', Hitler reiterated 'National Socialist Germany . . . needs peace and desires peace' (Baynes, 1942, Vol. 2, pp. 1218–20 and 1239). He even dismissed the idea of '*Anschluss*', union with his own homeland of Austria. These were the words of a responsible statesman.

During the early years of the Third Reich, modest foreign policy triumphs, which were quite in line with the improvements to her position which Germany had experienced between 1926 and 1932, gave a respectable sort of élan to Hitler's regime. The Saarland was a coal mining area which had been part of Germany's western borders until the Treaty of Versailles placed it under the governance of the League of Nations. In January 1935 a plebiscite determined its future; 90% of voters chose to return to Germany. The event filled the populations of both the Saarland and the rest of Germany with genuine enthusiasm. Hitler turned the event into a rather benign propaganda coup. Here is how a Reich minister remembered the return of the region to Germany.

Document 5.3 Saarland

We were all gathered around Hitler at the celebrations of the reincorporation [of the Saarland into the Reich], when he personally was present at that time in Saarbrücken [the regional capital] in the middle of March 1935. In pouring rain, and standing in his open car (as always was his practice), he took the march past of his columns, and for hours on end the Saarlanders surged around him as their liberator, liberated by a reluctantly forbearing regiment of the League of Nations. It was an auspicious start. Hitler gave a speech that was very reasonable, quiet and, above all, which was directed towards France in terms of peace and reconciliation. That afternoon, and then the whole night through, I travelled back to Munich with him in his special train. The attitude of us all was thoroughly happy and satisfied. In the dining car he invited me to sit next to him. He ate, as always, his vegetarian meal and drank apple juice. He was in fine spirits. He was especially happy about the solution of this problem (about which the whole world had been holding its breath for months) in a relatively peaceful manner and without any foreseeable trouble. . . .

At all of the stations there were tightly packed crowds, which had waited for hours for the Führer. And when his train slid through a railway station, going quite slowly at 30–40 km/h, he appeared at the window. And as soon as he was recognised, and for so long as he was seen, the people called, waved and shouted to him. Hats were waved, little children were lifted up by their mothers. Greeting everybody cheerfully, Hitler remained standing at the window, leaning out until no one was to be seen any more, and then he sat down, often just to stand up again after a few minutes when the same happened as we passed through a new town or village. Hitler never tired during this time and took great care that he didn't leave a single station on which there were people waiting to greet him without greeting them himself. But when the train stopped in a larger town – from this journey I remember stopping late in the evening in Mannheim – then there was a stormy jostling all around him and shouts of *Heil*. The masses rushed together around his window and grabbed for his hand. One lot of flowers after another rained down on him through the window, and there was no end to the enthusiastic celebration. He spoke with the people in simple, heart-felt words, always, asking if they were happy with him and his work. And the approval filled with thanks swelled up to the national hymn, which rang far and wide above and beyond the shining railway platform. It was the most genuine contact of a national leader with his nation which anyone can imagine. We experienced it. No one can persuade us otherwise, for we were his dumb eye and ear witnesses who were most deeply moved time and again.

Source: H. Frank, Im angesicht des Galgens, *1953, pp. 209–11*

The dominant themes of peace and respect ran through the international agreements made during the early years. Hitler's first important understanding signed with another national government was the Non-Aggression Treaty concluded with Poland on 26 January 1934. Based on the contention that 'the maintenance and security of a lasting peace' between the two states was 'an essential prerequisite for general peace in Europe', the treaty laid the basis for 'a good neighbourly relationship' which would prove 'a blessing' not only to the two countries directly involved, but to all other nations as well (*Reichsgesetzblatt*, 1934, p. 118). It was a master-stroke. Potential hostility over the Polish Corridor had been a feature of international life throughout the Weimar years, but was done away with in one fell swoop. As if to emphasise the *bona fides* of Germany, in June 1936 the Anglo-German Naval Agreement was reached, restricting the German fleet to 35% of the tonnage of the British. True, this has been identified as a horrid diplomatic blunder by Britain, since it acknowledged Germany's right to rearm beyond the limits specified at Versailles, but still it left the impression that Hitler was prepared to act in co-ordination with the demands of other nations. Relations with Austria were also addressed. The possibility of 'Anschluss' may have been expressly forbidden by the Treaty of Versailles, but remained a live issue. This was especially so after the murder of the Austrian Chancellor Dollfuss by Austrian Nazis in 1934. To allay fears, the 'Gentleman's Agreement' between the two governments was concluded on 11 July 1936.

Document 5.4 Gentleman's Agreement

In the conviction of being able to make a valuable contribution to the pan-European development for the preservation of peace, as in the belief thereby of best serving the manifold and reciprocal interests of the two German states, the governments of the German Reich and of the Federal State of Austria have decided to formulate their relations once again on a normal and friendly basis.

1. In the sense of the statements of the Führer and Reich Chancellor of 21 May 1935, the German Government recognises the full sovereignty of the Federal State of Austria.
2. Each of the two governments considers the domestic political situation which exists in the other land (including the question of Austrian National Socialism) to be a domestic affair of the other land, which it will try to influence neither directly nor indirectly.
3. The Austrian Federal government will, in general, maintain its policy (as in particular in respect of the German Reich) constantly on those fundamental lines which correspond to the fact, that Austria recognises itself as a German State.

Source: K. Hohlfeld, Dokumente. Vol. 4, *1953, p. 296*

During this period, even when potentially aggressive actions were undertaken, Hitler surrounded them in a fog of ambiguity. The Disarmament Conference of the League of Nations met on 16 March 1933. Hitler's first risky foreign policy gambit came six months later. In July 1932 the German delegation had walked out of the disarmament negotiations temporarily, but on 14 October 1933 Hitler removed Germany from both Conference and League once and for all (Schöllgen, 1995, p. 48). On the same day, he spoke to the world audience. Germany was said to have joined the League and participated in disarmament talks in a genuine desire to continue removing weapons from Europe. It had believed it would be treated with 'a just equality of rights'. Consistently, however, the nation had suffered 'disillusionment' and 'discrimination'. It had been 'humiliated'. As a result it was now 'forced' to leave these institutions. At the same time Hitler stated Germany retained an 'unalterable will for peace' (Baynes, 1942, Vol. 2, pp. 1088–9). In other words, faced with institutions he stigmatised as ineffectual and unjust, Hitler was trying to capture the moral high ground. His reintroduction of conscription, which came eighteen months later and flouted the Versailles prescriptions, fitted this context perfectly. The step was proclaimed on 16 March 1935 and was made to appear less a warlike step than something which was compelled by the intransigence of the rest of Europe. Formally speaking, Hitler's army was dedicated to the preservation of peace, not the pursuit of war.

Document 5.5 Law for the Construction of the Wehrmacht, 16 March 1935

The Reich government has decided the following law which is hereby proclaimed:

1. Service in the Wehrmacht is based on a general defensive obligation [Wehrpflicht].
2. The German army of peace [Friedensheer] (including the incorporated police troops) is structured in 12 command corps and 36 divisions.
3. The supplementary laws about the regulation of general defensive duty will be presented at once by the Reichswehr Minister to the Reich Ministry. . . .

Source: Reichsgesetzblatt, *1935, p. 375*

The remilitarisation of the Rhineland was a complicated event. At the time, the members of the League of Nations were preoccupied with the Italian invasion of Abyssinia. Britain in particular feared that Italian ascendancy in the Horn of Africa might threaten her imperial interests. With the world looking in the other direction, on 7 March 1936 Hitler sent troops into the demilitarised zone. German soldiers were restored to their place on the French border by an action which violated the Treaties of Versailles and Locarno (the latter was made in 1925 and ratified the existing frontiers in western Europe) (Rich, 1992, p. 86; Hiden, 1996, p. 222). It was a flagrant breach of international law, but Hitler set out to justify his actions. He first deployed his argument in a meeting with his Reich cabinet ministers at 9.15 p.m. the day beforehand.

Document 5.6 Justifying Remilitarisation

The Führer explained at length that the pact between France and the Soviet Union, which the French chamber had already approved, constituted a clear breach of the Locarno Treaty. He had therefore decided to reoccupy the demilitarised Rhineland with German troops. All preparations for this had been made; some of the German troops were already on the march. He had summoned the Reichstag for tomorrow – Saturday – and, for the benefit of the German people and of other countries he would set forth to it in detail the reasons for his action. . . .

The meeting ended at 10:15 pm.

Source: Documents on German Foreign Policy 1918–1945. Series C. Vol. 5, *1966, p. 27*

It was typical that Hitler tried to put himself in the right by blaming, quite unjustly, France for violating the international status quo. That nation had every right to complete its pact with the Soviet Union on 27 February 1936. There was really no violation of Locarno here. The last document also shows well that in this case Hitler was not consulting his cabinet, but only informing it of a *fait accompli*. Remilitarisation would happen regardless of what the meeting thought and was the plan of Hitler alone. The man demanded complete, unquestioned control over such an important matter (Lewin, 1984, p. 8).

When the German generals learned of remilitarisation, initially they were shocked. They knew that their forces could not withstand concerted opposition by the international community and only moved their units on the understanding that at the first hint of hostility they would be withdrawn. On the day of remilitarisation, Hitler made sure he provided all the noises the world wanted to hear. Emphasising that Germany had no territorial demands in Europe, and denying that international tensions could ever be solved through war, he told the Reichstag that the reoccupation of the Rhineland removed the first obstacle to Germany re-entering Europe's collective security institutions (Hohlfeld, 1953, Vol. 4, pp. 121–2). With Britain concerned over her empire and France lacking the confidence to act alone, it was a message everyone wanted to believe (Knopp, 1995, p. 213). Hitler's mixture of gamble and dissimulation worked.

After the Rhineland initiative, Hitler embarked on a major peace offensive. Joachim von Ribbentrop was head of the NSDAP's foreign affairs office and became Hitler's Ambassador to Britain. He conveyed the following proposal to the British government.

Document 5.7 Ribbentrop's Peace Proposal

PEACE PLAN OF THE GERMAN GOVERNMENT OF MARCH 31, 1936, HANDED TO THE BRITISH GOVERNMENT BY AMBASSADOR VON RIBBENTROP ON APRIL 1, 1936.

It was with hearty approval that the German Government learnt from Ambassador von Ribbentrop that it is the wish of the British Government and the British people to begin as soon as possible the practical work for a real pacification of Europe. This desire is in full accord with the inmost intentions and hopes of the German people and their leaders. . . .

To this end the German Government proposes the following peace plan:

(1) In order to give the future agreements to ensure the peace of Europe the character of inviolable treaties, those nations participating in the negotiations shall do so only on an entirely equal footing, and as equally esteemed members. The sole compelling reason for signing these treaties can only lie in the generally recognised and obvious suitability of these agreements for the peace of Europe, and thus for the social happiness and the economic prosperity of the nations.

(2) In order to abbreviate, as far as possible, the period of uncertainty, in the economic interests of the European nations, the German Government propose a limit of four months for the first period, up to the signature of the non-aggression pacts, and thus covering a guaranteed European peace.

(3) The German Government give the assurance that they will not undertake any reinforcement whatsoever to the troops in the Rhineland during this period, always provided that the Belgian and French Governments act similarly.

(4) The German Government give the assurance that they will not move during this period the troops at present stationed in the Rhineland closer to the Belgian and French frontiers.

(5) The German Government propose to set up a commission composed of representatives of the two guarantor Powers, England and Italy, and of a disinterested third neutral Power, to guarantee these assurances to be given by both parties.

(6) Germany, Belgium and France are each entitled to send a representative to this commission. If Germany, Belgium and France think that, for any particular reason, they can point to a change in the military situation having taken place within this period of four months, they have the right to inform the Guarantee Commission of what they have observed.

(7) Germany, Belgium and France declare their willingness, in such a case, to permit this commission to make the necessary investigations through the British and Italian military attachés, and to report thereon to the Powers participating.

(8) Germany, Belgium and France give the assurance that they will give the fullest consideration to the objections arising therefrom. . . .

(15) In order to stamp this peace pact, voluntarily entered into between Germany on the one hand and France on the other, with the character of a reconciliatory settlement of centuries-old variance, Germany and France shall pledge themselves to see that in the education of the young people of both countries, as well as in publications, everything is avoided which might be calculated to poison the relationship between the two peoples, whether it be the adoption of a derogatory or contemptuous attitude, or improper interference in the internal affairs of the other country. They shall agree to set up, at the headquarters of the League of Nations in Geneva, a joint commission whose function it shall be to submit to the two Governments, for their information and investigation, all complaints received.

Source: Documents on German Foreign Policy 1918–1945. Series C. Vol. 5, *1966, pp. 355ff.*

The more Hitler broke international agreements and rearmed, the more he emphasised a desire for peace (Rich, 1992, p. 84). At face value his message was common sense. Claims to peace, control of one's own land, the right to self-determination and equality with other sovereign states were not so controversial. So which signals were European statesmen to believe: what Hitler said, or what he did? The very ambiguity of things militated against a decisive confrontation between statesmen and nations. So soon after the First World War, other Europeans were reluctant to think the worst. Hitler was lulling a willing continent into a false sense of security (Hofer, 1989, p. 170).

What was Hitler really about? From the outset, many of Germany's neighbours, which often harboured substantial German minority populations, viewed him as a threat. As he put it in the second paragraph of *Mein Kampf*, 'One blood demands one Reich'. He added 'German-Austria must return to the great German mother country' (Hitler, 1985, p. 3). The contrast with the Gentleman's Agreement was total. It is hardly surprising that Austrian Prime Minister Schuschnigg told the Christian Social Party Day as early as 8 May 1933 that while it was acceptable for Germany to campaign for the restoration of colonies confiscated at Versailles, 'Austria is not a colony, never, never at all' (Ingrim, 1938, p. 69). Despite the Non-Aggression Treaty, Poland was worried too. On 17 November 1934 the Polish Ambassador to Berlin, Lipski, met his American counterpart, Dodd. Lipski stated his belief that good German–Polish relations were only temporary and that Germany intended to re-annex part of his country, not to mention Alsace-Lorraine, Austria and Czechoslovakia (Dodd and Dodd, 1941, pp. 201–2).

The record shows how well-founded were these concerns. Territorial expansion through war was always on Hitler's mind. He spoke to his senior generals in the Reich Chancellery as follows as early as 3 February 1933.

Document 5.8 The Briefing

2. Abroad. Battle against Versailles. Equality in Geneva; but without purpose if the *Volk* is not focused on the will to defend. Care for federal colleagues. [Bundesgenossen]. . . .
4. Build-up of the Army. Most important pre-requisite for achievement of the goal: regaining of political power. General military service must start again. First of all, however, the state leadership must take care that those obliged to serve have not been poisoned by pacifism, Marxism, bolshevism or fall prey to this poison after their service time.

How should political power be used when it is won? Not to be said yet. Perhaps securing of new export possibilities, perhaps – and really preferable – conquest of new Lebensraum in the east and ruthless Germanisation of it. Certain that present economic conditions can only be changed with political power and battle. Everything that can be done now – settlement – a means of helping this.

Source: T. Vogelsang, 'Neue Dokumente zur Geschichte der Reichswehr 1930–1933', pp. 434ff.

Hitler's overturning of the provisions of Versailles had been deliberate and concerted. Regardless of what he said in document 5.2, from the earliest days major expansions eastwards and Germanisation of the captured lands were both in the balance. Lipski read things correctly. According to Hermann Rauschning, Hitler always said he had no intention of maintaining a long-term friendship with Poland (Rauschning, 1939b, p. 123). Just four days after signing his treaty with that country, he told his generals there was a need for strikes in the East to create living space (Funke, 1996, p. 139). The East simply gripped his mind. On 21 May 1935 Hitler spoke to Berlin's foreign diplomats at the Kroll opera house. He expressed a veiled intention to annex Lithuania, western Poland and Estonia. Wild hurrahs resulted from the Nazis present (Dodd and Dodd, 1941, pp. 253–4). The impression is of a seamless connection between the ideas outlined in *Mein Kampf*, those recorded by Rauschning and the foreign policy thinking held by Hitler after he became Chancellor (Hofer, 1989, p. 170; also documents 2.16 and 2.17). An overall interpretation of Hitler's political career cannot escape this point (see Chapter 9, thesis 1).

So how are we to evaluate the treaties signed with Poland and Austria? Before coming to power, Hitler had indicated his attitude to international agreements in a meeting attended by Hermann Rauschning.

Document 5.9 Hypocrite

'I am willing to sign anything. I will do anything to facilitate the success of my policy. I am prepared to guarantee all frontiers and to make non-aggression pacts and friendly alliances with anybody. It would be sheer stupidity to refuse to make use of such measures merely because one might possibly be driven into a position where a solemn promise would have to be broken. There has never been a sworn treaty which has not sooner or later been broken or become untenable. There is no such thing as an everlasting treaty. Anyone whose conscience is so tender that he will not sign a treaty unless he can feel sure he can keep it in all and any circumstances is a fool. Why should one not please others and facilitate matters for oneself by signing pacts if others believe that something is thereby accomplished or regulated? Why should I not make an agreement in good faith today and unhesitatingly break it tomorrow if the future of the German people demands it?'

'I shall make any treaty I require', Hitler repeated. 'It will never prevent me from doing at any time what I regard as necessary for Germany's interests.'

Source: H. Rauschning, Hitler Speaks, 1939, p. 114

In his *Second Book* he said the same: alliances should be signed to achieve foreign policy aims even if it was well known they would have to be broken one day (Hitler, 1961, p. 116). Dishonesty was also clearly in evidence when von Ribbentrop prepared a set of notes for Hitler defining how Britain should be treated.

Document 5.10 Dishonesty as Policy: Notes for Hitler by Joachim von Ribbentrop, 2 January 1938

5. The consequences we are to draw:

1) To outward appearances further understanding with England under [conditions of] safeguarding the interests of our friends.
2) Manufacture in all silence, but with all tenacity, of an alliance constellation against England – i.e. the practical strengthening of our friendship with Italy and Japan – further winning over of all states, whose interests conform either directly or indirectly with ours – close and confidential co-operation of the diplomats of the three great powers to this end.

Only in this way can we counter England, whether one day it comes to reconciliation or to conflict. England will be a hard and skilful opponent in this diplomatic game.

Source: Akten zur auswärtigen Politik 1918–45. Series D. Vol. 1, *1964, pp. 132–7*

The appearance of co-operation with Britain had to be balanced by the reality of working against her. In this light Germany's alliances with Japan and Italy concluded on 25 November 1936 (the Anti-Comintern Pact) and 22 May 1939 (the Pact of Steel) were as much directed against Britain and her world empire as against the Soviet Union.

Now we have the overall pattern. As Jarman put it long ago, 'Nazi Germany was two-faced', its leader was engaged in 'plausible hypocrisy' (Jarman, 1955, p. 203). Robert Cecil puts it only slightly differently. Hitler was 'a master of deception, he succeeded in leaving a number of false trails, some of which have continued to confuse historians' (Cecil, 1972, p. 24). The point of the strategy is easy to see. In the words of Jarman, 'Peace – it was a useful theme for Hitler. It served its purpose; it deluded his enemies' (Jarman, 1955, p. 205). It allowed him to start rearming with minimal chance of foreign intervention in the form of a preventive strike (Funke, 1996, p. 138; Hofer, 1989, p. 170). Hitler told his cabinet as much on 7 April 1933. His policy was designed to 'avoid foreign political conflicts, until we have strengthened ourselves' (Funke, 1996, p. 139). From the outset Hitler was a deceiver lying to achieve foreign policy objectives which had long been integral to his ideological pronouncements.

This interpretation conflicts completely with that adopted by some historians. Most notably Hans Mommsen has denied that the foreign policy of the Third Reich constituted the pursuit of pre-existing priorities. He prefers to see it as the expression of a boundless dynamism, a kind of 'expansion without object' which ultimately knew no limits. He says that in 'reality, the regime's foreign policy ambitions were many and varied, without any clear aims'. Only with the benefit of hindsight is there consistency in Hitler's actions (Mommsen, 1976, p. 177). But if Hitler had no real aims, why did he bother with such a consistent pack of lies?

Deception as such a concerted strategy really only makes sense if he was trying to divert attention from sets of actions which reflected a genuine set of political aims and objectives.

Hitler had his own understanding of the forces driving international relations. This determined the fact that while, during the 1930s, Britain and France were desperate to preserve the *status quo* in Europe, Hitler was desperate to change it (Rich, 1992, p. 81). He laid out his philosophy of foreign policy in his *Second Book* (for the origins of this, see Chapter 2). History, it says, is a people's 'struggle for existence', a 'struggle for daily bread' (Hitler, 1961, p. 5). Hitler argued that people are conditioned by laws of nature which drive them to acquire food and reproduce. Given that the world has only finite space available to both individuals and nations, competition for land (or living space) has to result sooner or later. Politics, foreign policy and domestic policy take their characters from this truism of life.

Document 5.11 Definitions

If the task of politics is the execution of a people's struggle for existence, and if the struggle for the existence of a people in the last analysis consists of safeguarding the necessary amount of space for nourishing a specific population, and if this whole process is a question of the employment of a people's strength, the following concluding definitions result therefrom:

Politics is the art of carrying out a people's struggle for its earthly existence.

Foreign policy [Domestic policy] is the art of safeguarding the momentary, necessary living space, in quantity and quality, for a people.

Domestic policy is the art of preserving the necessary employment of force [power content] for this in the form of its race value and numbers.

Source: A. Hitler, Hitler's Secret Book, *1961, p. 24*

It followed logically that a people was only sure of preserving itself when its living space and population size stood in a healthy relationship (Hitler, 1961, p. 24). But sooner or later some sort of disequilibrium was certain to develop. Hitler explained why this would happen, and what the consequences would be.

Document 5.12 Fight

[T]he regulation of the relation between population and territory is of tremendous importance for a nation's existence. Indeed, we can justly say that the whole life struggle of a people in truth consists in safeguarding the territory it requires as a general pre-requisite for the sustenance of the increasing population. Since the population grows incessantly, and the soil as such remains stationary, tensions perforce must gradually arise which at first find expression in distress, and which for a certain time can be balanced through greater industry, more ingenious production methods or special austerity. But there comes a day when these tensions can no longer be eliminated by such means. Then the task of the leaders of a nation's struggle for existence consists in eliminating the unbearable conditions in a fundamental way, that is in restoring a tolerable relation between population and territory.

In the life of nations there are several ways for correcting the disproportion between population and territory. The most natural way is to adapt the soil, from time to time, to the increased population. This requires a determination to fight and the risk of bloodshed. But this very bloodshed is also the only one that can be justified to a people. Since through it the necessary space is won for the further increase of a people, it automatically finds manifold compensation for the humanity staked on the battlefield. Thus the bread of freedom grows from the hardships of war. The sword was the pathbreaker for the plough.

Source: A. Hitler, Hitler's Secret Book, *1961, pp. 13–15*

In paranoid fashion, Hitler believed Germany was on the brink of having to fight. The nation's territory was just too small to secure its people. The threat was evidenced in bald statistics. Berlin was only 175 km from the Polish border and 190 km from the Czech. It could be reached by aeroplane in less than an hour. The Czechs could reach Munich in the same time. The key industrial zone of the Rhineland was in a worse position. It could be reached by the French air force in barely 30 minutes. Hardly any of Germany could not be bombed by an enemy within an hour's flying time (Hitler, 1961, pp. 126–7). A nation of this size just was not defensible.

What could Germany do? Hitler identified four foreign policy options. The first was to do nothing. This he dismissed since whoever 'will not be a hammer in history, will be an anvil'. Secondly, the nation could try to strengthen itself through trade. The alternative he believed was utopian. Britain would protect her large share of the world market too jealously. Thirdly, an attempt could be made to re-establish the borders of 1914. Hitler dismissed this as 'insufficient from a national standpoint, unsatisfactory from a military point of view, impossible from a folkish standpoint . . ., and mad from the viewpoint of its consequences' (Hitler, 1961, pp. 142–5). This left him with option four.

Document 5.13 Option Four

4) Germany decides to go to war over . . . a clear, far-seeing territorial policy. Thereby she abandons all attempts at world-industry and instead concentrates all her strength in order, through the allotment of sufficient living space for the next hundred years to our people, also to prescribe a path of life. Since this territory can be only in the east, the obligation to be a naval power also recedes into the background. Germany tries anew to champion her interests through the formation of a decisive power on land.

This aim is equally in keeping with the highest national will as well as folkish requirements. It likewise presupposes great military power means for its execution.

Source: A. Hitler, Hitler's Secret Book, *1961, pp. 144–5*

Hitler recommended that Germany win half a million square kilometres of extra territory. The 'monstrous bloodshed' of the campaign would be offset by giving land to those who fought at the front. Eventually there would be homesteads for millions of new German peasants who would provide the nation with a fresh reserve of soldiers (Hitler, 1961, pp. 74 and 78). Once the land became German, the nation's economic problems would pale into history (Hitler, 1961, p. 210).

Martin Broszat has argued that Hitler's talk of winning land in the East was really little more than utopian, propagandist talk which functioned as a rallying cry to pull the German population behind the Führer and his movement (Broszat, 1970). Bill Carr has agreed (Carr, 1978, p. 129). But Hitler's ideas as expressed in the *Second Book* undeniably form a coherent whole with both those explained in *Mein Kampf*, and those noted by Rauschning in 1932–4 (see documents 2.16 and 2.17). Comparable talk of such utopias was relatively common among radical nationalist groups in Germany in the 1920s and took on a 'biblical authority' when expressed by Hitler (Graml, 1995, p. 150). During the First World War, there had been talk of carrying out settlement experiments in the occupied East (see Chapter 2). Given the consistency of Hitler's ideas and the historical context in which he expressed them, there is actually no good reason to doubt that he was stating genuine intent. So when Hitler removed Germany from the League of Nations, reintroduced conscription and remilitarised the Rhineland, he may have been overturning Versailles, re-establishing Germany's power of self-determination and placing her on an equal footing with other nations, but this was only part of the picture. These were not the first steps towards a lasting peace, but were always directed towards an ideologically dictated and massive campaign for the living space deemed necessary to feed the German population and to allow it room to procreate. In his own mind, Hitler was laying the foundations for racial war as early as 1933–6.

As a statesman, Hitler was capable of operating on different levels according to the needs of the time and situation. But as the years of his Reich Chancellorship passed, his true ambitions became less veiled. An acceleration of his aims occurred in the period 1936–7. Hitler wrote the memo of the Four Year Plan on the Obersalzberg in 1936. It was produced against a background of growing national economic problems. In line with his ideology, Hitler never considered increasing international trade to tackle the matter. He stuck to his long chosen path: preparation for war.

Document 5.14 Four Year Plan

The development of our military capacity is to be effected through the new Army. *The extent of the military development of our resources cannot be too large, nor its pace too swift.* It is a major error to believe that there can be any argument on these points or any comparison with other vital necessities. However well-balanced the general pattern of a nation's life ought to be, there must at particular times be certain disturbances of the balance at the expense of other less vital tasks. *If we do not succeed in bringing the German Army as rapidly as possible to the rank of premier army in the world so far as its training, raising of units, armaments, and, above all, its spiritual education also is concerned, then Germany will be lost!* In this the basic principle applies that omissions during the months of peace cannot be made good in centuries. . . .

Just as the political movement among our people knows only one goal, the preservation of our existence, that is to say, the securing of all the spiritual and other prerequisites for the self-assertion of our nation, so neither has the economy any other goal than this. The nation does not live for the economy, for economic leaders, or for economic or financial theories; on the contrary, it is finance and the economy, economic leaders and theories, which all owe unqualified service in this struggle for the self-assertion of our nation. . . .

. . . I . . . consider it necessary for the Reichstag to pass the following two laws:

1. A law providing the death penalty for economic sabotage, and
2. A law making the whole of Jewry liable for all damage inflicted by individual specimens of this community of criminals upon the German economy, and thus upon the German people. . . .

I thus set the following tasks:

I. The German armed forces must be operational within four years.
II. The German economy must be fit for war within four years.

Source: J. Noakes and G. Pridham, Documents on Nazism, 1919–1945, *1974, pp. 401–8*

The memo exuded urgency. Europe was said to be on the brink of a crisis which could break out at any time. In particular Bolshevik Russia was threatening 'the annihilation of the German people' (Noakes and Pridham, 1974, p. 402). The memo promised the reorientation of the entire economy as appropriate to rearmament: the mobilisation of the workforce, the conservation of foreign exchange, the heightening of German fuel production as well as that of synthetic rubber and iron, not to mention a general drive towards autarky (Noakes and Pridham, 1974, pp. 405–6). The whole nation had to be ready to fight by 1940. The full implications of Hitler's ideas were becoming reality.

Hitler held a singularly important meeting of the chiefs of the armed forces on 5 November 1937. Minutes were kept by an officer called Hossbach. For the first time Hitler openly characterised both France and Britain as Germany's enemies. He also focused on the timing at which the balance of forces in a European conflict would be most favourable to Germany.

Document 5.15 Hossbach Memorandum

Contingency I: Period 1943–45

After this date only a change for the worse, from our point of view, could be expected.

The equipment of the Army, Navy and Luftwaffe, as well as the formation of the officer corps, was nearly completed. Equipment and armaments were modern; in further delay there lay the danger of their obsolescence. In particular, the secrecy of 'special weapons' could not be preserved for ever. The recruiting of reserves was limited to current age groups; further drafts from older untrained age groups were no longer available.

Our relative strength would decrease in relation to the rearmament which would by then have been carried out by the rest of the world. If we did not act by 1943–45, any year could, owing to a lack of reserves, produce the food crisis, to cope with which the necessary foreign exchange was not available, and this must be regarded as a 'warning point of the regime'. Besides the world was expecting our attack and was increasing its counter-measures from year to year. It was while the rest of the world was still fencing itself off [sich abriegele] that we were obliged to take the offensive.

Nobody knew today what the situation would be in the years 1943–45. One thing was certain, that we could wait no longer.

On the one hand there was the great Wehrmacht, and the necessity of maintaining it at its present level, the ageing of the movement and of its leaders; and on the other, the prospect of a lowering of the standard of living and of a limitation of the birth-rate, which left no choice but to act. If the Führer was still living, it was his unalterable determination to solve Germany's problems of space by 1943–45 at the latest.

Source: J. Noakes and G. Pridham, Documents on Nazism, 1919–1945, *1974, pp. 522–9*

The importance of the meeting was manifold. It made clear that Hitler 'wanted war and was deliberately working towards it' (Heiber, 1961, p. 136). He was planning it by 1943–5 at the latest. From this foundation Hitler outlined what should be done to central Europe in advance of a final reckoning with the Soviet Union. So long as developments in France allowed, as foreseen in the Rauschning discussions (document 2.17) and as feared by central European statesmen, Hitler recommended the overthrow and annexation of Austria and Czechoslovakia (Noakes and Pridham, 1974, pp. 527–8). This would benefit the German economy through plunder. Foodstuffs for 5–6 million extra people would be seized as a result.

From this point on, Hitler embarked on a phase of territorial expansion at the core of Europe. Notwithstanding the Gentleman's Agreement, Austria was first. Hitler met the Austrian Chancellor, Schuschnigg, at the Berghof on 11 February 1938. For two hours Hitler ranted and raved. He threatened military action by calling General Keitel into the room. He screamed: 'You will wake up one morning

in Vienna to find us there – just like a spring storm. And then you'll see something'
(Schuschnigg, 1947, p. 367). Then he produced a document demanding that a Nazi
be made Austrian Minister of the Interior, that Austrian Nazis in prison be released,
and that there be closer economic and military co-operation between the two
states. Schuschnigg was so staggered that he signed. When German pressure on his
country continued, Schuschnigg decided to hold a plebiscite about Austrian
independence on 13 March. In response, on 11 March 1938 Hitler issued the
following military order, called 'Operation Otto'.

Document 5.16 Operation Otto

Top Secret

1. If other means do not lead to the end, I intend to invade Austria with
   armed forces and to establish constitutional conditions there and to
   prevent further violent actions against the German-minded [i.e. pro-
   German nationalist] population.
2. I exercise command over the whole undertaking. . . .
3. Tasks:

   a) Army: the invasion of Austria must follow the way outlined by me.
      The goal for the army first of all is the occupation of Upper Austria,
      Salzburg, Lower Austria, the Tyrol, the rapid seizure of Vienna and
      the securing of the Austrian–Czech border.
   b) Airforce: the airforce must exercise and discharge propaganda material,
      occupy Austrian airports for eventual subsequent troops, support the
      army in the necessary measure and also keep troops at the ready for
      special commissions.

4. The forces of the army and the airforce earmarked for the undertaking
   must be operational and ready for invasion from 12 noon on 12.3.38 at
   the latest. I reserve for myself the authorisation for flying across and
   marching across the border and the establishment of the moment for this.
5. The behaviour of the troops must give the appearance that we do not want
   to wage war against a nation of brothers. It is in our interest that the whole
   undertaking takes place without the application of force, in the form of a
   peaceful entrance which is welcomed by the population. As a result, any
   provocation is to be avoided. Should there be any resistance, however, then
   it is to be broken with the least consideration by armed force. Austrian
   military units which come over to us, come under German control at once.
6. No security measures are to be undertaken on the German borders with
   other states.
   Adolf Hitler

Source: 102–C, Trial of the Major War Criminals before the International
Military Tribunal. Vol. 36, *1947, pp. 336–7*

German troops invaded on the morning of 12 March 1938. It was not a carefully planned operation. Some of the tank corps didn't have any road maps (Knopp, 1995, p. 220). But the same day Hitler travelled from Braunau to Linz and the road was straddled by cheering crowds. Buoyed up by his perception of the popular atmosphere, on 13 March the Führer announced the annexation of Austria.

In Vienna alone 70,000 people were arrested. The action reflected the fact that the city had the third largest Jewish population in Europe (Cross, 1973, p. 265; Jarman, 1955, p. 233). In the former national capital, Jews were brought onto the streets and made to scrub and clean. Annexation brought benefits to German industry. There was plenty here for Germany's war economy to ravage, for example substantial deposits of iron ore, lignite, manganese (important in aviation construction) and timber. There was a significant steel industry plus foreign currency and gold reserves worth RM 400 million (Hiden, 1996, p. 236; Rich, 1992, p. 101). The take-over also improved Germany's access to raw materials and agricultural lands in south-eastern Europe. *Anschluss* left Greater Germany with a stranglehold on another part of the former Habsburg Empire – Czechoslovakia. The situation was exacerbated by the existence of a 3 million strong ethnic German population in the state's western border area known as the Sudetenland. The group had become so well mobilised that in 1935 the Sudeten German Party won 44 seats in the Czech parliament. Thereafter Hitler subsidised it secretly with RM 12,000 per month. According to Hermann Rauschning, the foreign policy of National Socialism consisted 'of universal unsettlement' (Rauschning, 1939a, p. 262). The aim was to foment unrest in a country before intervening to bring about its downfall. The strategy was visible in the agreement cooked up between Hitler and the leader of the Sudeten Germans, Konrad Henlein. A fortnight after *Anschluss*, on 29 March 1938 the two met in Berlin. Hitler was already conspiring to detach the Sudetenland for Germany. The official minutes of the meeting were as follows.

Document 5.17 Henlein

The conversation lasted almost three hours, and present, apart from the Führer, were Deputy Führer, Reich Minister Hess, Foreign Minister v. Ribbentrop and Obergruppenführer Lorenz. The Führer explained he intended to solve the Czechoslovakian problem in the not too distant future. . . .

The intention of the order which the Führer has given Henlein is that the SdP [Sudeten German Party] should establish demands which are unacceptable to the Czech government. Despite the favourable position in respect of the Austrian events, Henlein intends not to go too far, but rather only to put the old demands for self-administration and reparations to the Party Day (23 and 24 April 1938). He wants to reserve until later a suggestion of the Führer to demand special German regiments with German officers and German as a language of command. The Reich will not get involved off its own bat. Henlein himself is first and foremost responsible for events. But close co-operation would have to follow. Henlein has summarised his attitude to the Führer: we must demand so much that cannot be settled peacefully. The Führer agreed to the view.

Source: Akten zur auswärtigen Politik 1918–45. Series D, Vol. 2, *1964, p. 158*

Over the weekend of 21–22 May 1938 the Czech army began concentrating along the frontier with Germany. Hitler took this as a provocation. On 30 May 1938, he issued 'Operation Green' which declared his 'unalterable decision to destroy Czechoslovakia in the foreseeable future through a military action' (*Akten zur auswärtigen Politik 1918–45, Series D, Vol. 2*, 1964, p. 281).

With mounting tension on the border and the continuation of destabilising activities by Henlein and his crew, September 1938 saw a serious international crisis develop over the Sudetenland. Hitler met the British Prime Minister, Chamberlain, on 15 September and demanded the absorption into the Reich of the 3 million Sudeten Germans. After much diplomatic activity, the four most powerful nations of western Europe, Germany, Britain, France and Italy (but not Czechoslovakia herself), met at Munich on 29 September to solve the problem. Even in this forum, as the minutes of the meeting show, Hitler adopted a tone that was little short of bullying.

Document 5.18 Munich

The Führer opened the discussions at 12.45 and thanked the government chiefs present for agreeing to his invitation. He added that first of all he wanted to give a brief outline of the Czech question as it was at the moment. The existence of Czechoslovakia in its present form threatened the peace of Europe. The German, Hungarian, Slovak, Polish and Carpatho-Russian minorities, who had been squeezed into this state against their will, were revolting against the survival of this state. He, the Führer, could only appear as spokesman of the German minorities.

In the interests of European peace, the problem would have to be solved quickly, and indeed by cashing in the promise made by the Czech government for surrender. Germany could no longer overlook the misery and suffering of the Sudeten German population. Reports are arriving in increasing numbers about the destruction of property. The population is exposed to a barbaric persecution. Since he, the Führer, spoke with Mr Chamberlain last, the number of refugees has mounted to 240,000, and there seems to be no end to the stream. In addition it is necessary to bring to an end the political, military and economic tension which has become unbearable. This tension makes it necessary to solve the problem in a few days, since one can no longer wait for weeks on end. At the wish of the Italian government chief, Mussolini, he, the Führer, has explained that he is ready to postpone mobilisation [of the armed forces] in Germany for 24 hours. Further hesitation would be a crime. In order to solve the problem, the responsible statesmen of Europe have come together here, and he establishes that the differences [between them] really are minimal. First of all there is general agreement that the area must be ceded to Germany; secondly [there is general agreement] that Germany claims nothing other than this area. It cannot be left to a commission to decide exactly which area is at issue. Much rather a plebiscite is necessary, especially since free elections have not taken place in Czechoslovakia for 20 years. Now he has explained in his speech at the Palace of Sport that come what may he will invade on 1 October. It has been said to him, that this action would have the character of an act of violence. He has the task of taking seriously the character of this action. But it must be carried out immediately, on the one hand because the persecutions can no longer be overlooked, and on the other hand because he can no longer tolerate the delays resulting from the vacillating views in Prague. Militarily, occupation is no problem, since the low-lying lands are pretty insignificant everywhere. As a result, with any good will it would have to be possible to clear the area in ten days, in fact he was convinced even in six or seven days. . . . It is not to be endured for the long term that armed powers stood face to face in Europe.

Source: H. Michaelis and E. Schraepler, Ursachen und Folgen. Vol. 12, *1965–1968, pp. 443ff.*

It was an extraordinary way for a statesman to speak, but Hitler's biased characterisation of the situation was accepted by Britain and France. Czechoslovakia was forced to give up the Sudetenland. On 1 October 1938, German troops marched into the area unopposed. Plunder continued as Czechoslovakia lost (and Germany's war machine gained) 16,000 sq km of territory, 70% of her iron and steel production capacity, 80% of her textiles and 86% of her chemicals industry as well as 70% of her electric power capacity and her entire lignite industry (Rich, 1992, pp. 109–10). Important frontier fortifications were lost too.

Why was Hitler allowed this victory? On the one hand, the moral point about allowing the Sudeten Germans to join fellow Habsburg Germans in a Greater Germany seemed a strong one. On the other hand, it was assumed that once this sacrifice was made, Hitler would be satisfied. Days before the Munich meeting, Hitler had spoken at the Palace of Sport. Of the Sudetenland, he said 'when this problem is solved there is no further territorial problem in Europe for Germany' (Baynes, 1942, Vol. 2, p. 1526). He followed up these words with a personal note to Chamberlain sent on 27 September 1938.

Document 5.19 Hitler reassures Chamberlain

Dear Mr Chamberlain,
 . . . That Czecholsovakia will lose a part of its defence system is naturally an unavoidable consequence of the separation of the Sudeten German area brought about by the government in Prague itself. If one wanted to wait for the final enactment of the final regulation until Czechoslovakia has prepared

new defence sites in the remaining area, it would take months and years without doubt; but this is also the only purpose of all Czech objections. Above all it is perfectly wrong to maintain that Czechoslovakia would be threatened in this way in its national existence or political and economic independence. From my memo it is clear that German occupation will only stretch up to the given line [separating the Sudetenland from the rest of Czechoslovakia] and that the final establishment of borders should follow in the way which I have already described [i.e. by international agreement]. The government in Prague has no right to doubt that the military measures will stop inside these borders. If it wants to express such doubts, then the British and eventually also the French government may accept an explicit guarantee for the strict maintenance of my recommendations. Incidentally I can refer to my speech of yesterday in which I declared unequivocally *that I decline any attack on the Czechoslovakian territory*, and that I am even prepared under the conditions laid down by myself, to accept a formal guarantee for the rest of Czechoslovakia. So there can be not the least talk of a threat to the independence of Czechoslovakia. It is just as wrong to speak of an economic danger. In contrast it is a notorious fact that Czechoslovakia, after the separation of the Sudeten German area, will represent a healthier and more unified economic unit. . . .

Adolf Hitler

Source: H. Michaelis and E. Schraepler, Ursachen und Folgen. Vol. 12, *1965–1968, pp. 424ff.*

To the great nations of Europe, the appeasement of Hitler seemed the best option. Pacification based on one last success was preferable to the consequences of confrontation. The part of Europe at issue seemed a long way from London and could not be defended without descent into a massive conflict. Unfortunately the peace won in this way was only as durable as Hitler was honest. Three weeks after his invasion of the Sudetenland, he showed once again how little his word was worth. On 21 October 1938, he issued the following military order.

Document 5.20 Liquidate Bohemia and Moravia

I will lay down in a later directive the future tasks of the Wehrmacht and, in connection with these, the preparations for the conduct of war.

Until this directive comes into force, the Wehrmacht must be prepared, at any time, for the following eventualities:

1. the securing of the borders of the German Reich and protection against surprise air attacks.
2. the liquidation of the remainder of Czechoslovakia [Rest-Tschechi]
3. the occupation of Memel. . . .

2. The Liquidation of the remainder of Czechoslovakia

It must be possible to be able to defeat at any time the remainder of Czechoslovakia, if it perhaps would [attempt] to pursue an anti-German policy.

The associated preparations by the Wehrmacht for this will be considerably less extensive than at the moment for 'Green'; but they must (forgoing planned mobilisation) guarantee a constant and essentially higher [level of] readiness.

Source: W. Hofer (ed.), Der Nationalsozialismus Dokumente 1933–1945, *1989, p. 219*

Steps to deal with Bohemia and Moravia proceeded apace. In February 1939 the German Propaganda Ministry was instructed to launch a major campaign. It was said that troops were massing on the border and ethnic Germans were being terrorised (Rich, 1992, p. 114). On the night of 14–15 March, Hitler met the President of the Czech lands, Hacha, and bullied him brutally. When he demanded that Germany be allowed to annex Prague the next day, the ageing President collapsed. He was revived to sign a document promising Hitler everything he demanded (*The French Yellow Book*. No.73. Report of Coulondre, 15.3.39. 1939). On 15 March 1939 German troops crossed the border into Bohemia and Moravia. The very next day Hitler justified the move in a speech given in Prague. The area, he said, had always been part of Germany's living space (Baynes, 1942, Vol. 2, pp. 1586–7). It did not worry him that the Third Reich had just absorbed lands inhabited not by ethnic Germans, but by Czechs.

The economic benefits were considerable. The absorption of the Czech lands brought Germany £16 million in foreign currency. There was the Skoda armaments works too. There were 43,000 machine guns, 1 million rifles, 2,676 artillery pieces, 469 tanks, 1,582 aircraft and 3 million artillery rounds (Rich, 1992, p. 118). The conquest of the area sealed Germany's ascendancy over the south-east of Europe. By 1939 the following countries received the following percentage of their imports from Germany: Bulgaria 65%, Turkey 51%, Hungary 48.4%, Yugoslavia 47.6% and Romania 39.2% (Milward, 1976, p. 440). Hitler had managed to create a massive economic space dominated by Germany which could contribute to his rearmament drive as required. Out of the industrial areas of central Europe, he had managed to plunder resources and to create 'a powerful economic springboard for his military adventures' (Overy, 1994, p. 222).

But the move finally left the impression that no one in Europe could do business with Hitler. In Britain there was a fundamental change of attitude. The German Embassy in London sent an unequivocal report to Berlin.

Document 5.21 Re-evaluation

The Ambassador in Great Britain to the Foreign Ministry
London, March 18, 1939

. . . It is improbable that the incorporation of Czechia into Germany will result in German–British relations becoming increasingly strained to a point at which there is a danger of war. It is just as certain, however, that the present crisis will have deep and lasting repercussions; deeper, in any case, than those resulting from the Austrian *Anschluss*, the September crisis, and the anti-Jewish movement in November 1938.

For political circles in Britain, including the Prime Minister himself, the picture formed of National Socialist Germany has been radically altered. The following circumstances have contributed towards this:

1) The Führer's statement that he had no further territorial claims to put forward in Europe had been interpreted in too drastic and unpolitical a manner. Those who – like Chamberlain – had relied on this, felt that they had been misled in their confidence in the Führer's word.

2) It had been concluded from the National Socialist ideology and the words of the Führer that Germany was only aspiring to the annexation of Germans and not that of members of alien races. The incorporation of seven million Czechs has exploded this idea, especially as the press had purposely minimized the significance and extent of the autonomy granted.

3) It had been assumed that the 'Munich policy' would prepare the way for, and bring about, an arrangement and a delimitation of spheres of interest with Germany by means of friendly discussions. Germany's course of action in Czechia has been understood as a fundamental and curt repudiation.

4) Nor had the real significance of the incorporation of Czechia been understood. In Britain, this state had, in any case, been looked upon since Munich as a vassal of Germany, and one which, in case of emergency, was exposed to the latter's military attack without the chance to resist. Why, therefore, the 'annexation' and the military invasion with all its attendant political risks abroad? Merely – so it was further concluded – because Germany had reverted purely to power politics.

From the fullness of these disappointments and shattered hopes, there has arisen complete uncertainty regarding the aims of Germany and the policy to be adopted towards her. Does Germany aspire to 'world domination', or at least to the hegemony of Europe? Will her next undertaking be the overpowering of Rumania or an attack on Poland? What policy can be adopted towards so incalculable a State? These and similar questions are discussed here in London today by people who wish to be taken seriously. . . . Dirksen

Source: Documents on German Foreign Policy 1918–1945. Series D. Vol. 6, *1956, pp. 36–9*

At last Hitler had put himself decisively in the wrong. He had risked this knowingly and with contempt for the other statesmen of the continent. As he later put it himself, 'Our opponents are little worms. I saw them in Munich' (Jarman, 1955, p. 222; document 6.2). But deception as a strategy had run its course. Hitler achieved just one more territorial expansion under conditions of peace. It was the annexation of Memel on 23 March 1939. Looking back, in the Four Year Plan Hitler had asked for the army to be ready for war by 1940. According to the Hossbach memorandum he had chosen the period 1943–5 as ideal for the start of hostilities. But finally Hitler had tried to deceive with such crassness that even the 'little worms' could no longer ignore him. If he pressed ahead with expansionist aims now, Hitler risked war ahead of schedule.

Should Adolf Hitler's foreign policy be defined as revolutionary in the terms of this study (see Chapter 1)? Convinced of the *injustice* of the settlement reached at the end of the First World War and the way it was applied to Germany, Hitler took the *initiative* to bring about a fundamental change in the *constitution of power* at the international level in Europe. Regardless of deceptive public declarations of peaceful intent and honest principle during especially the earlier years of his government, Hitler's policy always involved a concerted and sensational overturning of the provisions of the Treaty of Versailles and the authority of the League of Nations. There is no other way to understand the drama of his leaving of the disarmament conference, his resignation from the League, the reintroduction of conscription, the remilitarisation of the Rhineland, the *Anschluss*, the absorption of the Sudetenland and the annexation of Bohemia and Moravia. All of this happened in just six years. The means chosen to bring about change were completely appropriate. Eschewing the reasonable approaches of his sophisticated predecessors such as Stresemann, he bullied, *threatened* and lied to Europe's statesmen *ruthlessly*. Quite *illegally* he supported 'fifth columns' abroad (as in the case of Henlein). He was always ready to disregard a treaty which others regarded as legally binding and had no scruples about the application of *violence* in the international arena. In the end, Hitler espoused a whole new *legitimating principle* and *myth* for the conduct of foreign policy. Economic success through trade was not enough for him, nor was the goal of growth through limited war. As the *Second Book* made plain, he understood the international environment to be riven by a type of competition which could only be settled once and for all by the most extensive territorial expansion pursued by military means. If anyone ever had a revolutionary understanding and practice of foreign policy, it was Adolf Hitler.

Warlord | 6

Was the Second World War led by Adolf Hitler as a revolutionary conflict? One thing is clear, the expression of Hitler's thinking and personality reached its apogee between 1939 and 1945. In the unrestrained atmosphere of warfare, he found a more complete scope for self-realisation than could ever have been the case during peacetime. For Hitler, war was something to be welcomed as a downright necessity of life. In 1927 he wrote that land could fall only to those with 'the courage to take possession' of it (Hitler, 1961, p.15). Fifteen years later he declared that 'we must wish for a war every fifteen or twenty years', since wars 'drive people to proliferation, they teach us not to fall into the error of being content with a single child in each family' (Trevor-Roper, 1961, pp. 55–6). War was an essential means both to the extension of Germany's borders (see also Chapters 2 and 5) and to the strengthening of the racial constitution of the nation. All of this meant that Hitler had to be able to rely on Germany's military men. The early signs had indicated that he could (see Chapter 4), and to consolidate the bond between government and the military he introduced an oath in which soldiers promised him their unconditional obedience (Strawson, 1971, pp. 43–4). More important still, in early 1938, just weeks after stating his warlike intent at the Hossbach meeting (document 5.15), he dismissed the Commander in Chief of the Wehrmacht, von Blomberg, and the Commander in Chief of the Army, von Fritsch, on trumped-up charges of moral failings. Thereafter Hitler took control of defence affairs more directly and personally than ever (Welch, 1998, pp. 60–2). The army was no longer a partner of National Socialism in the Third Reich; it had become an instrument of policy (Weissmann, 1997, p. 278). This was a decisive step in preparation for an even more aggressively expansionist foreign policy (Müller, 1989, pp. 91–2).

War came just eighteen months later, and for Hitler it was like a return to the womb. He bristled with pride when he addressed the Reichstag on the morning of the invasion of Poland, 1 September 1939. He would ask no sacrifice of any German which he had not been prepared to make himself. He had 'again put on that tunic' which made him 'the first soldier of the German Reich' (Michalka, 1996, p. 177). But at this time Germany had not managed to achieve the economic targets set in the Four Year Plan (document 5.14). Oil production was only about 20% of the required level, rubber production was less than 5% (Noakes and Pridham, 1974, pp. 411–12). In fact the economy was short of about 1 million workers (Mason, 1981, pp. 296–7). It goes too far to say the economy was in crisis, but still we have to account for why Hitler precipitated war at a time apparently unfavourable to himself? (Fest, 1973, p. 609; Overy, 1994, pp. 200, 222). After all, in November 1937 he had chosen 1943–5 as ideal for the commencement of hostilities (see document 5.15), so why should he have changed his mind now? Discussion of the point can work through two related questions: when exactly did Hitler decide on military action versus Poland; and did he realise at the time that this would unleash not just a localised conflict, but something much greater?

Hitler was desperately concerned about north east central Europe. In Autumn 1938, and then again in Spring 1939 after the annexation of Bohemia and Moravia, he demanded that Danzig (a formerly German Baltic port under the governance of the League of Nations since 1920) be ceded to Germany and that extra-territorial road routes be constructed across the Polish Corridor linking East Prussia with the German heartland. On 25 March 1939 Hitler informed his senior military commanders as follows.

Document 6.1 The Polish Question, 25 March 1939

Danzig quesion
L[ipski] [a Polish diplomat] is returning from Warsaw on Sunday, March 26. His mission was to enquire there whether Poland was ready to make an arrangement about Danzig. The Führer left Berlin on the evening of March 25 and does not wish to be there when L[ipski] returns. For the present R[ibbentrop] [Hitler's foreign policy chief] is to conduct the negotiations. The Führer *does not* wish to solve the Danzig question by force however. He does not wish to drive Poland into the arms of Britain by this.

A possible military occupation of Danzig could be contemplated *only* if L[ipski] gave an indication that the Polish government could not justify voluntary cession of Danzig to their own people and that a *fait accompli* would make a solution easier to them.

Polish question
For the present the Führer does not intend to solve the Polish question. However, it should now be worked upon. A solution in the near future would have to be based on especially favourable political preconditions. In such a case Poland would have to be so beaten down that, during the next few decades, she need not be taken into account as a political factor. In a solution of this kind the Führer envisaged an advanced frontier, extending from the eastern border of East Prussia to the eastern tip of Silesia. The questions of evacuation and resettlement still remain open. The Führer does *not* wish to enter the Ukraine. Possibly a Ukrainian State might be established. But these questions too still remain open.

Source: Documents on German Foreign Policy. Series D. Vol. 6, *1956,* *p. 117*

For all his worries, in late March 1939, Hitler planned military intervention over neither Danzig nor the Polish Corridor. When and why did he change his mind? On 31 March 1939, the British Prime Minister, Chamberlain, announced to the House of Commons that Britain would give full support to the defence of Polish independence. France did likewise. In April both countries concluded guarantees of mutual assistance with Poland, and Britain reintroduced conscription. Britain's commitment to eastern Europe was a 'significant evolution of policy' on her part and indicated the transformation of a readiness to appease Germany's demands into a determination to resist (Strang, 1996, p. 744). The change was in harmony with the new attitude which existed in London following Hitler's duplicitous absorption of Bohemia and Moravia (see Chapter 5 and document 5.21). It showed that Britain now understood her national interests to be intimately related to those of eastern Europe. The development caused a short-circuit in Hitler's brain (Heiber, 1961, pp. 147–8). He abrogated the Anglo-German Naval Agreement and the Non-Aggression Treaty with Poland. More decisively still, on 3 April he commissioned the military operation 'Case White'. It ordered the German armed forces to prepare for operations against Danzig and Poland as of 1 September 1939. If Poland adopted a threatening attitude, there would be a need to remove 'any threat from this direction for ever'. The aim would be to 'destroy Polish military strength, and create in the East a situation which satisfies the requirements of national defence' (*Documents on German Foreign Policy, Vol. 6*, pp. 186–7 and 223–5).

It is true that the directive said the operation against Poland should not be viewed as 'the necessary prerequisite' to conflict with the West. Hitler might have hoped this was the case, but under the circumstances of the British and French guarantees to Poland, he knew it was not something he could rely on. When Hitler spoke to his military men on 23 May 1939 he chose uncompromising rhetoric. Germany, he said, needed to extend its living space in the East, further foreign policy success was contingent only upon invasion, and there was a need 'to attack Poland at the first suitable opportunity'. But most significantly he concluded: 'This time there will be fighting. . . . The war with England and France will be a life-and-death struggle' (Garlinski, 1985, p. 6). A speech given early in 1939 by the Chief of the General Staff, General Halder, provides additional evidence about the thinking at the head of the Reich at this time. Halder spoke to senior military men and must have taken a line approved by Hitler. In the event of France and Britain entering the conflict, he said German troops would stay behind their fortifications on their western border until Poland was liquidated. Then they would storm out to destroy Paris and London. He even foresaw German soldiers being ready to take on Stalin's troops if the Soviet Union decided to enter the picture (Hartmann and Slutsch, 1997, pp. 489 and 495). In other words, when he decided to attack Poland, Hitler was ready for all eventualities.

Taking everything into account, Norman Rich's contention that Hitler only became clear he was going to war over Poland in August 1939 does not look so convincing. He was laying appropriate foundations from a much earlier date.

Nonetheless, on 22 August he outlined his intentions to his military men. The following are notes made by an officer who was present.

Document 6.2 22 August 1939

The relationship to Poland has become unbearable. My previous Polish policy stood in opposition to the view of the *Volk*. My recommendations to Poland (Danzig and the Corridor) were disrupted by the intervention of England. Poland altered its tone towards us. Condition of tension unbearable as a lasting situation. Law of action may not be passed over to the opponent. The time is more favourable now than in 2–3 years. Assassination of me or Mussolini could alter our position adversely. One cannot let things lie for ever with cocked weapons pointing at each other. A compromise solution recommended by us would have demanded a fundamental change of mind and a good gesture. One spoke to us in 'Versailles-speak' again. The danger of a loss of prestige existed. At the moment the appearance is still great that the West will not get involved. With complete decisiveness we must take the risk upon ourselves. The politician must take just as much of a risk upon himself as the supreme commander. We stand before the hard alternative of striking or sooner or later of being annihilated with certainty.

. . . The opponent still had the hope that Russia would appear as an opponent after the conquest of Poland. The opponents have not reckoned with my great decisiveness. Our opponents are little worms. I saw them in Munich.

I was convinced that Stalin would never enter into the English offer. Russia has no interest in the preservation of Poland. . . .

The publication of the non-aggression pact with Russia has exploded like a grenade [see document 6.3]. The effects are not to be foreseen. Even Stalin has said that this course will benefit both lands. The effect on Poland will be huge.

Source: 798-PS. Trial of the Major War Criminal before the International Military Tribunal. Vol. 26, *1947, pp. 338ff.*

Why was Hitler heading towards war now? The picture is complicated. Having been galled by British and French actions that April, and given confidence by an improved relationship with the USSR (see below), Hitler was prepared to delude himself over the prospect of western intervention in the event of an invasion of Poland. He was gambling and miscalculating in equal measure. As document 6.2 also shows, he wanted to act sooner rather than later for fear that time was not on his side. This, incidentally, may relate not only to fears of assassination. He told the British Ambassador, Henderson, during a fit of rage that he preferred the prospect of war now, when he was 50 years old, rather than when he was 55 or 60 (Jarman, 1955, p. 259). Worries over the economy also played their part. On the same day as the above speech was given, Hitler commented that due to developments in

Germany's economic position there was nothing for it; he had to act sooner rather than later (Carr, 1978, pp. 58–9). In other words Hitler did not regard economic difficulties as a restraint to action, but as grounds to accelerate it. With the passage of time, things could always get worse, not better. (This was an interesting way of thinking, see Chapter 9, thesis 4.) All of these factors fed into Hitler's reasoning and nourished a determination to set to one side his timetable of November 1937.

Hitler's speech of 22 August ended with the demand that Case White commence earlier than planned, namely on 26 August. On 23 August he received a letter from the British Prime Minister stating that in the event of hostilities, Britain would honour her commitments to Poland (Strawson, 1971, pp. 84–5). On 25 August Britain and France both ratified their treaties with that country. Disconcerted, on the same day Hitler ordered Case White to be suspended just 12 hours before it was due to run. There was a period of intense diplomatic activity. This soon showed there was no chance of Germany receiving territorial gains on her eastern borders, and so early on the morning of 31 August Hitler ordered the attack on Poland for 4.45 a.m. the next day. The order specified that Germany should open no hostilities in the West. If Britain and France did so, they should be met in such a way that the German armed forces conserve their strength until the Polish campaign was settled (Trevor-Roper, 1966, pp. 37–40). Hitler knew what he was facing. General Franz Halder wrote in his diary, 'Intervention of West said to be unavoidable: in spite of this the Führer has decided to attack' (Rich, 1992, p. 130). Hitler was knowingly bringing about a situation he had foreseen since at least early April 1939: war against Poland, with Britain and France joining in.

Under these dangerous circumstances, Hitler had to stand his ideologically dictated attitudes towards the USSR on their head (see document 2.11). He needed to ensure at least the neutrality of that country. An initial economic agreement was signed between Germany and the USSR on 19 August 1939. It guaranteed the delivery of Soviet supplies of lumber, cotton, grain, oil cake, lead, zinc, phosphates, platinum, furs, cotton and petroleum (Rich, 1992, p. 128). Three days later, on 22 August (the same day as the speech noted in document 6.2), the understanding was extended in the form of the Molotov–Ribbentrop Pact. The public sections of the document amounted to a non-aggression pact between two states. Of more importance was the secret protocol.

Document 6.3 Secret Protocol

Secret Supplementary Protocol
On the occasion of the signing of the non-aggression pact between the German Reich and the Soviet Union, the undersigned, who are authorised of the two parties, have discussed in strictly confidential talks the question of the delimitation of the mutual spheres of interest in eastern Europe. This discussion has led to the following result:

1. In the case of a territorial–political reorganisation in the areas which belong to the Baltic States (Finland, Estonia, Latvia, Lithuania), the northern

border of Lithuania forms the border of the spheres of interest of Germany and the USSR. In this connection, the interest of Lithuania in the Vilnius area is recognised by both sides.

2. In the case of a territorial–political transformation of the area belonging to the Polish state, the spheres of interest of Germany and of the USSR will be delimited approximately by the line of the rivers Narew, Vistula and San.

The question of whether mutual interests allow the maintenance of an independent Polish state to appear desirable, and how this state would be delimited, can only be clarified once and for all in the course of further political developments.

In each case both governments will solve this question via a friendly understanding.

3. Regarding the South East of Europe, the interest of the Soviet side in Bessarabia is emphasised. From the German side, complete political disinterest in these areas is declared.

4. This protocol will be treated as strictly secret by both sides.

Source: Akten zur auswärtigen Politik 1918–1945. Vol. 7, *1964, pp. 205ff.*

In a supplementary section of 28 August, Lithuania was added in its entirety to the Soviet sphere of interest. The two nations had divided eastern Europe into areas within which each would pursue her ends without hindrance. The USSR had allowed Germany a free hand to deal with western Poland.

The interesting thing is that even though he was facing war against Poland, Britain and France, Hitler still nursed much greater ambitions. In early August he had spoken to the League of Nations Governor of Danzig, Jakob Burckhardt, saying: 'Everything I do is directed against Russia; if the West is too stupid and too blind to understand this, I will be compelled to reach an understanding with the Russians, defeat the West, and then ... turn against the Soviet Union' (Burckhardt, 1967, p. 272). This was no idle chatter. The pact of 22 August and supplementary agreement of 28 August 1939 had seen the Baltic States bequeathed to Stalin's sphere of influence. In the long term, to 'give away' an area of such economic and strategic importance made little sense, as former diplomat Ulrich von Hassell explained in his diary.

Document 6.4 The Baltic States

The resultant intellectual confusion is already very noticeable in the Party. We sacrificed the most important positions, the Baltic Sea and the security of our eastern boundary – in order to rescue ourselves momentarily from a dire emergency that we brought upon ourselves. Not to speak of the politically unethical abandonment of the Baltic countries which now seriously endangers our *dominium maris Baltici.* In case of a conflict with Russia even the transportation of ore from Sweden is imperilled. But all this pales in comparison with the nonchalant handing over of a large and important part of the Occident – in part of German–Lutheran culture, in part old Austrian – to that same bolshevism against which we ostensibly fought to the death in distant Spain [in the Spanish Civil War, 1936–9]. The bolshevisation of the hitherto Polish sections has already started on a broad front.

It is quite possible – according to Hitler's speech before the Reichstag [August 27, 1939], and even probable – that Hitler secretly plans to attack Soviet Russia later. If this be the case the criminal character of his policies is only corroborated.

Source: Entry of 11.10.39, U. von Hassell, The von Hassell Diaries, 1948

In agreeing the Molotov–Ribbentrop Pact, with his invasion of Poland on 1 September 1939, and as his ideology of *Lebensraum* dictated (see Chapter 2, especially documents 2.16 and 2.17), Hitler knew full well he was starting a train of events that ultimately could only lead to a much wider conflagration. If he hoped it could be accomplished without the involvement of the West, he *knew* that eventually it would have to include Russia.

From the outset, Hitler's war was never going to be conventional. One set of minutes kept to his speech of 22 August 1939 instructed his military men to wage war as follows: 'Close hearts against sympathy. Brutal action. . . . The stronger has the right. Greatest harshness' (*Trial of the Major War Criminals*, Vol. 2, 1947, p. 157). According to another record of the same speech, Hitler admitted he was sending special units east 'with the order to kill without pity or mercy all men, women and children of Polish race or language' (Breitman, 1991, p. 43). Once war was under way, brutality on the part of special police units swiftly became a reality as they pursued a secret radical racial agenda (Housden, 1997, pp. 149–50). At least some senior military men complained to Hitler about dreadful actions which they perceived as completely arbitrary and unacceptable. The following document shows how he received one set of objections.

Document 6.5 Blaskowitz

18.11.39
Reich Chancellery
Siewert [Adjutant of v. Brauchitsch] orders me to him and gives me a memo from General Blaskowitz about conditions in Poland; greatest worries on account of illegal shootings, imprisonments and confiscations, worries about discipline of the troops who experience these things first hand; local arrangements with SD and Gestapo without success, they refer to orders from Rf-SS [Reichsführer-SS Himmler]; please restore lawful conditions, in particular only have executions implemented through lawful judgements. – Lay the memo (which is put together in a perfectly factual way) before the Führer the same afternoon. First of all he takes note of it calmly, but then begins again with serious accusations against 'childish attitudes' in the leadership of the army; one does not lead a war with Salvation Army methods. Also

a long harboured aversion is confirmed, he has never trusted General Bl. He was also against commissioning him to lead an army. It is maintained as correct to remove Bl. from this post since he is unsuitable. Orientate Supreme Commander of the Army and Siewert of the same. OQu IV.

Source: Tagebuch Wehrmachtsadjutant Hauptmann Engel, *Institut für Zeitgeschichte. Cited complete in M. Broszat*, Nationalsozialistische Polenpolitik, 1939–1945, *1961, p. 41*

Hitler knew what was going on and approved. Blaskowitz was removed from his post. The really senior military figures, such as the Commander in Chief of the Army, Field Marshal von Brauchitsch (who had received this post after the removal of Blomberg and Fritsch), were left to stick their heads in the sand (Graml, 1997, pp. 374–5).

The Polish campaign was tied up with the concept of 'resettlement'. Substantial elements of the Polish population, Poles and Jews alike, were to be displaced from their homes. This was especially the case in the Polish lands incorporated directly into the German Reich, as well as the area of Lublin which was found in the Government General (i.e. the area of southern Poland which was not incorporated into the German Reich, but which was run by the Governor General Hans Frank). The homes were to be taken over by ethnic Germans assembled from around eastern Europe, for instance from the Baltic States which came under Soviet occupation. Although much chaos was associated with resettlement, and while it eventually became a smokescreen behind which the Holocaust was enacted, still it was a genuine policy in its own right. On 7 October 1939 Hitler issued the Decree for the Consolidation of German Folkdom. In it he authorised the *Reichsführer-SS*, Heinrich Himmler, to return to the Reich all Germans living abroad, and 'to eliminate the harmful influence of such alien parts of the population as constitute a danger to the Reich and the German community' (Koehl, 1957, pp. 247–9). But Hitler kept pulling the strings of policy. When, on 25 September, a Baltic German called Erhardt Kroeger, told Heinrich Himmler that all Germans living in the Baltic States would be threatened by the impending Soviet invasion, Himmler asked that the matter be left with him for discussion with the Führer. On the next day, the *Reichsführer-SS* related that Hitler had agreed to evacuate the whole Baltic German population (Kroeger, 1967, pp. 48–54). At the start of October 1939 Hitler told the Reichstag he had decided to create a new order of ethnographic relations in the East and to resettle 'untenable splinters of the German nation' found there. The policy was put into effect and by the end of the year most Baltic Germans (66,866 people) had been resettled to the Reich from Estonia and Latvia (Taube *et al.*, 1995, p. 91). In due course, tracts of Polish territory were cleared of their indigenous populations to make way for incoming ethnic Germans (Madajczyk, 1977, 1987, chapter 22).

From the outset of the Polish campaign, it was clear that the Slavic peoples under German edict had little future. In May 1940 Himmler penned a memorandum which Hitler authorised as 'very correct'. It included the following sections.

Document 6.6 Memo about the Treatment of Foreign Peoples in the East, May 1940, by Heinrich Himmler

Secret Matter of the Reich
Some Thoughts about the Treatment of the Foreign Peoples in the East
In the treatment of the foreign peoples in the East we must seek as much as possible to recognise and nurture individual ethnic groups [*Völkerschaften*], that is to say (apart from Poles and Jews) Ukrainians, White Russians, Gorals, Lemks and Kashubians. If any other national splinter groups are to be found anywhere, these too.

I want to say that we have the greatest interest not in structuring the eastern population into one unit, but rather, in contrast, into as many parts and splinters as possible.

But also inside the ethnic groups themselves we do not have the interest of leading these to unity and greatness, and perhaps to bring them gradual national consciousness and national culture. Rather [we want] to dissolve them into innumerable small splinters and particles. . . .

In a very few years – I imagine 4 to 5 years – the concept of, for example, the Kashubians must be unrecognised, since there will no longer be a Kashubian *Volk* (that refers in particular to the West Prussians too). I hope to see the perfect obliteration of the concept of the Jews through the possibility of a great emigration of all the Jews to Africa or otherwise into a colony. In a rather longer time it must also be possible to allow the ethnic concepts of the Ukrainians, Gorals and Lemks to vanish. The same that is said for these splinter peoples, is valid in the larger context for the Poles.

Source: H. Krausnick, 'Denkschrift Himmlers über die Behandlung der Fremdvölkischen im Osten (Mai 1940)', pp. 195–8

The identities of the eastern peoples were to vanish; the Jews were to vanish more completely still. The memorandum also stated that the eastern peoples should receive only basic education. They should learn to count to just 500, write only their names, respect God's laws and be loyal to Germans. The population of especially the Government General was to be sifted for children with 'valuable' Germanic blood who would be removed from their families.

The eastern peoples were to be used up according to the needs of Germany and her war machine. General Halder explained in his diary on 18 October 1939 that the eastern population was a rabble which might best be used as a supply of slaves (Schramm, 1972, pp. 100–1). Hitler's thinking was not so different and was expressed in the concept of *Grossraumwirtschaft* (literally, 'economy of the large area') (Gruchmann, 1962; Chodorowski, 1972). It held that whole tracts of Europe could be allocated particularly appropriate economic functions. The next memorandum was compiled by the head of the Party Chancellery, Martin Bormann, and shows at greater length how Hitler saw the use of the Government General and its population developing.

Document 6.7 Poland and *Grossraumwirtschaft* – the Thinking in 1940

The people of the Government General, the Poles, are not qualified workers like our German comrades [Volksgenossen] and nor should they be; in order to be able to live they must export their own capacity for work, that is to say themselves. In order to earn their living, the Poles must come to the Reich and work in agriculture, on the roads and in other lowly types of work; but their place of abode remains Poland, because we do not want them in Germany and do not want their blood mixed with that of our German comrades.

The Führer stressed further that the Pole, in contrast to our German worker, is precisely born to lowly work; but we must guarantee every opportunity for betterment to our German worker. This does not come into question at all for the Pole. The standard of life in Poland must be low, and must be kept that way.

The Government General should in no case be a self-contained and unified economic area, which produces completely or in part the industrial products it needs. Rather the Government General is our labour reservoir for lowly labour (brickworks, road construction etc. etc.). The Führer emphasised you could not put anything different into the Slav than what he is by nature. While our German worker by nature as a rule is industrious and diligent, the Pole by nature is lazy and must be forced to work. Incidentally the prerequisites are lacking for the Government [General] to be able to form its own economic area. The natural resources are lacking, and even if these existed the Poles are incapable of exploiting these resources.

The Führer explained we needed large agricultural estates in the Reich so that we could feed our large cities. The large estate, like other agricultural enterprises, needs a labour force for preparing the ground and for the harvest, and a cheap labour force at that. . . . When the harvest is over, the workforce can return to Poland. If the workers were active in agriculture the whole year long, then they would themselves eat a large part of whatever is harvested. It is quite right, therefore, for the Poles to come as seasonal labour for the sowing and harvest seasons. – We have on the one hand over-inhabited industrial areas, but on the other hand a shortage of labour in agriculture and so on. It is thoroughly correct if in the Government [General] there is a serious surplus in the workforce, so that all year long the necessary labour force comes from there to the Reich. – Care is to be taken absolutely that there may be no 'Polish Masters'. Wherever Polish masters exist, so hard though it may sound, they should be killed.

Naturally in terms of blood we may not mix with the Poles; so it is right if in addition to the Polish reapers, Polish reaperesses come to the Reich. What these Poles do among themselves in their camps can be all the same to us. No Protestant zealot should stick his nose into these things.

Once again the Führer must stress that there may be only one master for the Poles and that is a German one; there cannot be two masters side by side, and so all representatives of the Polish intelligentsia are to be killed. This sounds hard but it is the law of life.

The Government General is a Polish reservation, a big Polish labour camp. Even the Poles profit from it, since we keep them healthy and see to it that they don't go hungry. But we may never raise them to a higher level, for otherwise they would simply become anarchists and communists. . . .

In summary the Führer wants to establish:

1. The least German worker and least German farmer must be 10% better off economically than any Pole.
2. A possibility must be sought and found so that a Pole living in Germany does not receive his whole pay, but rather that a part of his pay goes to the families in the Government [General].
3. The Führer stresses that as a rule he does not want the German worker to work longer than 8 hours when relations return to normal [i.e. after the war has ended]. Even if the Pole works 14 hours still he must earn less than the German worker.
4. The ideal picture is: the Pole may only possess small parcels of land in the Government General which secure reasonably his own food needs and those of his family. What other money he needs for clothes, additional food etc. etc. he must earn through work in Germany. The Government [General] is a supply centre for unskilled labour, in particular for agricultural labour. The existence of these labourers is an assured thing since they will always be needed as cheap labour.

Source: K.M. Pospieszalski, Documenta Occupationis. VI, *1958, pp. 31–5*

Poles had a long history of choosing to migrate to Germany in search of work. Some had even been drafted as forced labour during the First World War (Herbert, 1997, chapter 2). But Hitler's planning was something else again. An area with a population of about 13 million people was to become a camp for cheap itinerant labour. It was a fantastic idea, but one which was at least partially realised. By August 1944, 1,688,080 Poles (civilians and prisoners of war) had been taken to Germany to work. The majority (1,125,632) were employed in agriculture, but others were in mining, metal work, the chemical industry, construction and transport. Their numbers were outstripped only by Soviet civilians, of whom 2,758,312 were labouring in Germany (Herbert, 1997, p. 298).

The Polish campaign was more than a war to bring about resettlement, the destruction of national identities and the slavery of the Poles. As the previous document indicates, it was also a war of racial annihilation. Resettlement, national fragmentation, *Grossraumwirtschaft* and mass murder formed an indissoluble whole. Because the Poles had to be rendered a completely servile mass, they were to be deprived of their leadership cadre. From the end of October 1939 German authorities were active in exterminating Polish intellectual and leadership circles. Hitler ordered this himself. On 21 September 1939 a letter was issued by the Supreme Commander of the Army concerning 'Activity and Tasks of the Police Special Action Groups in the Operational Area'. It specified that these police units were to act 'in commission of the Führer' and carry out 'certain national-political tasks' the detail of which was not described (Radziwonczyk, 1996, pp. 94–118). The agenda included mass murder. In November 1939 Polish academics at the Jagiellonian University in Cracow were rounded up (Batowski, 1978–9, p. 113). This was only the beginning.

On 30 May 1940 Hans Frank, the Governor General of the Government General, cited the principle which was to operate in his territory and which had been given to him by Adolf Hitler: 'Whatever leading stratum we have now identified in Poland must be liquidated; whatever moves up into its place must be secured by us and again removed after an appropriate space of time' (Haffner, 1988, p. 134). The comments came at the same time an 'extraordinary pacification action' was running. The following document is taken from the minutes of a meeting of the Government General's main police authorities also held on 30 May 1940. The fate of the people being seized hardly needed to be spelled out.

Document 6.8 Extraordinary Pacification

The extraordinary pacification action embraces two circles [of people]: on the one hand [there is] the circle of people in the Government General who are politically dangerous, the political intellectual leadership layer of the Polish resistance; and on the other hand, [there is] the circle of criminal elements, who, by reason of their earlier actions and their earlier life, have proved that they will never comprise any useful element of society, even of Polish society.

About 2,000 men and several hundred women were in the hands of the security police at the beginning of the extraordinary pacification action. They had been imprisoned on the grounds of being some kind of functionaries of the Polish resistance movement. Actually they comprised an intellectual leadership layer of the Polish resistance movement. Naturally this leadership layer is not limited to the 2,000 people. The names of perhaps another 2,000 people who are to be numbered among this circle were found in the documents and card indexes of the security service. They are people who, by virtue of their activity and behaviour, without exception fell under the summary law order which is valid for the Government General. The summary judgement of these people began at the moment the extraordinary pacification action was ordered. The summary judgement of the 2,000 people in custody is nearing its end, and there are only a few people still to be tried.

After the implementation of this summary court proceeding, an arrest action also began which should lead to the seizure of the circles of people known to the security service who are not yet imprisoned. This should lead to their summary court martial. The result of this arrest action is not yet known. We estimate it will be 75% successful. All in all, the action should embrace a circle of about 3,500 people. There can be no doubt that with these 3,500 people we will seize the most dangerous political part of the resistance movement.

Source: W. Präg and W. Jacobmeyer, Das Diensttagebuch des deutschen Generalgouverneurs in Polen 1939–1945, *1975, pp. 214–15*

The actual military defeat of Poland took barely 5 weeks. Hitler began to turn his attention westwards. On 23 November he told his military commanders he would 'attack France and England at the most favourable and quickest moment'. In the new campaign, the infringement of the neutrality of Belgium and Holland would be 'without meaning' (*Trial of the Major War Criminals*, Vol. 26, 1947, pp. 32 ff.). The assault did not begin until 10 May 1940 and followed a successful campaign against Denmark and Norway. On 21 June 1940, the French capitulated.

The speed of victory left Hitler contemplating the invasion of Great Britain. No plans had been drawn up for the operation. Not until 16 July 1940 did Hitler commission a suitable one, Operation Sealion. He foresaw a wide front of landings to stretch from Ramsgate to the Isle of Wight (Trevor-Roper, 1966, pp. 74–6). Preparations for attack were made during the remainder of the summer, but shelved due to bad weather and a failure to dominate the air space over the English Channel. On 12 October Operation Sealion was cancelled for 1940. Hitler responded to his failure with a spate of terrorist bombing initiatives against British urban areas. In September he bombed London and Liverpool. On 15 November 1940 he carried out Operation Moonlight Sonata against Coventry (Knopp, 1995, pp. 252–3).

Why didn't Hitler invade Great Britain? At times he appeared doubtful whether a successful landing operation was technically possible (Jacobsen, 1963, p. 46). But had he really been dedicated to the idea, the handicaps would have been overcome, or at least discounted (Heiber, 1961, p. 157). More fundamentally we should question the depth of his desire for invasion. Operation Sealion may have been less the product of real intention, and more a manifestation of chagrin at Britain's refusal to fit in with his plans: i.e. its failure to allow him to invade Poland unopposed (Fest, 1973, p. 638). At precisely the time Hitler should have been planning for invasion, he had actually been extending peace feelers to Britain. This he did on 6 October 1939 (Knopp, 1995, p. 243). More bizarrely still, on 19 July 1940, just three days after commissioning Operation Sealion, he repeated the offer during an address to the Reichstag (Hofer, 1989, p. 241). Hitler always felt that war against Great Britain was a mistake. He said of the British on numerous occasions, 'They are our brothers. . . . Why fight our brothers?'(Sereny, 1995, p. 218).

When he spoke to his generals, increasingly Hitler linked the need to overwhelm Britain to a perceived requirement to attack his ally of 1939 – the USSR. During 1940, the USSR had aided Germany in its attack on Norway and had provided its war economy with much needed supplies (Weinberg, 1995, pp. 178–9). But from the middle of that year, in private Hitler was signalling his true intentions. In a talk recorded by General Halder on 31 July 1940, he argued that Russia was the 'factor on which England places most store'. He continued, 'If Russia is defeated, then England's last hope is eradicated' (Jacobsen, 1963, pp. 46 ff.). Just as he had found reasons to rush to war in 1939, so he found grounds to expand hostilities once more (for an explanation of this way of thinking, see Chapter 9, thesis 4). Hitler emphasised the point again in January 1941. The defeat of Britain could best be achieved by the crushing of Russia. This was recorded in the diary of the Supreme Command of the Armed Forces.

Document 6.9 Hitler on Russia and Britain, 9 January 1941

The possibility of a Russian attack keeps the English going. They will only give up the race when this final continental hope is smashed. He – the Führer – does not believe that the English are 'senselessly crazy'; if they saw no more prospect of winning the war, then they would stop. For if they lost, they would no longer have the moral strength to keep their empire together. . . .

The question of time is particularly important in respect of the defeat of Russia. The Russian Armed Forces are indeed a clay colossus without a head, their future development is, however, not to be foreseen clearly. Since Russia must be defeated in any case, then it is better to do it now, when the Russian Armed Forces are obliged to no [particular] leader and are badly armed, and when the Russians have great difficulties to overcome in their armaments industry which has been developed with foreign help. . . .

The massive Russian spaces are hiding immeasurable riches. Germany must dominate them economically and politically, but not annex them. Then anything would be possible, even to lead battle against continents in the future. No one could defeat [us] any more. When this operation is implemented, Europe will hold its breath.

Source: H.A. Jacobsen (ed.), Kriegstagebuch des Oberkommandos der Wehrmacht. Band 1: 1 August 1940 – 31 Dezember 1941, 1965, *pp. 257–8*

But there is an oddity here. Although Hitler was talking about the need to attack Russia from July 1940, the Supreme Command of the Armed Forces was instructed to do nothing for a further six months. In some respects this represents a parallel lapse to the lack of planning to invade Britain. Whatever explanations we offer of these two episodes, it may be that when Hitler faced both these moments of monumental importance, even he froze with indecision.

On 18 December Hitler commissioned the attack on Russia, Operation Barbarossa. It had to be ready for implementation by 15 May 1941. He stated, 'The final objective of the operation is to erect a barrier against Asiatic Russia on the general line Volga–Archangel'. The bulk of Russian troops stationed to the west of the Urals was to be destroyed in a 'rapid campaign' (Trevor-Roper, 1966, pp. 93–7). Whether Hitler really believed that he could do this so easily is another matter. On one occasion he commented 'the Russian colossus will be proved a pig's bladder; prick it and it will burst' (Warlimont, 1964, p. 140). International intelligence services knew Stalin had purged his officer corps mercilessly during the 1930s (Beevor, 1999, p. 23). The strategy could only have reduced the professional competence of the Russian military. On another occasion, however, Hitler also admitted that the 'beginning of each war is like opening a great door into a dark room. You never know what is hiding in the dark' (Eitner, 1994, p. 188). The arguments dictating action rather than patience won the day (again see Chapter 9, thesis 4). Once planning was under way for this decisive campaign, Hitler's interference in it became 'more radical and more continuous than in any that had gone before' (Strawson, 1971, p. 139). It was his decision to ignore the basic military rules of singleness of objective and concentration of forces, and to split the military objectives between Moscow, the Ukraine and Leningrad. By overextending his capabilities so drastically, he was planning for disaster.

Of course the war in the East was more than just a way to round off the campaign against Britain. It was both an ideologically determined quest for *Lebensraum* (the possibility of which had been in his mind since the 1920s, see documents 2.16 and 2.17) and an ideological crusade against the related enemies of Communism and Jewry. Hitler went out of his way to convince his generals of the latter point. (For the ideologically defined relationship which existed in Hitler's mind between Marxism and Jewry, see document 2.10.) On 3 March 1941 General Jodl issued a circular summarising special instructions Hitler had given him. The forthcoming assault was characterised as 'a collision between two different ideologies' in which the 'Bolshevist–Jewish intelligentsia must be eliminated' (Warlimont, 1964, pp. 150–1). On 30 March 1941 Hitler delivered a keynote speech to over 200 senior military men (Beevor, 1999, p. 15). This was to be no war between comrades. The Communist could not be accorded any such status. It was to be 'a battle of annihilation' in which Bolshevik Commissars and the Communist intelligentsia were to meet with 'annihilation'. Hitler said in 'the East severity [now] is mildness for the future' (Jacobsen, 1963, pp. 336–7).

With Hitler at the absolute height of his power, and the likes of Blaskowitz removed after the Polish campaign (document 6.5), Germany's generals did not object when a whole series of criminal orders was passed among them. Several even issued their own instructions which were as radical as anything their Führer envisaged (Beevor, 1999, pp. 16–17). In the Jurisdiction Order of 13 May 1941, General Keitel exonerated German soldiers in advance of *any* crime (whether murder, rape or looting) which they might commit against Russian civilians (Beevor, 1999, p. 14). Most famous, however, was the 'Commissar Order' which was produced at Hitler's instigation just a fortnight before the start of the campaign. The timing should have ensured that all German officers had its contents fixed firmly in their minds as the offensive began. Orders like this were unprecedented in the annals of German military history (Sereny, 1995, p. 246).

Document 6.10 Commissar Order

Guidelines for the Treatment of Political Commissars (Commissar Order),
6.6.41
In the battle against Bolshevism, it cannot be reckoned that the enemy will
behave according to the principles of humanity or of international law.
A hate-filled, cruel and inhuman treatment of our prisoners is to be expected,
in particular by the political commissars of every kind who are the real bearers
of resistance.

The troops have to be conscious:

1. In this battle, to extend consideration and international legal consider-
    ations towards these elements is mistaken. They are a danger for one's
    own security and the rapid pacification of the conquered area.
2. The political commissars are the originators of barbarian Asiatic methods
    of fighting.

As a result, actions of all severity must be taken against them at once and
without any more ado.

As a result, if they are seized in battle or in resistance, in principle they are
to be dealt with at once with weapons [i.e. shot].

Source: H. Laschitza and S. Vietzke, Geschichte Deutschlands und der
deutschen Arbeiterbewegung 1933–1945, *1964, pp. 258f.*

Operation Barbarossa was launched on 22 June 1941. It had been delayed
several weeks because Germany invaded Yugoslavia and Greece the preceding
spring. That summer, 3.2 million men, or 75% of the German armed forces, attacked
into Russia along a front 2,400 km long stretching from the Black Sea to the Baltic
(Eitner, 1994, p. 188). Victories came so quickly that after just 14 days senior military
men believed they could not be defeated (Dülffer, 1996, p. 127). They would be
proved wrong. Within months the campaign degenerated into a slog from which
there was no escape. But how did this vital military undertaking relate to the
most important event of twentieth-century European history? How did Operation
Barbarossa relate to the Holocaust?

Faced with such a massive military initiative, we might have expected the
persecution of the Jews to have slowed. Hitler needed every man he could muster
for other tasks. But his anti-Semitic obsession was not to be sidelined (Jäckel, 1981,
p. 67). Persecutions continued and grew into the attempted extermination of the
whole Jewish race. Why? One view says the key period was October to December
1941. Before this, attacks on the Jews in the newly invaded areas were substantial,
but still are assessed as indicative of something other than an intention to annihilate
the whole race across the entire continent. Only very late in the year did something
change fundamentally (Pohl, 1998, p. 114; Sandkühler, 1998, p. 133; Gerlach, 1998a,
pp. 289–90). Recently Christian Gerlach has argued that Hitler only gave a series
of speeches adopting a clearly genocidal policy after he declared war on the USA

on 11 December 1941 (Gerlach, 1998b, pp. 785–92). In his study of East Galicia, Thomas Sandkühler argues there is no sign among local Nazi officials of an order to kill *every single* Jew in the area until May 1942 (Sandkühler, 1998, pp. 143 and 147). But the most fateful of steps has been interpreted most famously by Martin Broszat (Broszat, 1985, pp. 390–429). Plausibly it was linked with the military campaign becoming bogged down first in mud and then in snow. It became certain there would be no quick military victory over the Soviet Union. Military failure created an organisational blind alley for the resettlement projects which were supposed to affect Slavs and, especially, Jews. One resettlement plan was to send all Europe's Jews to Siberia, but obviously the stagnation made this impossible. Another idea had been to send them to Madagascar. But an unbeaten Britain in charge of the high seas ruled this out too. Nonetheless, during autumn and winter 1941, Himmler kept trying to make resettlement work. Jews were deported from German-controlled lands in western Europe to locations in the East. The result was chaos. Resettlement centres and ghettos across eastern Europe became hopelessly overcrowded, food became horrendously scarce and disease became rife. In the depths of winter, the local administrators of the East just could not cope with their Jews. They believed the only option was to start killing them. They took this step on their own initiative. Localised killing projects spiralled throughout the winter until they coalesced into the Holocaust. To this way of thinking, Hitler never ordered the event. He just let the local bureaucrats bring it about and revised his own thinking accordingly. At the height of this winter, Hitler addressed the Reichstag. The severity of his language was striking. Could there really have been a 'sea change' in his attitude towards Jewry at this point?

Document 6.11 Hitler on the Jews, 30 January 1939

We are clear that the war can only end with either the Aryan peoples being rooted out or else that Jewry vanishes from Europe.

On 1 September 1939 [in fact it had been 30 January 1939 (see document 4.19) – the war started on 1.9.39] in the German Reichstag I already announced – and I guard myself before rash prophecies – that this war will not turn out as the Jews imagine, namely with the rooting out of the European–Aryan peoples, but rather that the result of this war will be the annihilation of Jewry.

For the first time it will not be other peoples which are bled to death, but rather for the first time the genuinely old Jewish law will be applied: an eye for an eye, a tooth for a tooth.

Source: 2664-PS. Trial of the Major War Criminals before the International Military Tribunal. Vol. 31, *1947, pp. 64–5*

Others argue that Hitler did specifically order annihilation and that it happened at an early point in the Russian campaign, namely when Germany stood at the height of her military victories. In this connection, Christopher Browning has analysed the pattern of Jewish killings carried out by German police units (Browning, 1992, pp. 86–121). For example, on 4 July 1941, Special Action Group 'A' operating in Lithuania reported killing 416 Jews, which included just 47 women. But on 29 August 1941 the same unit reported killing 582 Jewish men, 1,731 Jewish women and 1,469 children. In other words, between early July and late August the overall numbers killed increased dramatically, and the killing of women and children became far more common. It may be that during Summer 1941 there was a fundamental rethink by Hitler: he decided not just to persecute Jewish communities severely, but to wipe them out. Both Browning and Eberhardt Jäckel believe a speech given by Hitler on 16 July 1941 functioned as an order for total annihilation (Jäckel, 1984, p. 33). On this day he told his most senior military and party officials that the Crimea and Galicia had to be cleared of all foreigners and settled by Germans; also that there should never be a foreign military power west of the Urals again. More significantly, to the minds of Browning and Jäckel, Hitler declared, 'We must make a Garden of Eden out of the newly won eastern territories; they are important for our existence' (*Akten zur auswärtigen Politik*, Vol. 13.1, 1964, pp. 127–8). This is taken as a sign that no Jews could be tolerated in Eden.

Others again believe the Holocaust was conceived and set up during the planning stage of Operation Barbarossa. After all, the very nature of Hitler's prejudice, which saw Jewry as a worldwide matter, always predisposed him to a deliberate and extensive solution to the 'problem' (document 2.9). Certainly there are signs Hitler was involved in *something* odd in this connection during Spring 1941. Alfred Rosenberg came to lead the administration of German-occupied Russia and met Hitler days after he had given a bloodthirsty address to the generals on 31 March. On 2 April 1941, Rosenberg confided to his diary that they had discussed something 'I do not want to write down today, but will never forget' (Fest, 1973, p. 680). The head of the SS, Heinrich Himmler, was the man Hitler put in charge of the Holocaust. Drawing on a text written by Gitta Sereny, we can see from the quoted meeting with Himmler's secretary that he had a devastating personal meeting with Hitler at about the same time.

Document 6.12 Four Eyes

I have asked a number of these people [those who had been around Hitler] what they would have done if they had known of Hitler's plans for the murder of Poland's élites and of the Jews. It is a measure of their honesty that none of them simply said they would have departed in horror. I think several of them spoke the truth when they said they would have felt horrified. But I believe that all of them would have tried to put it out of their minds: not because any of them were monsters, but because they were totally convinced that Hitler wasn't, and that, therefore, whatever they might have heard couldn't have been quite as bad as it sounded – not 'if the Führer knew'.

The group I speak of here was, of course, very small and, with few exceptions, such as again Speer and Brandt, lived in virtually cloistered conditions, as we have shown. It was only rarely, almost by accident, that they learned what had been the subject of Hitler's meetings 'under four eyes' [i.e. completely private, confidential meeting on a one-to-one basis].

Christa Schröder, Hitler's second senior secretary, told me of one such occasion when I talked with her in 1977. I mentioned that one of Bormann's former adjutants, Heinrich Heim (to whom he entrusted the daily recording of Hitler's *Table Talk*), had told me that *he* didn't think Hitler knew about the extermination of the Jews. Schröder laughed. 'Oh Heimchen –', she said, 'he's too good for this life. Of course Hitler knew! Not only knew, it was *all* his ideas, his orders.

'I clearly remember a day in 1941, I think it was early spring', she said. 'I don't think I will ever forget Himmler's face when he came out after one of his long "under four eyes" conferences with Hitler. He sat down heavily in the chair on the other side of my desk and buried his face in his hands, his elbows on the desk. "My God, my God", he said, "what am I expected to do?"

'Later, much later', she said, 'when we found out what had been done, I was sure that this was the day Hitler told him the Jews had to be killed.'

When I told this story to Speer a year later, he considered it highly probable. 'Himmler was a very paradoxical personality', he said.

Source: G. Sereny, Albert Speer, *1995, pp. 248–9*

Then there is a speech given by Gauleiter Bracht of Upper Silesia in May 1941. Bracht spelled out that as far as the Führer was concerned, he could 'eliminate' [*ausmerzen*] everything in his *Gau* which was not German in a way which would be both more painful and quicker than resettlement (R 52 II/ 182, Federal Archive). He could only have meant an option of mass killing. Nor should we forget that from the very outset of Barbarossa, Jewish women and children were potential murder victims. Right at the start of July 1941, Zlotow (in the Ukraine) was invaded. An eye witness remembers a security policeman shooting a young Jewish woman and her three-year-old child after first denouncing her as a Communist (Rep. 502 VI M 38, Nuremberg State Archive). In eastern Galicia during the first half of July 1941 alone 10,000 Jews were killed in pogroms and organised shootings (Sandkühler, 1998, p. 128). Daniel Goldhagen has documented an array of comparable atrocities committed across the area invaded by German troops from the earliest days of Operation Barbarossa (Goldhagen, 1996, pp. 150–2). Something so extensive must have been authorised at the most senior level before the military operation began.

The creation of Special Action Groups (*Einsatzgruppen*) is another reason to focus on spring. These were four groups of 750 men each which were set up and trained between March and May 1941 on commission of Adolf Hitler by Himmler and his right-hand man, Reinhardt Heydrich. During 1941–2, these groups killed 500,000 Jews in eastern Europe. The original order dictated by Hitler on 13 March 1941 described their function as 'certain special tasks' which stemmed from 'the necessity to settle finally the conflict between two opposing political systems'. By the end of April they had been empowered to take 'executive measures' against 'the civilian population'. At least one participant in the groups later recalled that in June 1941 Heydrich told the Special Action Group Commanders that Judaism, as the source of Bolshevism in the East, had to be 'wiped out' (Krausnick and Broszat, 1982, pp. 77–8). If we can believe testimony such as this, it looks like these groups were established deliberately as agents of the Holocaust.

The precise truth about the relationship of Hitler to the origins of the Holocaust will never be put beyond all possible doubt. We lack the sort of evidence which supports decisively only a single interpretation of events (Benz, 1995, p. 118). But the balance of probability in the light of the unfolding of events, Hitler's speeches to the military in Spring 1941, the context of annihilatory actions that had already been undertaken against the Poles together with what we know of his personality and ideas, suggests the following reading of events. In the weeks before the launching of Operation Barbarossa Hitler was shut away in his mountain idyll in Berchtesgaden brooding on plans for wholesale annihilation (these were not just directed against Jews – see below) (Knopp, 1995, p. 295). In Spring 1941 he decided to implement a mass anti-Semitic killing process in the East that was tantamount to the Holocaust. Even if he was not exactly sure at such an early point how the whole initiative would develop, he was clear enough about the direction in which he wanted to proceed. Thereafter he worked towards his goal in a series of operational stages. Initially the idea that the Jews were expendable was introduced into the minds of men like Himmler, Rosenberg and Bracht. They became clear that the attack in the East would see massive Jewish fatalities. At the same time, the *Einsatzgruppen* were set up as a murderous executive. Anti-Semitic killing as a deliberate policy started along with Operation Barbarossa in late June/early July 1941. Its intensity was increased on the Führer's urging in mid-summer. During the chaos of winter, motivated by both ideological reasoning and practical considerations (not to mention in response to more initiatives urged by the Führer), German administrators got used to the idea of state-sponsored genocide. As a result the process became ever more widespread. By January 1942 Hitler felt sufficiently confident to voice in public the new radical racial line.

The Holocaust did not stand isolated from other policies Hitler pursued in the East. We have already discussed the annihilation of Polish intellectuals and document 6.6 shows that as early as 1940 Hitler had agreed the de-nationing of eastern peoples as a whole. In July 1941 he authorised the clearing of all foreigners from Galicia and the Crimea. Some months earlier, in March 1941, he had demanded the clearing of the Government General too. Governor General Hans Frank said as much in a speech delivered on 25 March 1941. It was to happen over the next 15 to 20 years, leaving his territory '*a purely German land*' (R 52 II / 181, Federal Archive). Over 10 million Poles and Jews were to be removed from the Government General alone.

The changes involved dramatic depopulation in the East, and in this connection the Holocaust was intimately related to Hitler's policy as it developed towards the Slavic peoples (Aly and Heim, 1993; Housden, 1995). Apocalyptically, in January

1941, Himmler had told an SS gathering at Weselburg that the destruction of 30 million Russians was a prerequisite to German planning for the East and that the impending Operation Barbarossa was to be promote this end (Koehl, 1957, p. 146). In similar fashion, State Secretary of Food and Agriculture Backe commented on 23 May 1941 that in the near future, 'Tens of millions of people will become superfluous in this area [i.e. the East] and will die or have to emigrate to Siberia' (Dülffer, 1996, p. 158). Before Operation Barbarossa was launched, it became an accepted principle of policy, which was explicitly approved by Hitler, that 30 million people in the occupied Soviet Union would be allowed to starve so that more food would be available for the German population and army (Gerlach, 1998a, pp. 266–71).

A profound will to destruction was evident in the way Hitler commanded the campaign against the Slavs. By September 1941 his troops were outside Leningrad and he was considering how best to deal with the city. He decided on the complete destruction of property and people alike. In conversation he justified this by stating that the German 'species' was 'in danger' (Trevor-Roper, 1961, pp. 69–70). In October 1941, on Hitler's say so, the starvation of everyone living in Leningrad became a military aim.

Document 6.13 Starving Leningrad

Order of the Supreme Command of the Army
Supreme Command of the Army
Führer HQ, 7.10.41
Only through an officer
Secret Command Matter
In connection with: OKH (Operations Dept) Nr.41244/41 g.K. of 18.9

The Führer has decided anew that the surrender of Leningrad, or later of Moscow, is not to be accepted, even if the other side offers it.

The moral justification for this measure is clear before all the world. Just as the most severe dangers arose in Kiev for troops as a result of time bombs, we have to reckon with the same problem to an even greater extent in Moscow and Leningrad. Soviet Russian radio itself has said that Leningrad is mined and will be defended to the last man.

Serious outbreaks of disease are to be expected.

As a consequence, no German soldier is to enter these cities. Whoever wants to leave the town through our lines is to be turned back by fire. Smaller gaps [in our lines] which are not blocked, and which enable the population to stream out into the Russian interior, are only to be welcomed. It is true that all other towns are to be worn down by artillery fire and air attack before being captured, and their population caused to flee.

It is not justified to set the life of German soldiers against a danger of fire in order to save Russian towns; likewise it is not justified to feed their population at the cost of the German homeland.

Chaos in Russia will become so much greater, our administration and exploitation of the occupied territories so much easier, the more the population of the Soviet Russian towns flees to the Russian interior.

This will of the Führer must be made known to all commanders.

Chief of the Supreme Command of the Army

Signed: Jodl

Source: Akten zur auswärtigen Politik 1918–45. Vol 13.2, *1964, pp. 509–10*

There was a savage irony here. The eastern peoples, and especially non-Russians, often welcomed the Germans with open arms. They saw them as liberators from Soviet oppression. Often only Communists fled before German troops and industrial complexes were taken over undamaged. All that would have been necessary for a successful occupation would have been 'a soft hand and a soft word' (Lewin, 1984, p. 132). Instead, and on Hitler's direct instructions, the war in the East was pursued with the utmost barbarity.

Once Barbarossa was under way, extensive plans were drawn up for the Germanisation of vast tracts of the East. Most famous among these was General Plan East. It was written by the Reich Security Head Office at the end of 1941 as a plan for the Germanisation of the whole of the East – the Baltic States, Poland, Czechoslovakia, the Ukraine and White Ruthenia. The plan was to be enacted over 20 years or so, but also foresaw the whole of the area up the Urals becoming populated by 600 million Germans in a matter of centuries. There were plans to sift through the eastern populations to find individuals suitable for Germanisation, but still it was assumed that between 40 and 45 million Slavic people would be removed from Europe (one way or another) to make way for the settlement of Germans. These people were to be derived from the following sources: 3.8 million from Germany itself; 100,000 from resettlement camps; 500,000 from ethnic German communities scattered throughout southern Europe; 150,000 from ethnic German communities in northern Europe; 750,000 Estonians, Latvians, Lithuanians and Goralians (who were all to be Germanised) plus 150,000 Germans who were expected to return from overseas (for example from the USA) (Dülffer, 1996, p. 157; Heiber, 1958; Benz, 1990; Giordano, 1991, p. 154). A plan such as this could only have been developed under the patronage of Adolf Hitler. Its scope was too great for anything else.

The year 1941 proved a turning point in the Second World War. Helped by indecisive leadership on Hitler's part (he found it hard to decide conclusively on military objectives), Germany failed to take advantage of her early victories and did not defeat the Soviet Union before the onset of winter (Beevor, 1999, p. 33). It was an eventuality Hitler had not wished to contemplate: he had not even authorised in good time the allocation of winter clothing for his troops (Beevor, 1999, p. 44). In December the USA entered the war, lending its huge material resources to both Great Britain and the Soviet Union. Hitler now faced a phenomenal coalescence of enemies. According to General Jodl, as early as the winter of 1941–2 the Führer realised that the sort of victory he was interested in was not attainable (Schramm,

1972, p. 26). Warfare became a matter of attrition. With the weight of forces against him, Hitler worsened his position by making a variety of strategic blunders. Drunk on the idea of his own infallibility, he frittered away soldiers in operations that were too ambitious (Beevor, 1999, p. 68). During the offensive of 1942 he sent troops to defeat Russian forces in the Caucasus, at Stalingrad and at Leningrad. Any one objective would have sufficed; he was asking the impossible. Hitler was too impatient and too inclined to overestimate the capacities of his own men relative to the enemy to be an effective general (Strawson, 1971, pp. 232–5; Halder, 1950, pp. 6–7). He ignored the sort of practical issues that constitute the reality of military campaigns (Beevor, 1999, p. 33). The longer the war went on, the more Hitler showed he lacked the lucid, rational mentality of a great military leader. He had only 'a stubborn will guided by dark intuition' (Halder, 1950, p. 14). It became increasingly obvious he had no well-thought-out plan about how exactly to achieve final victory (Eitner, 1994, p. 186).

As defeat approached, Hitler became increasingly obstinate and inflexible. He intervened in lower and lower level military affairs. With his health becoming ever more frail, he showed all the characteristics of being an old man sustained by medication. He could barely evaluate information soberly. He fitted the facts to his preconceived ideas (Maser, 1973, pp. 277, 281, 307). After a catastrophic defeat at the second battle of Stalingrad in the winter of 1942–3, more than ever Hitler lived in a land of make-believe. Orders to his troops became increasingly doctrinaire, not to say bizarre.

Document 6.14 Ideology for the Military

Order of the Day   15 April 1945

Soldiers of the German Eastern front!

For the last time our deadly enemies the Jewish Bolsheviks have launched their massive forces to the attack. Their aim is to reduce Germany to ruins and to exterminate our people. Many of you soldiers in the East already know the fate which threatens, above all, German women, girls, and children. While the old men and children will be murdered, the women and girls will be reduced to barrack-room whores. The remainder will be marched off to Siberia.

We have foreseen this thrust [i.e. the most recent Soviet offensive], and since last January have done everything possible to construct a strong front. The enemy will be greeted by massive artillery fire. Gaps in our infantry have been made good by countless new units. Our front is being strengthened by emergency units, newly raised units, and by the *Volkssturm* [homeguard]. This time the Bolshevik will meet the ancient fate of Asia – he must and shall bleed to death before the capital of the German Reich. Whoever fails in his duty at this moment behaves as a traitor to our people. The regiment or division which abandons its position acts so disgracefully that it must be ashamed before the women and children who are withstanding the terror of bombing in our cities. Above all, be on your guard against the few treacherous officers and soldiers who, in order to preserve their pitiful lives, fight against us in Russian pay, perhaps even wearing German uniform. Anyone ordering you to retreat will, unless you know him well personally, be immediately arrested and, if necessary, killed on the spot, no matter what rank he may hold. If every soldier on the Eastern front does his duty in the days and weeks which lie ahead, the last assault of Asia will crumple, just as the invasion by our enemies in the West will finally fail, in spite of everything.

Berlin remains German, Vienna will be German again, and Europe will never be Russian.

Form yourselves into a sworn brotherhood, to defend, not the empty conception of a Fatherland, but your homes, your wives, your children, and, with them, our future. In these hours, the whole German people looks to you, my fighters in the East, and only hopes that, thanks to your resolution and fanaticism, thanks to your weapons, and under your leadership, the Bolshevik assault will be choked in a bath of blood. At this moment, when Fate has removed from the earth the greatest war criminal of all time [i.e. President Roosevelt], the turning-point of this war will be decided.

Signed: ADOLF HITLER

Source: H.R. Trevor-Roper, Hitler's War Directives 1939–1949, *1966, pp. 300–1*

In Hitler's mind ideological fixity became tied to an urge to destruction which, in the final stages of the war, threatened to affect the whole nation. With the Allies poised to invade German territory from both East and West, on 19 March 1945 Hitler issued his infamous Nero Order – everything in the country was to be destroyed in the face of the advancing troops. The order was not implemented because Hitler's personal architect and the Minister for Armaments, Albert Speer, toured Germany countermanding it.

The radicalisation of Hitler's orders ran parallel to the radicalisation of his personal racism. His lines of argument suddenly, and quite grotesquely, would culminate in anti-Semitic diatribes. In the final stages of the war there was only one way Hitler could defy what he saw as a 'Jew-infested' world: he wrote. His *Testament* opens a window to a tortured mind. Rediscovering the radicalism of *Mein Kampf*, he turned out phrases stigmatising the Jews as abscesses (Genoud, 1959, pp. 55–7). His enemies were vilified. Roosevelt became a 'Jew-ridden man' (Genoud, 1959, pp. 90–1). As if admitting culpability for the Holocaust, he stated that 'National Socialism can justly claim the eternal gratitude of the people for having eliminated the Jew from Germany and Central Europe' (Genoud, 1959, p. 105). Hitler started his political career with a hate-filled anti-Semitic diatribe (document 2.2), and ended it the same way.

Document 6.15 The Testament, 2 April 1945.

[I]n this cruel world into which two great wars have plunged us again, it is obvious that the only white peoples who have any chance of survival and prosperity are those who know how to suffer and who still retain the courage to fight, even when things are hopeless, to the death. And the only peoples who will have the right to claim these qualities will be those who have shown themselves capable of eradicating from their system the deadly poison of Jewry.

Source: F. Genoud (ed.), The Testament of Adolf Hitler, *1959, p. 109*

Did Adolf Hitler pursue a war that was revolutionary in the terms of this study (for a definition of 'revolutionary', see Chapter 1)? It is certain he did. Hitler took the *initiative* to precipitate war in September 1939. He did so *ruthlessly* in the conscious risk that a relatively localised campaign against Poland could escalate into a much wider conflict. In equally *ruthless* fashion he stood his political ideology on its head and entered into a pact with Russia which carved up the political order of central and eastern Europe. From the outset the war sought to *transform the social structures* of occupied nations. An attempt was made to eradicate the Polish intelligentsia and a plan was hatched to introduce a new Germanic layer to Polish lands by the resettlement of ethnic Germans. In fact the whole social purpose of the Polish population was redefined: it became a slave people at the behest of Germany. Hitler took the *initiative* again in 1941 to escalate conflict by the attack on the USSR. The military's rules of engagement were redefined by a number of brutal orders most armies would regard as *illegal*. Operation Barbarossa was accompanied by more revolutionary actions. The Jews (long believed a *social evil*) began to be exterminated. The war was waged in such a way as to reduce Slavic populations dramatically. There were massive plans, such as General Plan East, to redefine the whole population of the East. Obviously these steps had the most radical consequences for the *social structures* in the lands affected. New systems were being established which were *legitimated by myths* of race. Just as important, Europe saw a fundamental *change in the constellation of political power* across most of its mass. The single-party nation was giving way to the single-party continent and overturning the whole order of European nations along the way. *As leader of the process, Hitler used war as a means to export National Socialism's revolutionary principles. He took the opportunity to implement them in their most radically murderous form.*

Adolf Hitler fought and lost the Second World War as he had lived his life: as a violent anti-Semite and racist (see Chapter 9, thesis 2). Where hostilities mattered to him most, in eastern Europe and Russia, this had not been a traditional conflict aiming to subdue an enemy by killing or defeating his troops. It had been a great race war fought in favour of racial re-ordering through annihilatory means and ultimately against a perceived universal Jewish enemy. This reflected the vivid ideological fantasies spun in the mind of Adolf Hitler and went a long way towards creating a wasteland out of the East. Ironically Hitler's ultimate impact on the world was the precise opposite to what he had hoped. Far from annihilating Communism, the Second World War brought the Soviet Union into the heart of Europe. Far from eradicating Jewry (and not withstanding the fact that Hitler killed about 6 million Jews), an independent Jewish state was created. At the Nuremberg Trials in 1946, the Third Reich's leading henchmen were convicted by an international tribunal of hideous crimes against peace, crimes against humanity and of war crimes. Hitler's politics was discredited as criminal (see Chapter 9, thesis 5) (Friedrich, 1996, pp. 20–1). As a warlord, Hitler failed completely – but what suffering he caused in the process.

Artist and architect | 7

How did Adolf Hitler's interest in art and architecture relate to the possibility of his being a revolutionary? The question may seem out of place following so closely a discussion of the Second World War – after all society generally views artists in positive ways (Stierlin, 1995, p. 88). They enrich the world with their creations; they pose questions about prevailing realities; and they make available new ways of experiencing that which is familiar. By contrast, so much about Hitler's life was destructive. But still Hitler had much of the artist about him; even aspects of his war effort were touched by artistic ambitions (see below). The artistic facet of Hitler's personality must be explored to provide a wider context for his political and military career.

The truth about Hitler was realised by a literary giant of the 1920s and 1930s, Thomas Mann. He attributed a whole host of characteristics to Hitler which are held common to artists: laziness, a tendency to reject reasonable activity due to arrogance, anger at the world, a feeling of being especially chosen, an indefinability of his work – the list goes on and on (Mann, 1989, pp. 26–7). It has even been said that Hitler's intuitive, artistic characteristics were the most important thing about him (Cross, 1973, p. 14). Hitler did always believe himself to be an artist and on a number of occasions implied he had only entered politics to implement creative designs (Waite, 1993, p. 64). There was a definite relationship between the drive with which the man approached politics and his desire to remodel the physical environment (Taylor, 1974, pp. 28–9). Hitler believed that in himself the roles of artist and politician flowed together and said as much when, in 1932, he identified the skill of managing the state as an art form (Eitner, 1994, p. 61). Under the circumstances, it is quite an oversight that many standard biographies make little attempt to take account of Hitler 'the artist and architect'.

As a youth, Hitler expressed artistic characteristics especially clearly. When his father pressed him to secure a career in the Habsburg civil service, Adolf decided on a career in art instead. August Kubizek knew the teenage Hitler. His memoirs were originally commissioned by the NSDAP and occasionally incorporate elements that were invented to support what Hitler wrote in *Mein Kampf*. Nonetheless, so long as they are used carefully, the memoirs make for a valuable historical source (Kershaw, 1998, p. 20). For example, they show the extent to which the young Adolf adopted the mannerisms of an aspiring artist. The two met for the first time in about 1905, at the opera in Linz (Kubizek, 1955, p. 7). Hitler's self-presentation was affected as if to emphasise individuality and creative potential. He carried a black ebony cane topped by an elegant ivory shoe, and wore a broad-brimmed hat, black coat, black (silk-lined) overcoat and black kid gloves (Kubizek, 1955, p. 10; Heiber, 1961, p. 13). There is no doubting the way this Bohemian dandy impressed Kubizek, who was an apprentice upholsterer (Kubizek, 1955, p. 11). His memoirs contain the following passage.

Document 7.1 A Poem

One day when we were taking a walk he suddenly stopped, produced from his pocket a little black notebook – I still see it before me and could describe it minutely – and read me a poem he had written.

I do not remember the poem itself any longer; to be precise, I can no longer distinguish it from the other poems which Adolf read to me in later days. But I do remember distinctly how much it impressed me that my friend wrote poetry and carried his poems around with him in the same way that I carried my tools. When Adolf later showed me his drawings and designs which he had sketched – somewhat confused and confusing designs which were really beyond me – when he told me that he had much more and better work in his room and was determined to devote his whole life to art, then it dawned on me what kind of a person my friend really was. He belonged to that particular species of people of which I had dreamed myself in my more expansive moments; an artist, who despised the mere bread-and-butter job and devoted himself to writing poetry, to drawing, painting and to going to the theatre. This impressed me enormously. I was thrilled by the grandeur which I saw here. My ideas of an artist were then still very hazy – probably as hazy as were Hitler's. But that made it all the more alluring.

Source: August Kubizek, The Young Hitler I Knew, *1955, p. 11*

Even in his elder years listening to music could transform the dictator, and it was the opera which the young Adolf revered in particular (Waite, 1993, p. 64). The experience of a full-blown Wagnerian performance was formative for him, and once again this point has rarely been given its due in mainstream studies of the man (Hitler, 1985, p. 16; Eitner, 1994, p. 83). Wagner's world was powerful. It rejoiced in visual spectacle. It conjured up a potent environment of ancient Germanic myth. It consisted of melodrama and sensuousness, battle and catastrophe, vengeance and death. There were dreadful crimes and heroes sent to combat them. Terrible brutality found a counterpoint in some of the most innocent characters to walk the stage. Throughout his life, Hitler loved to hurl himself into this twilight world. Wagnerian performances became akin to religious services. They stimulated him to brood and dream. After experiencing them, he would leave the theatre deep in fantasy (Smith, 1979, p. 103). Later in life, Hitler wrote that Wagner had turned him into an artistic revolutionary (Hitler, 1985, p. 16).

Young Adolf actually tried to pen his own opera based on a story which Wagner had only begun. It was called Wieland the Smith, a gory tale of hunger for gold, the murder of sons and the rape of daughters. Hitler planned to compose the music himself but, since he could not read the medium, he wanted Kubizek to write it down (Kubizek, 1955, pp. 194–6). No relic remains of the undertaking. In fact we have just a single extract from one of Hitler's forays into the field of opera. It is a lone paragraph which sets the scene for a drama.

Document 7.2 Setting the Scene

Holy Mountain in the background, before it the mighty sacrificial block surrounded by huge oaks; two powerful warriors hold the black bull which is to be sacrificed, firmly by the horns, and press the beast's mighty head against the hollow in the sacrificial block. Behind them, erect in light-colored robes, stands the priest. He holds the sword with which he will slaughter the bull. All around solemn, bearded men leaning on their shields, their lances ready, are watching the ceremony intently.

Source: Robert G.L. Waite, The Psychopathic God, *1993, p. 69*

Hitler was absorbed by myth. He may even have cultivated his appearance after a painting of a fantastic scene. Robert Waite has noticed a picture by Franz von Stuck called 'Wild Chase'. It hangs in the Municipal Gallery in Munich and so probably was seen by Hitler when he lived in that city immediately before the First World War (Waite, 1993, p. 68). In it, wolves look on intently as the Germanic god Wotan, who personified death and destruction, rides forth as a mad huntsman brandishing a bloody sword. He sports a lengthy forelock hanging over his left temple together with a small moustache. The similarity to Adolf Hitler is striking.

Art and opera expose the way Hitler lusted after the fantastic. But his real, most lasting, deepest obsession was architecture. As a fifteen-year-old, and in the company of Kubizek, Hitler would climb to vantage points overlooking Linz and discuss how the city should be redesigned. Later, recalling their conversations, Kubizek indicated that the architectural plans which Hitler commissioned after the *Anschluss* of 1938 were the same as those hatched in the mind of the teenager in 1906–7. Kubizek said, 'What the fifteen-year-old planned, the fifty-year-old carried out . . . as faithfully as though only a few weeks instead of decades lay between planning and execution' (Kubizek, 1955, pp. 85–6). This is how young Adolf wanted to develop the Austrian city.

Document 7.3 Linz

And now for the rebuilding of Linz! Here his ideas were legion, yet he did not change them indiscriminately, and indeed held fast to his decisions once they were taken. That is why I remember so much about it. Every time we passed one spot or another, all his plans were ready immediately.

The wonderfully compact main square was a constant delight to Adolf, and his only regret was that the two houses nearest to the Danube disturbed his free vista on to the river and the range of hills beyond. On his plans, the two houses were pushed apart sufficiently to allow a free view of the new, widened bridge without, however, substantially altering the former aspect of the square, a solution which later he actually carried out. The Town Hall, which stood on the square, he thought unworthy of a rising town like Linz. He visualised a new, stately town hall, to be built in a modern style, far removed from the neo-Gothic style which at that time was the vogue for town halls, in Vienna and Munich, for instance. In a different way, Hitler proceeded in the remodelling of the old Castle, an ugly boxlike pile which overlooked the old city. He had discovered an old print by Merian depicting the castle as it was before the great fire. Its original appearance should be restored and the castle turned into a museum.

Another building which never failed to rouse his enthusiasm was the Museum, built in 1892. We often stood and looked at the marble frieze which was 110 metres long and reproduced scenes from the history of the country in relief. He never got tired of gazing at it. He extended the museum beyond the adjoining convent garden and enlarged the frieze to 220 metres to make it, he asserted, the biggest relief frieze on the continent. The new cathedral, then in course of construction, occupied him constantly. The Gothic revival was, in his opinion, a hopeless enterprise, and he was angry that the Linzers could not stand up to the Viennese. For the height of the Linz spire was limited to 134 metres out of respect for the 138-metre-high St Stephen's spire in Vienna. Adolf was greatly pleased with the new Corporation of Masons which had been founded in connection with the building of the cathedral, as he hoped it would result in the training of a number of capable masons for the town. The railway station was too near the town, and with its network of tracks impeded the traffic as well as the town's development. Here, Adolf found an ingenious solution which was far ahead of his time. He removed the station out of the town into the open country and ran the tracks underground across the town. The space gained by the demolition of the old station was designated for an extension of the public park. Reading this, one must not forget that the time was 1907, and that it was an unknown youth of eighteen, without training or qualification, who propounded these projects which revolutionised town planning, and which proved how capable he was, even then, of brushing aside existing ideas.

In a similar way, Hitler also reconstructed the surroundings of Linz. . . . Quite a different project, of absolutely modern design, was the tower on the Lichtenberg. A mountain railway should run up to the peak, where a comfortable hotel would stand. The whole was dominated by a tower three hundred metres high, a steel construction which kept him very busy. The gilded eagle on the top of St Stephen's in Vienna could be seen on clear days through a telescope from the highest platform on the tower. I think I remember seeing a sketch of this project.

The boldest project, however, which put all the others in the shade, was the building of a grandiose bridge which would span the Danube at a great height. For this purpose he planned the construction of a high-level road. This would start at the Gugel, then still an ugly sandpit, which could be filled in with the town's refuse and rubbish, and provide the space for a new park. From there, in a broad sweep, the new road would lead up to the Stadtwald. (Incidentally, the city engineers went thus far some time ago, without knowing Hitler's plans. The road which has meanwhile been built corresponds exactly to Hitler's projects.)

Source: August Kubizek, The Young Hitler I Knew, *1955, pp. 86–8*

The thinking was comprehensive, showed some originality, and there really were consistencies across the years. After 1938, although he did not route the railway beneath Linz, Hitler did authorise extensive work on the city – including the bridge.

In September 1907 Hitler moved to Vienna. His sat the entrance examination of the General School of Painting at the Academy of Fine Arts. Only 28 out of 113 applicants passed, and he was not among them. The outcome struck him 'like a bolt from the blue' (Hitler, 1985, pp. 18–19). Apparently Hitler had not included enough heads in the batch of sketches he submitted to the school (Maser, 1973, pp. 40–1). Requesting a proper explanation from the rector, he was told that without doubt his real talent lay in architecture. Hitler later remembered the impact of the opinion: 'In a few days I myself knew that I should some day become an architect' (Hitler, 1985, pp. 18–19). In 1908 Hitler applied to the Academy again, this time to study architecture. Lacking basic school matriculation qualifications, he was rejected once more.

Although Hitler received a small stipend from his family to support his life in Vienna, still he was left to face the basic difficulty of life: how to earn a living? His answer in due course was to set himself up as a painter. He worked first in the Austrian capital (between 1909 and 1913) and then Munich (from 1913 to 1914). He painted numerous small pictures, perhaps seven per week, mostly of buildings, which could be sold as postcards. These were 'not unpleasing copies of reality, proportionally accurate renderings of photographs projected in two dimensions' (Heiber, 1961, p. 24). Occasionally he produced landscapes or illustrations for advertisements for cosmetics, shoe polish and underwear. During his stay in Vienna, Hitler's work was hawked around the city's second-order art shops by an acquaintance, Reinhold Hanisch, with whom Hitler shared his income (Maser, 1973, p. 47).

It should be no surprise that Hanisch complained that Hitler produced his works too slowly (Hanisch, 1939a, p. 240). These small jobs were of only minor concern for a mind which strived after grandeur. As if rejecting the harsh reality of his failure at the Academy, while still in Vienna Hitler's first response to rejection was to embark on a course of self-directed study which was designed to enable him one day to become an architect. Hitler would walk around the city engrossed in its buildings. Kubizek described these excursions.

Document 7.4 Ringstrasse

All the more enthusiastic was he about what people had built in Vienna. Think only of the Ringstrasse! When he saw it for the first time, with its fabulous buildings, it seemed to him the realisation of his boldest artistic dreams, and it took him a long time to digest this overwhelming impression. Only gradually did he find his way about this magnificent exhibition of modern architecture. I often had to accompany him on his strolls along the Ring. Then he would describe to me at some length this or that building, pointing out certain details, or he would explain to me its origins. He would literally spend hours in front of it, forgetting not only the time but all that went on around him. I could not understand the reason for these long drawn out and complicated inspections; after all, he had seen everything before, and already knew more about it than most of the inhabitants of the city. When I occasionally became impatient, he shouted at me rudely, asking whether I was his real friend or not; if I was, I should share his interests. Then he continued with his dissertation. At home he would draw for me ground plans and sectional plans, or enlarge upon some interesting detail. He borrowed books on the origin of various buildings, the Hof Opera, the House of Parliament, the Burg Theatre, the Karlskirche, the Hof Museums, the Town Hall; he brought home more and more books, among them a general handbook of architecture. He showed me the various architectural styles, and particularly pointed out to me that some of the details on the buildings of the Ringstrasse demonstrated the excellent workmanship of local craftsmen.

Source: August Kubizek, The Young Hitler I Knew, *1955, pp. 163–4*

Vienna captivated Hitler, and soon he was planning to redevelop this city, just as he had done Linz. He spent hours in the public library working on street patterns. His travails were haphazard. Dozens of plans were begun, but none ever finished. After drafting out ideas for one project, he would divert his attention to the next. Most of his time went on designs for monumental buildings (Smith, 1979, pp. 118–19). Despite all his shortcomings, he brought a strange kind of dedication to his task. On one occasion he decided to redevelop whole working class areas of the capital. He told Kubizek he would be away for three days, and was. It seems he left the city, just to walk back to its centre to gain an idea of the way its land was used. Then he planned out simple workers' flats (including space for baths – an innovation at the time) and drew pictures of low-rise, light and airy homes which would be surrounded by trees and gardens, and hold between four and sixteen families. They would be served by an extensive railway network and replace the dingy tenements of the time (Kubizek, 1955, pp. 168–70).

Hitler regarded architecture as the highest form of art; through stone monuments he believed a nation could express its most essential values. Imposing buildings, triumphal arches, impressive housing projects – they all displayed the splendour and power of the state. In this quest for lasting glory, 'Hitler the child' was truly 'father to the man'. What is more, there was distinct continuity between his conceptions and their achievement. The case of Linz has already been mentioned, but other ideas Hitler coined, especially during the 1920s, also became reality during the 1930s. Drawings completed in the mid-1920s, were handed to the chief architect of the Third Reich, Albert Speer, a decade later as the basis for monumental public buildings for Berlin, Linz and Nuremberg (Speer, 1971, pp. 120–4). In 1927 Hitler sketched out a plan for the complete redevelopment of central Munich (Strasser, 1969, p. 72). Ten years later this became a task of state. In 1929 he declared his same intent for Berlin (Thies, 1976, p. 38). In January 1937 he appointed Speer 'General Building Inspector for the Transformation of the Capital of the Reich'. In 1929 Hitler declared Germany needed community focal points to last millennia and that his victories would require eternal memorials (Thies, 1976, p. 38). In the 1930s he initiated their planning and construction. This continuity of ideas needs to be integral to our understanding of Hitler's life (see Chapter 9, thesis 1).

Hitler had dealings with architects like Paul Ludwig Troost (whom he commissioned to renovate the Brown House and design the 'House of German Art'), Albert Speer and Hermann Giesler (Weissmann, 1997, p. 183). He showed himself constitutionally well-equipped for the task. He had the imagination necessary to grasp sketches quickly and could turn plans into three-dimensional conceptions (Speer, 1971, p. 128). In fact, he loved studying Speer's architectural drawings and would do so until two or three o'clock in the morning. Once serious plans were begun for the reconstruction of Berlin and Linz, scale models had to be made. These included a thirteen-foot-high model of a victory arch for the capital which in reality was to be 400 ft. high (Speer, 1971, p. 218). As late as April 1945, with the Russians at the 'city gates', he still took visitors to inspect the models (Zoller, 1949, p. 57). They simply transfixed Hitler, as Albert Speer relates in memoirs written after the war.

Document 7.5   Model Cities

Hitler's favourite project was our model city, which was set up in the former exhibition rooms of the Berlin Academy of Arts. In order to reach it undisturbed, he had doors installed in the walls between the Chancellery and our building and a communicating path laid out. Sometimes he invited the supper guests to our studio. We would set out armed with flashlights and keys. In the empty halls spotlights illuminated the models. There was no need for me to do the talking, for Hitler, with flashing eyes, explained every single detail to his companions.

There was keen excitement when a new model was set up and illuminated by brilliant spots from the direction in which the sun would fall on the actual buildings. Most of these models were made on a scale of 1:50; cabinetmakers reproduced every small detail, and the wood was painted to simulate the materials that would actually be used. In this way whole sections of the grand new avenue were gradually put together, and we could have a three-dimensional impression of the building intended to be a reality in a decade. The model street went on for about a hundred feet through the former exhibition rooms of the Academy of Arts.

Hitler was particularly excited over a large model of the grand boulevard on a scale of 1:1000. He loved to 'enter his avenue' at various points and take measure of the future effect. For example, he assumed the point of view of a traveler emerging from the south station or admired the great hall as it looked from the heart of the avenue. To do so, he bent down, almost kneeling, his eye an inch or so above the level of the model, in order to have the right perspective, and while looking he spoke with unusual vivacity. These were the rare times when he relinquished his usual stiffness. In no other situation did I see him so lively, so spontaneous, so relaxed, whereas I myself, often tired and even after years never free of a trace of respectful constraint, usually remained taciturn. One of my close associates summed up the character of this remarkable relationship: 'Do you know what you are? You are Hitler's unrequited love!'

These rooms were kept under careful guard and no one was allowed to inspect the grand plan for the rebuilding of Berlin without Hitler's express permission.

Source: Albert Speer, Inside the Third Reich, *1971, pp. 195–7*

An intimate relationship existed between Hitler's architectural and political visions. Berlin was to be renamed 'Germania', expanded to accommodate 10 million people and become *the* capital of a German-dominated Europe stretching from Ireland to the Urals (Thies, 1976, p. 82; Taylor, 1974, p. 46). He said it was his 'unalterable will and determination to provide Berlin with those streets, buildings and public squares which will make it appear for all time fit and worthy to be the capital of the German Reich', a 'millennial city' (Taylor, 1974, p. 46). It was to become a Mecca, a centre of pilgrimage for the Aryan race (Teut, 1967, p. 7). It was to rival the capital of ancient empires; as Hitler put it, 'without the city of Rome, there would never have been a Roman empire' (Lane, 1985, p. 189; Domarus, 1992, pp. 984–5). With Speer appointed head of the redevelopment project, in 1938 ground began to be bought up, demolition programmes were begun and barracks were constructed to house the tens of thousands of workers required by the massive work on the capital (Thies, 1976, p. 96). The timescale foresaw work continuing until 1950 (Maser, 1974, p. 126). So determined was Hitler that his phenomenal plans should be realised that he banned Speer from costing any of the projects (Weissmann, 1997, p. 184). Money was no object.

How was the Reich capital expected to turn out? According to Speer writing in 1939, it was to be based on ideas which had existed in Hitler's mind for 'many years'.

With Berlin the focus of 3,000 km of motorways spread around the empire, it was to be constructed around two axes able to accommodate traffic from 'the four corners of the earth'. The axes were to run north–south and east–west, beginning and ending at a ring road, and would necessitate 'a completely new layout in the heart of the city'. The north–south axis would be a totally new road measuring 38.5 km. Its central section would run between the two main railway stations and on it would be built 'the largest and most representative buildings of the German Reich'. At the intersection of the axes would be 'Berlin's greatest construction', namely 'the Great Hall of the German People' (Speer, 1939).

Speer's post-war memoirs flesh out these impressions. In Summer 1936 Hitler handed him a set of architectural sketches with the words, 'I made these drawings ten years ago. I've always saved them, because I never doubted that some day I would build these two edifices.' At issue were a domed structure (the Great Hall) and a triumphal arch of massive proportions standing at opposite ends of an avenue which would be 70 ft wider than the Champs Elysées – i.e. some 400 ft in total width – and 3 miles long. More amazing still, the diameter of the dome in question was to be 825 ft, and it would be mounted on a hall able to hold 150,000 people. In all, the building would be 725 ft high (Maser, 1974, p. 120). The triumphal arch was to be 400 ft high, granite, and carved with the names of the 1,800,000 German casualties of the First World War. Quite rightly Speer remembered being staggered not just by the proportions of the projects, but also that Hitler had conceived them at a time when their completion was purely a 'pipe dream' (that is to say, the mid-1920s). He had stuck to the fantasies obsessively (Speer, 1971, pp. 120–4).

The new buildings were to embody the principles of heavily ornamented classical architecture. There would be plenty of domes, columns and colonnades decorated with porticoes, heavy cornices, stone window casings, enormous piers and recessed arches (Speer, 1976, p. 112). In his post-war memoirs, Speer explains further the character of especially the dome.

Document 7.6 The Dome

This structure, the greatest assembly hall in the world ever conceived up to that time, consisted of one vast hall that could hold between one hundred fifty and one hundred eighty thousand persons standing. In spite of Hitler's negative attitude toward Himmler's and Rosenberg's mystical notions, the hall was essentially a place of worship. The idea was that over the course of centuries, by tradition and venerability, it would acquire an importance similar to that St Peter's in Rome has for Catholic Christendom. Without some such essentially pseudoreligious background the expenditure for Hitler's central building would have been pointless and incomprehensible.

The round interior was to have the almost inconceivable diameter of eight hundred and twenty-five feet. The huge dome was to begin its slightly parabolic curve at a height of three hundred and twenty-three feet and rise to a height of seven hundred twenty-six feet.

In a sense the Pantheon in Rome had served as our model. The Berlin dome was also to contain a round opening for light, but this opening alone would be one hundred and fifty-two feet in diameter, larger than the entire dome of the Pantheon (142 feet) and of St Peter's (145 feet). The interior would contain sixteen times the volume of St Peter's.

The interior appointments were to be as simple as possible. Circling an area four hundred and sixty-two feet in diameter, a three-tier gallery rose to a height of one hundred feet. A circle of one hundred rectangular marble pillars – still almost on a human scale, for they were only eighty feet high – was broken by a recess opposite the entrance. This recess was one hundred and sixty-five feet high and ninety-two feet wide, and was to be clad at the rear in gold mosaic. In front of it, on a marble pedestal forty-six feet in height, perched the hall's single sculptural feature: a gilded German eagle with a swastika in its claws. This symbol of sovereignty might be said to be the very fountainhead of Hitler's grand boulevard. Beneath this symbol would be the podium for the Leader of the nation; from this spot he would deliver his messages to the peoples of his future empire. I tried to give this spot suitable emphasis, but here the fatal flaw of architecture that has lost all sense of proportion was revealed. Under that vast dome Hitler dwindled to an optical zero.

From the outside the dome would have loomed against the sky like some green copper mountain, for it was to be roofed with patinated plates of copper. At its peak we planned a skylight turret one hundred and thirty-two feet high, of the lightest possible metal construction. The turret would be crowned by an eagle with a swastika.

Optically, the mass of the dome was to have been set off by a series of pillars sixty-six feet high. I thought this effect would bring things back to scale – undoubtedly a vain hope. The mountainous dome rested upon a granite edifice two hundred and forty-four feet high with sides ten hundred and forty feet long. A delicate frieze, four clustered, fluted pillars on each of the four corners, and a colonnade along the front facing the square were to dramatize the size of the enormous cube. Hitler had already decided on the subjects of these sculptures when we were preparing our first sketches of the building. One would represent Atlas bearing the vault of the heavens, the other Tellus supporting the globe of the world. The spheres representing sky and earth were to be enamel coated with constellations and continents traced in gold.

The volume of this structure amounted to almost 27.5 million cubic yards; the Capitol in Washington would have been contained many times in such a mass. These were dimensions of an inflationary sort.

Yet the hall was by no means an insane project which could in fact never be executed. . . . As early as 1939 many old buildings in the vicinity of the Reichstag were razed to make room for our Great Hall and the other buildings that were to surround the future Adolf Hitler Platz. The character of the underlying soil was studied. Detail drawings were prepared and models built. Millions of marks were spent on granite for the exterior. Nor were the purchases confined to Germany. Despite the shortage of foreign exchange, Hitler had orders placed with quarries in southern Sweden and Finland. Like all the other edifices on Hitler's long grand boulevard, the great hall was also scheduled to be completed in eleven years, by 1950. Since the hall would take longer to build than all the rest, the ceremonial cornerstone laying was set for 1940.

Technically, there was no special problem in constructing a dome over eight hundred feet in diameter.

Source: Albert Speer, Inside the Third Reich, *1971, pp. 222–4*

The project underlines an adolescent feature of Hitler's approach to architecture: whatever he designed had to be gigantic. His boulevard had to be wider than its counterpart in Paris. In Linz he wanted to extend a stone frieze to make it the longest in Europe. The same city's redesigned bridge had to rise 270 ft above the Danube – making it unrivalled in the world (Fest, 1973, p. 526). The Reich Chancellery was to have a corridor running from the main entrance to his study over a quarter of a mile long. Hitler wanted a visitor to feel he was 'visiting the master of the world' (Trevor-Roper, 1961, pp. 103–4). Even in his mountain retreat, the Berghof, he had to incorporate the largest lowerable window in existence. According to one commentator, this emphasis on scale covered up amateurish and unsatisfactory characteristics in the conception which stood behind many of the undertakings (Fest, 1973, p. 531). But what would it have been like to arrive in a capital city planned according to this way of thinking? Once again Albert Speer has explained how things would have looked to someone arriving in 'Germania' by train.

Document 7.7 The Station

Our happiest concept, comparatively speaking, was the central railroad station, the southern pole of Hitler's grand boulevard. The station, its steel ribbing showing through sheathings of copper and glass, would have handsomely offset the great blocks of stone dominating the rest of the avenue. It provided for four traffic levels linked by escalators and elevators and was to surpass New York's Grand Central Station in size.

State visitors would have descended a large outside staircase. The idea was that as soon as they, as well as ordinary travelers, stepped out of the station they would be overwhelmed, or rather stunned, by the urban scene and thus the power of the Reich. The station plaza, thirty-three hundred feet long and a thousand feet wide, was to be lined with captured weapons, after the fashion of the Avenue of Rams which leads from Karnak to Luxor. Hitler conceived this detail after the campaign in France and came back to it again in the late autumn of 1941, after his first defeats in the Soviet Union.

This plaza was to be crowned by Hitler's great arch or 'Arch of Triumph' as he only occasionally called it. Napoleon's Arc de Triomphe on the Place de l'Etoile with its one-hundred-sixty foot height certainly presents a monumental appearance and provides a majestic terminus to the Champs Elysées. Our triumphal arch, five hundred and fifty feet wide, three hundred and ninety-two feet deep, and three hundred and eighty-six feet high, would have towered over all the other buildings of this southern portion of the avenue and would literally have dwarfed them.

Source: Albert Speer, Inside the Third Reich, *1971, pp. 198–9*

A person arriving at the main station was to look through the triumphal arch, along the massive boulevard to the Great Hall. The vista would have been breathtaking.

In the early years of the war, over 25 cities were scheduled for redevelopment. They included Nuremberg, Munich, Hanover, Augsburg, Bremen, Weimar and Linz. By the end of 1941, planning had burgeoned to include 50 towns and cities, practically all large urban areas in Germany and Austria. Of these, five were to become exceptionally impressive 'Führer' cities (Thies, 1976, p. 99). Linz in particular was to be rebuilt until it surpassed Vienna's splendour. Hitler worked on the city with real passion late into the war. It was to be expanded in size three or four times over. There were extravagant ideas for locating houses along the banks of the Danube and for a major new observatory built in classical style. There would be a new hotel (built in the Renaissance style) for exclusive use of the 'Strength through Joy' movement, new municipal buildings, a Party House, a new army headquarters, an Olympic Stadium and (fulfilling the teenage vision) a massive suspension bridge (Trevor-Roper, 1961, pp. 421–3). At the heart of the city would be a central avenue running between two great squares. Along it would be new theatres, concert halls, restaurants, museums and libraries, not to mention a railway station, post office and an air-raid shelter (Taylor, 1974, pp. 50–1). Linz was even to house Hitler's tomb. This would be in a crypt beneath a tower (Lewin, 1984, pp. 30–1; Taylor, 1974, pp. 50–1).

The schemes for Germanic cities were visionary, but when Hitler considered the East (the *Lebensraum* to be captured during the Second World War), his thinking took on the quality of science fiction. Talking at military headquarters during wartime, Hitler and *Reichsführer-SS* Heinrich Himmler agreed on the need to establish *Wehrbauerndörfer*, that is villages for German farmers who were prepared to take up arms to protect themselves and Germandom. The villages would be developed as if they were parts of the German heartland. They would have ponds and greens; their farmhouses would be decorated with window boxes full of geraniums. There would be lime trees and streets lined with oaks (Speer, 1976, pp. 399–400). The East was to be made into a Teutonic rustic idyll. And this was not all.

Document 7.8 In the East

Along with the new towns, gigantic cemeteries were to be established, looking like the tumuli of the ancient world, but rising to heights of a hundred meters and more. . . . In addition to Himmler's fortress villages, many new towns were to spring up in the vicinity of the existing Russian towns. As models, Hitler would mention Regensburg, Augsburg, Weimar, or Heidelberg. These towns were to be as different as possible from each other. It was perfectly all right for us to copy familiar buildings, so that even in Russia a feeling for the homeland could develop. In antiquity, Hitler would say, no attempt was made to develop new forms of temples for, say, the colonial cities in Sicily. He also wanted to use a great deal of color. He recalled the 'Theresian yellow' to be found in any territory where the influence of the Hapsburg monarchy extended, even deep into the wilds of Montenegro. Our old buildings in the Ukraine, in White Russia, and as far as the Urals must always be identifiable as products of German culture.

One day, towards four o'clock in the morning, when all of us were completely worn out and scarcely listening, Hitler came out with the surprising thesis that these towns ought to reproduce the tight, crooked patterns of medieval German cities. It was a grotesque idea, to place huddled Rothenburgs or Dinkelsbühls in the broad Russian plains with their enormous available space. But Hitler could summon up reasons. The tighter the circumference of the city walls, the better the inhabitants could defend themselves. The density of medieval cities was a direct result of the insecurity and the feuds of those times, he argued, not cultural backwardness.

In the immediate vicinity of these German-style cities Hitler wanted to establish industries. All the raw materials and coal you wanted were available in ample quantities, he pointed out. Armament works also had to be planned for, so that our armies posted on the borders of Asia would have no supply problems. . . .

Late in the afternoon in the cell [at the time of writing this memoir, Speer was in prison after the war], I recall other items in Hitler's plans for the East. Above all, I realize how concrete and tangible it all must have been for Hitler. He often showed us sketches in which he had, for example, calculated how long it would take a German farmer living on an entailed estate in the southern Ukraine to drive to Berlin. Significantly, Hitler used a Volkswagen as the basis for his calculations; he wanted to build a million of these cars a year after the war. Porsche, at their last conference on tanks, had again assured him that the car would be able to keep up a steady speed of sixty miles an hour, he told me. That meant a farmer from Kiev or Odessa would need about thirty hours to reach Berlin. In every sizable village, Hitler commented on another occasion, there must be a stop that would always have the same name, Gasthof zur Post, as in Bavaria. That proposal was another example of his obsession that the German farmer lost in the expanses of Russia must find way stations where he could feel secure and in a homelike environment.

Illustrating his points with his own sketches, Hitler would sometimes talk to the minister of transportation, Dorpmüller, about a modern railroad system that was to have a track width of no less than four meters. In this way, he said, the trains would have a useful width of six meters; this would allow for really handsome sleeping compartments, virtual bedrooms, on both sides of the central aisle. He decided that the height of the cars would be from four and a half to five meters, so that two-story cars with compartments of two to two and a half meters in height would be possible. These are house measurements; and evidently that is how Hitler conceived the new railroad system for the East. It must be spacious, because whole families would have to live on the trains for days on end. 'But we'll make the dining car one story. Then, with six meters in width and thirty meters in length, we'll have a height of five meters. Even in a palace that would make a handsome banquet hall, as Minister Speer here will corroborate.' Hitler wanted separate lines for passenger cars and for freight cars; sometimes he wanted to make the lines four-tracked. There were to be two east–west lines across all of Europe, one beginning north at the Urals, the southern line beginning at the Caspian Sea. 'That's where we'll be in luck with our colonial empire. The maritime empires needed a fleet; building and maintaining a fleet costs thousands of millions.' Even while we were sitting together, Hitler ordered Dorpmüller to start working on the plans and figures at once.

Source: Albert Speer, Spandau. The Secret Diaries, *1976, pp. 156–7*

The massive train would travel at 150 mph and carry 480 people per carriage. Stations along its track would have an imposing authority. Throughout the war, 100 officials and 80 engineers continued to work on the project (Lewin, 1984, pp. 31–2). What is more, there were plans for gigantic motorway systems to stretch from Scandinavia to the Crimea (Lewin, 1984, p. 31). These would have lanes not the usual 7 m wide, but fully 11 m (Schramm, 1972, p. 99). They would make the East and South of Europe accessible. Hitler believed the Crimea would become Germany's riviera, and tourists would flock to Croatia too (Trevor-Roper, 1961, p. 35).

Hitler's public building projects were colossal, classical and breathing a Germanic spirit. Of course not all construction work undertaken in the Third Reich reflected these values. Housing projects did not always change from what might have been expected during the Weimar years (Lane, 1985, pp. 193–206). Göring's Air Ministry even commissioned very functional, modern-style buildings made of glass, steel and reinforced concrete (Taylor, 1974, p. 38). But Hitler's plans were something different. They were designed to dwarf the individual and put him in awe. How else can we interpret a sports stadium planned to hold 405,000 people (Schramm, 1972, p. 98)? As Hitler put it, 'I am convinced . . . that art, since it forms the most uncorrupted, the most immediate reflection of the people's soul, exercises unconsciously by far the greatest direct influence upon the masses of the people' (Taylor, 1974, p. 31). Hitler's community architecture was designed first to render the individual impotent, and then to mould his spiritual and psychological state according to the needs and values of National Socialism. Architecture and political mission were inseparable: this was construction as propaganda.

According to Hitler, part of the political purpose of architecture was to surpass the limitations of the bourgeois world, as he explained in a speech of 11 September 1935.

Document 7.9 Beyond the Bourgeois World

It is impossible to give to a people a strong sense of its stability if the great buildings erected by the community as a whole are not essentially superior to those which owe their origin and maintenance in a lesser or greater degree to the capitalistic interests of individuals. . . .

That which gave to the cities of antiquity and of the Middle Ages their characteristic features, those features which are most worthy of our admiration and our love, was not the greatness of the houses of their private citizens, but rather those evidences of the life of the community which towered high above them. It was not these public buildings which had to be sought out with difficulty, but the buildings of private citizens which lay deep down in their shadow. So long as the characteristic features of the great cities of our day, the outstanding points which catch the eye, are warehouses, bazaars, hotels, offices in the form of sky-scrapers, &c., there can be no talk of art or any real culture. Here it would be better to withdraw modestly into simplicity. Unfortunately in a *bourgeois* age the architectural development in public life was sacrificed to objects serving private capitalistic enterprise. The great task in the history of culture which lies before National Socialism consists above all in abandoning this tendency.

But it is not only artistic but also political considerations which must constrain us, as we look on the great models of the past, to give to the new Reich a worthy cultural incorporation. Nothing is better calculated to reduce to silence the small carping critic than the eternal language of great art. Before the expressions of such great art the millennia make their obeisance in awed stillness. May God grant to us the greatness so to conceive our tasks that they may not fall short of the greatness of the nation. That is indeed no easy undertaking.

. . . Our cathedrals are witness to the greatness of the past; the greatness of present will one day be measured by those creations of eternal value which it leaves as its legacy.

Source: N.H. Baynes, The Speeches of Adolf Hitler. April 1922 – August 1939. Vol. 1, *1942, pp. 582–4*

In medieval times, the landscape had been dominated by cathedrals around which the community rallied. In Weimar Germany, there had been only private, capitalist, Jewish department stores which few people felt a stake in, and which consequently left society fragmented. Hitler wanted to restore the old, community-based order of things. In 1937 he explained that the construction of massive monuments should encourage Germans to sink their petty differences and experience unity (Thies, 1976, p. 82). At the Party Day held in the same year he explained that great buildings awakened national consciousness and strengthened political unification (Lane, 1985, p. 188). On another occasion he said that great buildings could persuade people of where they belonged (Eitner, 1994, p. 79). They bound the nation together.

Building was a means of expressing and shoring up national pride. Hitler conceived a direct relationship between the size of a construction and the strength of a people. As he put it, if constructions 'are to have a lasting significance and value, they must conform to the largeness of scale prevalent in other spheres of national life' (Lane, 1985, p. 189). So when he thought about a bridge to span the Elbe in Hamburg, he did not want one on a scale with existing structures in the USA. He wanted the largest in the world. When he discovered the bridge in question could not have free-standing sections longer than the Golden Gate bridge, he specified that instead it should have a larger drivable surface area. Hamburg was also supposed to have received the largest skyscrapers in the world. Hitler wanted the largest airport ever in Berlin, the largest swimming baths, the largest and fastest ship and the largest radio transmitter (Thies, 1976, pp. 80–2). This emphasis on size certainly had a teenage ring (as noted already), but it also bolstered the nation's claims to global primacy and supported its claim to world domination.

Architecture also had a historical purpose. 'We must build as large as today's technical possibilities permit: we must build for eternity', so said Adolf Hitler (Lane, 1985, p. 189). Longevity was as important as scale. Hitler wanted materials to enable his buildings to last at least 10,000 years. Even if one day National Socialism should fall by the wayside, these would continue as reminders of what had been (Thies, 1976, p. 76). Hitler explained it himself.

Document 7.10 Granite and Marble

The small needs of daily life, they have changed through the millennia and they will continue to change eternally. But the great evidences of human civilization in granite and marble they stand through the millennia, and they alone are a truly stable pole in the flux of all other phenomena. In them, in periods of decline, humanity has ever sought and found afresh the eternal, magic strength which should enable it to master confusion, to restore out of chaos a new order. Therefore these buildings of ours should not be conceived for the year 1940, no, not for the year 2000, but like the cathedrals of our past they shall stretch into the millennia of the future.

. . . For it is precisely these buildings which will co-operate to unify our people politically more closely than ever and to strengthen it: for the Germans as a society these buildings will inspire a proud consciousness that each and all belong together; they will prove how ridiculous in our social life are all earthly differences when faced with these mighty, gigantic witnesses to the life which we share as a community; they will by their effect upon the minds of men fill the citizens of our people with a limitless self-confidence as they remember that they are Germans.

Source: N.H. *Baynes,* The Speeches of Adolf Hitler. April 1922 – August 1939. Vol. 1, *1942, pp. 593–4*

Ancient Egypt had left behind the Sphinx and pyramids; Greece bequeathed the Acropolis; Rome left the Colosseum. Hitler believed Berlin would one day be compared to the ancient imperial capitals, and that his heritage would over-power even these (Eitner, 1994, p. 78; Frank, 1953, pp. 320–1). So sure was he of the endurance of his constructions that he even sketched them as ruins in the forthcoming millennia!

But Hitler the dictator had designs not just for Germany's architecture. The Weimar years had seen radical alterations in the development of art. There had been a dramatic rise in expressionist schools such as Dadaism and Futurism. Hitler rejected these out of hand. He believed the quality of art had declined since about 1910 (Schramm, 1972, p. 65). After National Socialism seized power, the Bauhaus (the centre for the modern art movement in Germany) was closed down. Hitler disliked 'modern' trends so much that when an exhibition was staged at the House of German Art in Munich in Summer 1937, Hitler vetted the 1,450 pictures personally and banned fully 500 (Zoller, 1949, p. 52). An impressive array of artists were stigmatised as 'degenerate'. They included Cézanne, Gauguin, van Gogh, Kandinsky, Klee, Kokoschka, Matisse and Pablo Picasso. Hitler's personal aim was to get rid of all 'degenerate' specimens of art from all German museums and galleries (Hoffmann, 1955, pp. 180–1).

What sort of art did Hitler prefer? The short answer would be 'German art'. He went some way towards defining this at the opening of the major exhibition at the House of German Art on 19 July 1937.

Document 7.11 To be German

The question has often been asked what it really means 'to be German'. Among all the definitions which have been put forth by so many men throughout the centuries, there is one I find most fitting; one which makes no attempt whatsoever to provide any basic explanation, but instead simply states a law. The most marvellous law I can imagine as the lifelong task for my Volk in this world is one a great German once expressed: 'To be German means to be clear!' Yet that would signify that to be German means to be logical and above all to be true.

A splendid law – yet also one that puts every individual under an obligation to subordinate himself to it and thus abide by it. Taking this law as a starting-point, we will arrive at a universally applicable criterion for the correct character of our art, because it will correspond to the life-governing law of our Volk.

A deep-felt, inner yearning for such a true German art bearing the marks of this law of clarity has always been alive in our Volk. It inspired our great painters, our sculptors, those who have designed our architecture, our thinkers and poets, and perhaps above all our musicians. On that fateful sixth of June, 1931, when the old Glass Palace went up in flames, an immortal treasure of truly German art perished with it in the fire. They were called

'Romantics' and yet were the most splendid representatives of that German search for the real and true character of our Volk and for a sincere and decent expression of this inwardly-sensed law of life.

What was decisive in characterizing the German being was not only the choice of subject matter they portrayed, but also their clear and simple way of rendering these sentiments.

Source: M. Domarus, Hitler. Speeches and Proclamations. 1932–1945. Vol. 2. The Years 1935 to 1938, *1992, pp. 910–11*

Hitler wanted art which needed the minimum of intellectual interpretation. In the end, this was pretty much what he liked personally. It amounted to nineteenth-century landscapes, insipid pastoral views and peasant scenes such as those accomplished by Defregger and Eduard Grützner; it involved pictures of inebriated monks and priests, Falstaff figures and men historically clad. Hitler liked Grützner's work so much that he owned about thirty pieces (Eitner, 1994, p. 81).

To ensure his values would be passed down to future generations, Hitler began collecting paintings for a huge, eternal exhibition to be established in the new gallery planned for Linz. Thousands of works of art were purchased thanks to royalties from the sales of *Mein Kampf* and from stamps bearing the Führer's head. In 1943–4 alone, 3,000 works were bought at a cost of RM 150 million (Waite, 1993, p. 67). Acquisitions included a self-portrait by Rembrandt, Leonardo da Vinci's *Leda and the Swan* and Myron's most famous statue, *The Discus Thrower* (Hoffmann, 1955, pp. 182–3). At the end of the war, in the salt mines of Alt-Aussee alone, 6,755 paintings and 237 cases of books were discovered which were intended for Linz had Germany won the war (Waite, 1993, p. 67).

In so far as Hitler deliberately turned away from expressionism, arguably he was rejecting everything that was progressive, vital and creative (Lewin, 1984, p. 67). In artistic terms he was turning the clock back 30 years at least. This quality is clearly displayed in Albert Speer's characterisation of Hitler's architectural influences.

Document 7.12 Influences

Up to the end Hitler lauded the architects and the buildings which had served him as models for his early sketches. Among these was the Paris Opera (built 1861–74) by Charles Garnier: 'The stairwell is the most beautiful in the world. When the ladies stroll down in their costly gowns and uniformed men form lanes – Herr Speer we must build something like that too!' He raved about the Vienna Opera: 'The most magnificent opera house in the world, with marvellous acoustics. When as a young man I sat up there in the fourth gallery. . . . ' Hitler had a story to tell about van der Null, one of the two architects of the building: 'He thought the opera house was a failure. You know he was in such despair that on the day before the opening he put a bullet through his head. At the dedication it turned out to be his greatest success: everyone praised the architect.' Such remarks quite often led him to observations about difficult situations in which he himself had been involved and in which some fortunate turn of events had again and again saved him. The lesson was: You must never give up.

He was especially fond of the numerous theaters built by Hermann Helmer (1849–1919) and Ferdinand Felner (1847–1916), who had provided both Austria–Hungary and Germany at the end of the nineteenth century with many late-baroque theaters, all in the same pattern. He knew where all buildings were and later had the neglected theater in Augsburg renovated.

But he also appreciated the stricter architects of the nineteenth century such as Gottfried Semper (1803–79), who built the Opera House and the Picture Gallery in Dresden and the Hofburg and the court museums in Vienna, as well as Theophil Hansen (1803–83), who had designed several impressive classical buildings in Athens and Vienna. As soon as the German troops took Brussels in 1940, I was dispatched to look at the huge Palace of Justice by Poelaert (1817–79), which Hitler raved about, although he knew it only from its plans (which was true of the Paris Opera). After my return he had me give him a detailed description of the building.

Such were Hitler's architectural passions. But ultimately he was always drawn back to inflated neobaroque such as Kaiser Wilhelm II had also fostered, through his court architect Ihne. Fundamentally, it was decadent baroque, comparable to the style that accompanied the decline of the Roman Empire. Thus in the realm of architecture, as in painting and sculpture, Hitler really remained arrested in the world of his youth: the world of 1880 to 1910, which stamped its imprint on his artistic taste as on his political and ideological conceptions.

Source: Albert Speer, Inside the Third Reich, *1971, pp. 78–9*

Hitler's favourite road, the Ringstrasse in Vienna, had been built between 1858 and 1865 (Maser, 1973, p. 63). In artistic terms, and as document 7.12 says, Adolf Hitler was rooted in the late nineteenth century; this is an important point (see Chapter 9, thesis 3).

There was nothing so unusual in Hitler's styling for his main buildings. At the time, the renaissance of classicism was a pan-European movement. Different political systems took up classical architecture at the same time as they became authoritarian. Classicism was the architecture of dictators. Not only Hitler, but also Mussolini and Stalin favoured it (Thies, 1976, p. 68). Nor was the drive to establish a new empire in massive building projects anything new. The ancient empires had done so, and Napoleon had remodelled Paris. Hitler's comments on architectural theory were derivative in the extreme. When he liked something it was simply because it conveyed grandeur (Taylor, 1974, pp. 19–23). His enthusiasm for building remained that of the amateur sketcher rather than the professional technician. What is more, the environment Hitler cultivated within his own buildings was conventional in the extreme. He furnished the Berghof in a manner typical of a 'cultivated industrialist'. There was nothing 'to offend good taste', but nothing 'which rose above bourgeois conventionality' – nothing that was 'the slightest bit modern' or which showed 'any individuality on the part of the owner' (Schramm, 1972, pp. 60–1).

Despite all this conservatism, Hitler still managed to inject a new element into German art: racism. During the Weimar period Jews, he asserted, had tampered fundamentally with German art collections and artistic sensibilities. In 1942, Hitler explained the proposition in a mealtime conversation.

Document 7.13 Falling Standards

I've often had occasion, during recent years, to immerse myself in collections of the review *Die Kunst*.

It's striking to observe that in 1910 our artistic level was still extraordinarily high. Since that time, alas! our decadence has merely become accentuated. In the field of painting for example, it's enough to recall the lamentable daubs that people have tried to foist, in the name of art, on the German people. This was quite especially the case during the Weimar Republic, and that clearly demonstrated the disastrous influence of the Jews in matters of art. The cream of the jest was the incredible impudence with which the Jews set about it! With the help of phoney art critics, and with one Jew bidding against another, they finally suggested to the people – which naturally believes everything that's printed – a conception of art according to which the worst rubbish in painting became the expression of the height of artistic accomplishment. The ten thousand of the élite themselves, despite their pretensions on the intellectual level, let themselves be diddled, and swallowed all the humbug. The culminating hoax – and we now have proof of it, thanks to the seizures of Jewish property – is that, with the money they fraudulently acquired by selling trash, the Jews were able to buy, at wretched prices, the works of value they had so cleverly depreciated. Every time an inventory catches my eye of a requisition carried out on an important Jew, I see that genuine artistic treasures are listed there. It's a blessing of Providence that National Socialism, by seizing power in 1933, was able to put an end to this imposture.

Source: H.R. Trevor-Roper (ed.), Hitler's Secret Conversations. 1941–1944, *1961, pp. 354–5*

By offering spurious artistic criticisms, Jews had manipulated the German concept of art and had taken the opportunity to amass their own collections of truly quality pieces. Meanwhile, Germans came to accept degenerate art in the place of something better (Domarus, 1990, p. 927). Actually Hitler held that Jews by nature had little real artistic sensibility of their own. As early as August 1920, he described them as nomads lacking any inner cultural life (Phelps, 1968, p. 394). Later he explained that their only means for self-expression was in the system of capitalism and the enterprise it allowed (Baynes, 1942, Vol. 1, p. 577). He made a similar point to the Party Congress in Nuremberg in 1938. Jews only had any feeling for art by virtue of foreign blood which had penetrated their family trees. Most of their number were happier with the artistic expressions of 'primitive negro tribes' than German high culture (Wulf, 1963, p. 313).

The alienation of the German from his true artistic sensibility was believed dangerous. Hitler explained this in his *Second Book* (see Chapter 2).

Document 7.14 Subversion of the Race

Once a people no longer appreciates the cultural expression of its own spiritual life conditioned through its blood, or even begins to feel ashamed of it, in order to turn its attention to alien expressions of life, it renounces the strength which lies in the harmony of its blood and the cultural life which has sprung from it. It becomes torn apart, unsure in its judgment of the world picture and its expressions, loses the perception and the feeling for its own purposes, and in place of this it sinks into a confusion of international ideas, conceptions, and the cultural hodge-podge springing from them. Then the Jew can make his entry in any form, and this master of international poisoning and race corruption will not rest until he has thoroughly uprooted and thereby corrupted such a people. The end is then the loss of a definite unitary race value and as a result, the final decline.

Source: A. Hitler, Hitler's Secret Book, *1961, pp. 28–9*

In other words, loss of the real sense of culture laid a people open to abuse, including racial mixing. In this context, Hitler's fight against degenerate art (and the removal of those 500 pictures from the gallery in Munich) took on the character not of taste, but race war.

Hitler believed there was only one, eternal culture, namely that exhibited by Greek–Nordic peoples. He said, 'No art is founded in the period, but rather only in the peoples' (Thies, 1976, p. 74). True art was conditioned exclusively and statically by the way the Greek–Nordic race expressed itself. In other words, he believed Greeks and also Romans (i.e. the prime exponents of the classical schools of art he so admired) were intimately related through race to the Germans, who should express their own art appropriately and classically. He regarded it as 'mental decadence' to ignore these 'racial determinants' of art (Berliner Lokal-Anzieger, 2 September 1933). In 1930 Hitler put it as follows.

Document 7.15 Art and Race

There is no such thing as a Revolution in art: there is only one eternal art – the Greek–Nordic art, and all such terms as 'Dutch Art', 'Italian Art', German Art' are merely misleading and just as foolish as it is to treat Gothic as an individual form of art – all that is simply Nordic–Greek art and anything which deserves the name of art can always only be Nordic–Greek. . . . There is no such thing as Chinese or Egyptian art: the Chinese or Egyptian peoples were of a mixed composition, and upon a body belonging to a people of lower race there was set a Nordic head which alone created the masterpieces which to-day we admire as Chinese or Egyptian art. When this thin Nordic upper layer disappeared, e.g. the Manchus, then art in those countries came to an end.

Source: N.H. Baynes, The Speeches of Adolf Hitler. April 1922 – August 1939. Vol. 1, *1942, pp. 567–8*

No surprise, then, that Hitler believed Greek–Nordic artistic expressions, such as those of the human form, were not just arbitrary representations of shape (in the way he thought African art might be), but were absolutely correct (Hitler, 1934, pp. 233–4). Art was the product of the Greek–Nordic race and as such expressed truths about the world and life.

To be absolutely correct, architecture and the arts were more than just expressions of Hitler's racialism. Culture provided the answer to the question: what was the point of the thousand-year Reich? To facilitate the unfolding of the cultural innateness of the Nordic people became the whole purpose of Hitler's conception of the world. At the Party Congress of 1937 he identified only one true mission: 'we are not striving for the brute strength of someone like Genghis Khan, but instead for an empire of strength which is instrumental in shaping a strong and protected community as the support and guard of a higher culture!' (Domarus, 1992, p. 927). During the war he commented that the only justification for establishing empire was to spread culture (Trevor-Roper, 1961, p. 103). On another occasion he indicated it was vitally important that he leave behind cultural sites to survive him. 'In time', he said, 'wars are forgotten. Only the works of human genius are left' (Trevor-Roper, 1961, p. 215). Hitler wanted to make an eternal contribution to the development of mankind as reflected in the artistic record. Although it goes too far to suggest that he only entered politics to realise artistic achievements, he did regard political power as the only possible means to put his artistic ideas into practice (Maser, 1973, p. 60). Once again it is evident how closely Hitler's political and artistic missions hung together. And with what phenomenal imagination he set about both.

Whether this discussion defines Adolf Hitler as a revolutionary is much less certain. Hitler thought about art and architecture a great deal. He developed plans which he clung to over the years and which he tried to realise when he was in a position to do so. This point is important in its own right (see Chapter 9, thesis 1). Hitler brought the principle of racism into the arts as a new means of their *legitimation*. But what did he do beyond that? He took the *initiative* to establish projects demolishing whole urban areas and starting them afresh with buildings planned on a colossal scale. He also wanted to use construction to establish a national *myth* of community, greatness and the permanence of National Socialist values. If we interpret these actions solely as expressions of and means to bolster the wider *changes to political power* and *social structure* which Hitler wrought across Europe (i.e. as means to underlining the political superiority of National Socialism and racial superiority of the Germans), then perhaps there was something revolutionary here. Assessed in their own right, however, Hitler's *myths* and *initiatives* were not actually so new. Wanting to build big in itself is nothing novel. Hitler's own artistic tastes were conservative in the extreme and, by the 1920s, the classical style he revered so much was commonplace and twenty years out of date. In this sense, Hitler was not an artistic revolutionary, but a reactionary *opposing* perceived cultural *modernisation*. This limitation provides a significant insight into how we should understand Hitler's character (see Chapter 9, thesis 3). It also means that in the area of art and architecture, Adolf Hitler's revolutionary credentials were flawed.

8 | Mind

Did Adolf Hitler have a revolutionary personality; was he afflicted by an Oedipal complex or some other mental disturbance which predisposed him to radical behaviour? The answer calls for an investigation into often mundane aspects of Hitler's life in the hope of finding interesting perspectives on his political and military actions. Identifying a general style of thinking may help an understanding of how Hitler reached more important decisions; analysing health problems may contribute to an interpretation of important policy initiatives; his childhood experiences may have been related to later conduct. So who exactly was the dictator of Germany (Zoller, 1949, p. 9)?

Albert Speer, Hitler's architect and the nearest anyone came to being a friend after 1933, felt he never really knew the man. Rudolf Hess, deputy leader of the NSDAP, and General Alfred Jodl, senior member of the Supreme Command of the Armed Forces, both found his character distant. The Führer was aloof and contradictory, someone who protected his inner core (Schwaab, 1992, pp. 1–4). Few personal letters from Hitler exist and he kept no private diary. The gaps in our knowledge have left substantial room for speculation. Hitler's character has been 'hyped' and demonised by all-comers (Lewin, 1984, pp. 4–5). It takes a particular effort to break through the crust of ignorance to trace the living, breathing individual.

The characteristics of Hitler's intellectual life are important. Although he was supreme leader of Germany, with only one or two exceptions (e.g. Albert Speer), he failed to surround himself with the nation's original thinkers. As companions he chose party loyalists and military cronies who offered little creative stimulus. In a world devoid of critical challenge, Hitler was left to deliver lengthy monologues which only confirmed him in his fantasies (Weinstein, 1980, p. 150). His reading was at the level of trivia. It inclined towards popular pseudo-science, for example Hanns Hoerbiger's *World Ice Theory* (Schramm, 1972, p. 127). There is some evidence he liked sensationalist history too (Breitman, 1990). He would devour books like these in a day, skimming through them at top speed (Maser, 1973, p. 129). In this way he picked up a smattering of ideas that were half-baked in the first place. Hitler was used to taking dubious opinions and supposed facts which he interpreted according to his own set of prejudices and beliefs. These had much in common with popular attitudes in Austria and Germany during the late nineteenth and early twentieth centuries (see especially Chapter 2). So Hitler was a poseur (Rauschning,

1939b, p. 138). He aspired to profundity but remained an 'unsophisticated, self-taught thinker' (Cross, 1973, p. 12). Lacking the restraint and self-doubt which true education brings with it, he became perfectly positioned to make dire mistakes.

Hitler's personality may have been subject to a series of more unusual pathological influences. There is the matter of ill-health. From late 1942 he experienced shaking limbs. This has been interpreted as a symptom of Parkinson's disease. The condition can be accompanied by mental changes including intellectual deterioration, depression and paranoia. The onset of such a clinical state might help explain the radicalisation of National Socialist policy during the war, but a diagnosis of Parkinson's disease remains uncertain. Hitler experienced trembling on just one side of his body although the illness should afflict both sides. It is disputed whether Hitler experienced the rigor in his limbs which also accompanies the disease (Eitner, 1994, pp. 204–5; Redlich, 1999, p. 234). The balanced judgement is that at most Hitler suffered from a 'low to moderate' severity of the condition and that it probably had no implications for the way his mind worked (Redlich, 1999, p. 234).

Another possibility involves Hitler's heart. From 1932 he believed he had a cardiac condition. His symptoms involved a strong heart beat, troubled breathing, sweats, pressure in the chest and throat, and the sensation that the heart could stop (Eitner, 1994, p. 194). From 1937 Hitler became particularly anxious about this. He began to avoid exercise deliberately (Carr, 1978, p. 144). In a meeting with senior military men held in November 1937 (document 5.15) he raised the possibility of his death (Maser, 1973, p. 213). An examination by his personal physician in 1940 indicated high blood pressure associated with some damage to the heart (Maser, 1973, p. 214). In July 1941 Hitler may have suffered a mild stroke during a vigorous debate with Ribbentrop (Eitner, 1994, p. 199). The next month an electrocardiograph indicated progressive arteriosclerosis. It is reasonable to assume that fear of mortality related to worries about his heart must have intensified for Hitler as time passed. From 1937 at least, his political actions were motivated in part by a belief that his life expectancy might be limited.

Hitler's personal physician, Dr Morell, prescribed Hitler a substantial array of drugs. From 1937 to 1945 there were about thirty different medicines (Eitner, 1994, pp. 208–10). These included a variety of stimulants, among them amphetamines. Morell let Hitler take some of these as he required between 1939 and 1943, and it is highly likely he abused them (including the amphetamines) (Redlich, 1999, p. 243). Amphetamines reduce fatigue and provide a feeling of alertness, but they can be associated with increased aggression, recklessness, anxiety, anger, transient hallucinations, paranoid delusions, preoccupation with religious and philosophical themes and a feeling of cleverness (Redlich, 1999, p. 239). It is possible that amphetamine abuse increased Hitler's recklessness in August 1939 as he geared up to the invasion of Poland (Redlich, 1999, pp. 243–4). Either the direct consequences of amphetamine misuse, or character change brought on by it, may also have had an impact in Spring 1941 when he was planning Operation Barbarossa and thinking about racial annihilation. A historian describes how Hitler presented himself at the time.

Document 8.1 Addict?

Under the impact of the treatment, his patient's habitus would sometimes undergo a complete change. His eyes, which had always excited such fascination, would flash dangerously, he became peremptory if not actually aggressive, and would sometimes make outrageous remarks. . . . During discussions he would occasionally put forward projects so wildly unrealistic as to obliterate all memory of that grasp of technical detail which had once commanded the admiration of his expert advisers. For now he began to urge not only the realization of what was possible, as indeed he had been doing since 1935, but also the realization of what exceeded the bounds of possibility.

Source: W. Maser, Hitler, *1973, p. 215*

Drug abuse may have compounded psychological problems which various authors have tried to identify in Hitler. Walter C. Langer was involved in the Office of Strategic Studies in the USA during the Second World War and drew up a psychological profile of Hitler as part of his posting. It was published in the early 1970s. Langer believed the most significant thing about Hitler was that he felt omnipotent, akin to Jesus Christ (Langer, 1973, pp. 34, 35, 39, 54–5). This feeling of being specially 'chosen', was explained in terms of the relationships in Hitler's family when he was a child.

According to Patrick Hitler (Adolf's nephew), Adolf's father (Alois) used to beat his children mercilessly. In public, by contrast, he was a model citizen whom fellow villagers respected. This ambiguous father figure left Adolf lacking a suitable role model and in confusion (Langer, 1973, pp. 139, 145–7). Hitler's relationship with his mother (Klara) at first was close. Since a number of her offspring had died as infants, she lavished attention on Adolf who consequently began to feel 'chosen'. Unfortunately the relationship between mother and son was upset by two traumatic events. One was that the infant Adolf witnessed his parents having sex; the other was that a baby brother was born (Langer, 1973, pp. 149–52). Now Hitler was left confused about the relationship between himself and his mother. He responded by repressing his emotions throughout much of his childhood, especially his adolescence, and by transferring his feelings about his mother onto the German nation. When Germany was defeated in 1918, it was as if Hitler's mother had been subjected to a sexual assault once again and in Pasewalk hospital (where in October and November 1918 Hitler was treated for the effects of a gas attack) he suffered 'hysterical blindness and mutism' (Langer, 1973, pp. 155–7). Nonetheless, survival of the war confirmed Hitler in his feeling of being 'chosen'.

The military defeat mobilised all Hitler's psychic forces and he projected his hatreds and frustrations onto the traditional victim: the Jew (Langer, 1973, pp. 186 and 194). It is also theorised that at some point Hitler's libidinal development was disrupted leading to a perversion which was projected onto the same target. When Hitler described the Jew as a leech draining the life from the German nation, he really meant his perversion was draining his own life away. According to Langer, then, Hitler was moulded by a twin complex. On the one hand, it designated him a German Messiah; on the other hand, it determined he would preach anti-Semitism.

Another early analysis came from the prison psychologist at the Nuremberg Trials, G.M. Gilbert. Like Langer, he believed Hitler had grown up in an unhealthy environment. Quoting evidence from a half-brother, Gilbert establishes once again that Klara (the mother) was over-indulgent towards Adolf (Gilbert, 1950, p. 18). Once again Alois (the father) is described as a martinet. He made his children address him formally and became an embittered, ill-tempered alcoholic. Hitler's lawyer, Hans Frank, told Gilbert the following story.

Document 8.2 Alcohol

His father suffered from an uncontrollable addiction to alcohol which often led to the most painful family experiences for the boy, Adolf Hitler. How often did this boy have to fetch his father late at night out of the tavern, after the latter had been guzzling alcohol for hours on end. Hitler himself related to me in 1930 – when we were speaking about his family relationships (in connection with a blackmail threat), 'Even as a 10 or 12-year-old kid I always had to go late at night to this stinking, smoky dive. Without being spared any of the details, I would have to go to the table and shake him as he looked with a blank stare. Then I would say, "Father, you must come home! Come now, we've got to go!" And I often had to wait a quarter of an hour, begging, cursing, until I could get him to budge. Then I would support him and finally get him home. That was the most terrible shame I have ever experienced. Oh, Frank, I know what a devil Alcohol is! Through my father it became my greatest enemy in my youth!'

Source: G.M. Gilbert, The Psychology of Dictatorship, *1950, p. 19*

Adolf grew up 'a friendless, hostile child who would break out into temper tantrums at the slightest provocation' (Gilbert, 1950, p. 18). His personal development became skewed.

Document 8.3   Psychosexual Conflicts

We may thus sum up the psychodynamics and social interaction in Hitler's early emotional development: Beaten and repulsed by a somewhat degenerate old father, while dominating his indulgent young mother, Adolf Hitler grew up with a seething reservoir of suppressed hostility, unresolved psychosexual conflicts, and intense feelings of persecution and inferiority. The cultural influences were such as to provide some outlet through heroic fantasies and ethnic identification, while his aggression was displaced to the emperor-figure and a vague enemy out-group.

In early adolescence these were still largely unchannelized conflicts that could take any turn. The direction they finally took was partly predetermined not only by the emotionally toned symbols of his early life experience but by the further interaction of these personal conflicts with the socioeconomic conflicts of the society into which he grew.

Source: G.M. Gilbert, The Psychology of Dictatorship, *1950, p. 26*

The father's cruelty drove his son into a lasting world of fantasy. His retreat from reality was exacerbated and became increasingly neurotic during Hitler's frequently solitary time in Vienna (from 1907 to 1913) (Gilbert, 1950, p. 28). The situation became pathological when he fell in love with an artist's model but was rejected in favour of a Jew. Thereafter Hitler displaced his frustration and psychosexual aggression onto the same old scapegoat (Gilbert, 1950, p. 33). Anti-Semitic hatred accelerated after the First World War and the November revolution. Hitler explained his frustrations in terms of a Jewish conspiracy. As a result, there appeared the beginnings of true paranoid tendencies in an unmistakably neurotic personality seeking an outlet for aggression through the acquisition of political power (Gilbert, 1950, p. 51). Those with comparable psychologies flocked to Hitler's political movement and the National Socialist 'revolution became for them rather a psychological end than a means to any socialistic ideal' (Gilbert, 1950, p. 41). While in prison in 1924, Hitler felt persecuted to the point that a Messiah complex took root and he began to identify his own fate with that of the German nation. From this point on his political course was set.

The early theories of Langer and Gilbert found some support in subsequent research. For example, Alois Hitler often came in for particular criticism. Bradley F. Smith believes the father only compounded problems Adolf had at school. Smith sympathises with Adolf whom he considers 'a very human little boy' whose main problems were only 'laziness and his passion for romantic games'. He was a child 'we all know', because most people experience the same desires he did (Smith, 1967, p. 8). At primary school, Adolf had been self-assured and he achieved adequately. He escaped the rigours of his father's authority through fantastic games in the shape of 'cowboys and indians' played with friends in the fields around his home. Tragedy arrived when a new and unwelcome authority exerted at Adolf's *secondary* school was augmented by blunt paternal authority at home.

At precisely the point Adolf began experiencing educational problems, his father insisted his son pursue a career in the civil service. The twin assault led Hitler to withdraw. He refused to study and talked of a career as an artist. Then he encountered his history teacher, Mr Poetsch. While Adolf found most school lessons dull, drab and uninspiring, with vivid and imaginative tales of Germany's past Poetsch appealed to the 'unhappy and resentful' youngster (Smith, 1967, pp. 77, 79 and 80). This enjoyment of history represented a new type of withdrawal from the world, a trend which was intensified when Adolf was rejected by the Academy of Fine Arts in Vienna. Hitler never managed to recover a healthy relationship to reality.

Document 8.4 Something Grandiose

His personality and way of life prevented him from acknowledging his errors and accepting his rejection as a sign of the need for any change. His escapism was reinforced by his social affectations and his scorn for work which seemed dirty, degrading or tiring. He was a confused and snobbish young man who had indulged himself for so long that he would neither work at an unpleasant task nor consider anyone except himself and the manner of life he enjoyed. His solution to rejection by the Academy was to go back to the Stumpergasse [where he lived] and settle down as if nothing had happened. In this sanctuary, he resumed what he grandly called his 'studies', doodling and reading, with excursions around town or to the opera.

Hitler's disdain for reality had something grandiose about it.

Source: B.F. Smith, Adolf Hitler, *1979 ed., p. 110*

The most sophisticated psychological theory vilifying the father figure was developed by Robert Waite. Alois is characterised in the usual way: he beat his children, wife and dog alike. Adolf once told his secretaries that on one occasion he received 230 blows. It was just the sort of thing to turn a sensitive child into a murderer (Waite, 1993, p. 137). This was especially so for two reasons. On the one hand Adolf was monorchid: he had only one testicle. Typically such boys are hyperactive, develop learning difficulties, lack concentration, are prone to accidents, feel inadequate, are indecisive and believe in magical things (Waite, 1993, p. 153). In Hitler's case, fear of beatings exacerbated these tendencies by establishing a tremendous anxiety over the single testicle. Even in later life, time and again in public Hitler clutched his hands over his crotch, as if protecting himself. On the other hand, Waite believes the infant Hitler witnessed his father rape his mother. This is said to be reflected in the following passage, quoted from *Mein Kampf*.

Document 8.5 Primal Trauma Scene

Let us imagine the following: In a basement apartment of two stuffy rooms lives a worker's family. . . . Among the five children there is a boy, let us say, of three. This is the age at which a child becomes conscious of his first impressions. In gifted people, traces of these early memories are found even in old age. The smallness and overcrowding of the rooms do not create favourable conditions. Quarrelling and nagging often arise because of this. In such circumstances people do not live with one another, but push down on top of one another. Every argument . . . leads to a never-ending, disgusting quarrel. . . . But when the parents fight almost daily, their brutality leaves nothing to the imagination; then the results of such visual education must slowly but inevitably become apparent in the little ones . . . especially when the mutual differences express themselves in the form of brutal attacks on the part of the father towards the mother or to assaults due to drunkenness. The poor little boy at the age of six, senses things which would make even a grown-up shudder. Morally infected . . . the young 'citizen' wanders off to elementary school. . . .

The three year old has now become a youth of fifteen who [has been dismissed from school and] despises all authority . . . Now he loiters about and God only knows when he comes home.

Source: Mein Kampf, *cited in R.G.L. Waite,* The Psychopathic God, *1993, p. 163*

Ambivalence towards Alois left Adolf in search of a stable identity. He took up the image of an artistic dandy to infuriate his father. A new element in the conundrum was added by the death of his beloved mother from cancer on 21 December 1907. This happened despite the attendance of a Jewish doctor called Bloch. It may be that Hitler already wondered if he had Jewish blood in his veins. Apparently during the Weimar period he got his lawyer, Hans Frank, to investigate whether Alois's father had been sired by a Jew while his grandmother worked in a Jewish household in Linz. Waite believes that within a short time of Klara dying, Adolf became a convinced anti-Semite. In his memoirs of this period (during which Hitler was based in Vienna), Hitler's boyhood friend, August Kubizek, gives an account of what may have been one of the most formative events in Adolf's life.

Document 8.6 Anti-Semitic Union

Things got worse. One day, when I was very busy with preparations for my exam, Adolf stormed into our room full of excitement. He had just come from the police, he said: there had been an incident in the Mariahilferstrasse, connected with a Jew, of course. A Handelee had been standing in front of the Gerngross store. The word 'Handelee' was used to designate eastern Jews who, dressed in caftan and boots, sold shoe laces, buttons, braces and other small articles in the street. The Handelee was the lowest stage of the career of those quickly assimilated Jews who often occupied leading positions in Austria's economic life. The Handelees were forbidden to beg. But this man had whiningly approached passers-by, his hand outstretched, and had collected some money. A policeman asked him to produce his papers. He began to wring his hands and said he was a poor, sick man who had only this little trading to live on, but he had not been begging. The policeman took him to the police station, and asked bystanders to act as witnesses. In spite of his dislike of publicity, Adolf had presented himself as a witness, and he saw with his own eyes that the Handelee had three thousand crowns in his caftan, conclusive evidence, according to Adolf, of the exploitation of Vienna by immigrant eastern Jews. . . .

. . . one day Adolf came home and announced decidedly, 'Today, I joined the Anti-Semite Union and have put down your name as well'.

Source: August Kubizek, The Young Hitler I Knew, *1955, pp. 251–3*

The passage is broadly supportive of Hitler's own contention that he became an anti-Semite in Vienna (see document 2.3). Unfortunately there is a problem with it: the detail is wrong. There was no such organisation as the Anti-Semitic Union in Austria–Hungary before 1918 (Kershaw, 1998, p. 62). The example shows both how much care has to be used when assessing memoir material and how difficult it is to chart definitively Adolf Hitler's conversion to anti-Semitism.

Nonetheless, Waite's psychoanalysis can be summarised as follows: Adolf had an unsatisfactory relationship with his father which amounted to an unresolved Oedipal complex (Waite, 1993, p. 188). With the death of his mother, these tensions were transferred from Alois to the image of Dr Bloch. Further displacement and projection of hatred onto all Jews occurred in the years before the First World War.

Rudolph Binion approaches analysis rather differently. He focuses on Hitler's two-fold ideological fixation: anti-Semitism and living space (which Binion refers to frequently as 'feeding space'). The former is said to have grown out of a trauma specific to Adolf Hitler, the latter out of one suffered by the whole German people. Like Waite, Binion roots Hitler's anti-Semitism in the failure of the Jewish doctor to cure his mother's cancer, but unlike Waite he maintains that this prejudice remained latent until late 1918. Race hatred was only mobilised by the twin experience of Hitler's being gassed and the loss of the First World War. The nature of the psychological mobilisation explains Hitler's comments of 1925 that Germany's Jews should be held under gas. Binion also says that viewed 'in this light, the gassing of the Jews [undertaken during the Holocaust] looks like a massive revenge' (Binion, 1976, p. 13).

Hitler's fixation on living or feeding space, is interpreted in terms of Klara Hitler's breast feeding techniques. Because the mother had experienced three infants die, she over-indulged Adolf, with the result that his emotions fixed at a stage marked by oral craving. The resulting oral–aggressive characteristics certainly equipped him to be a fiery orator who found a kind of sexual gratification in talking, but there were further consequences. He came to see all history as a fight for feeding ground. When, after the First World War, Hitler perceived Germany as unable to feed her children, he expressed his psychological misdevelopment in an appropriate political way. The doctrine of *Lebensraum* melded Hitler's oral characteristics with the perception that Germany required more land.

Hitler brought together the 'anti-Semitic' and '*Lebensraum*' traumas in his particular view of the world which internationalised his anti-Semitism and tied it up with the fixation on space.

Document 8.7 Global Thrust

The argument from 'land and soil' spoke to Germany's traumatic purposes as he was programmed to sense and serve them in nursing his mother's trauma at his mother's breast. His racial-ideological argument was a device for according Germany's traumatic purposes with his own derived from 1907 [i.e. at the time of his mother's death]. . . . He met his own traumatic need concurrently through his global thrust against the Jew.

Source: Rudolph Binion, Hitler among the Germans, *1976, p. 64*

These analyses underline further the lack of agreement about when and why Hitler became anti-Semitic. While there is the failure of the Jewish doctor in 1907 (as highlighted by Waite), in *Mein Kampf* Hitler dates his own race hatred to an encounter with an Orthodox Jew in Vienna (see document 2.3). To this we can add Kubizek's rather shaky evidence (document 8.6). During his stay in the Austrian capital between 1907 and 1913, Hitler certainly encountered the anti-Semitic politics associated with Schönerer and Lueger, and sought out popular anti-Semitic publications (see Chapter 2). There may even have been a personal humiliation by a Jew (as highlighted by Gilbert). Hitler's confidant Albert Speer certainly believed the prejudice was a remnant from his Austro-Hungarian days which Hitler should have out-grown (Speer, 1976, p. 353). By contrast Binion says Hitler's hospitalisation in 1918 was key. Some evidence supports this by disputing whether Hitler really was anti-Semitic when he lived in Vienna (Hanisch, 1939b, pp. 271–2). Reinhold Hanisch used to sell Hitler's paintings for part of this period. He says the following.

Document 8.8 By no Means a Jew Hater

Now I want to make some remarks about Hitler's opinion about the Jews. In those days [in Vienna] he was by no means a Jew hater. He became one afterwards. . . .

In the Home [i.e. the hostel in which Hitler lived], Hitler had helpful advisers who were Jews. There was a one-eyed locksmith called Robinsohn who often assisted him, since he was a beneficiary of an accident-insurance annuity and was able to spare a few pennies. And in the Maennerheim Hitler often found Jews who listened to his political debates. The salesman Neumann became a real friend. Neumann was a business man by profession and didn't shrink from any work. At first he was with two signboard painters, one a very industrious man and the other a former lamplighter, Greiner. Later on Neumann worked with another Jew who was buying old clothes. He was a good-hearted man who liked Hitler very much and whom Hitler of course highly esteemed. Hitler told me once that Neumann was a very decent man, because if any of us had small debts Neumann paid them, though he himself was very much in want.

At that time Theodor Herzl and the Zionist question were very much discussed. Hitler and Neumann had long debates about Zionism.

Source: R. Hanisch, 'I Was Hitler's Buddy. II', pp. 271–2

Hitler knew Jews where he lived and through the art trade. He had no problem living in a multi-ethnic area. Hanisch even implies Hitler looked like a poor Jew at this time. He wore 'an incredibly greasy derby hat', his 'hair was long and tangled and he grew a beard on his chin such as we Christians seldom have' (Hanisch, 1939a, p. 242).

In other words, it is by no means certain that Hitler gave himself over decisively to anti-Semitism during his time in Vienna (Kershaw, 1998, p. 64). This is not so remarkable. Character traits are not necessarily formed all at once. They can just as well result from dynamic processes which develop over time. Hitler certainly witnessed anti-Semitism during the period 1907–13 and may have begun to nurse a personally motivated dislike for Jews then. It is perfectly plausible that as the months and years passed, as he read more and more trashy racist literature, and as he brooded on the injustices of a life which had denied him entrance to art school and consigned him (the son of a solidly middle-class family) to a life of increasing poverty (in the middle of Vienna where affluence was to be seen all around), the more he began to sympathise with ideological anti-Semitism. But there is still room to maintain that he only became a 'dyed in the wool', radical anti-Semite as a result of experiences at the end of the First World War. According to one way of thinking, a truly deep-seated hatred only developed after Hitler witnessed a decline in civilian morale in Germany during a period of leave from the army which he took in 1916 (Kershaw, 1998, p. 95). But there may be a more dramatic explanation still. This theme will be taken up below.

A psychological interpretation of Hitler which looks beyond the family has been put forward by Erich Fromm. He starts his analysis by wondering why people gave up personal freedom to fascist movements. The answer is provided by a basic human need: 'to avoid aloneness', since to 'feel completely alone and isolated leads to mental disintegration just as physical starvation leads to death' (Fromm, 1960, p. 15). Fromm believes that in the modern world people are given more scope than ever to stand on their own two feet. The rigid feudal system, in which everyone was allotted a given place in society, has broken down in favour of a capitalist system where everything is up for grabs. An individual can either embrace this freedom joyously, or give it up.

Freedom can be abrogated masochistically: a person can revel in powerlessness in the face of authority. Specifically somebody might have chosen loyalty to a fascist leader to satisfy this craving. He or she became an unthinking automaton carrying out the instructions of someone else (Fromm, 1960, pp. 131 and 160). There would also have been a feeling of security and retreat from aloneness through union with millions of other fascist followers. But the proposition has a reverse side. It implies that a person can revel in subordinating others to him- or herself: a characteristic called *sadism* (Fromm, 1960, p. 123). Fromm identifies sadistic elements in Adolf Hitler: he responded to the fear of aloneness by despising the powerless and by loving power.

Document 8.9 Sadism in Print

The *sadistic craving for power* finds manifold expressions in *Mein Kampf*. It is characteristic of Hitler's relationship to the German masses whom he despises and 'loves' in the typically sadistic manner, as well as to his political enemies towards whom he evidences those destructive elements that are an important component of his sadism. He speaks of the satisfaction the masses have in domination. 'What they want is the victory of the stronger and the annihilation or the unconditional surrender of the weaker.'

[Quoting *Mein Kampf*:] 'Like a woman, . . . who will submit to the strong man rather than dominate the weakling, thus the masses love the ruler rather than the suppliant, and inwardly they are far more satisfied by a doctrine which tolerates no rival than by the grant of liberal freedom; they often feel at a loss what to do with it, and even easily feel themselves deserted. They neither realize the impudence with which they are spiritually terrorized, nor the outrageous curtailment of their human liberties for in no way does the delusion of this doctrine dawn on them.'

Source: Erich Fromm, The Fear of Freedom, *1960, p. 192*

Fromm identifies a further characteristic in Hitler: destructiveness (Fromm, 1960, p. 155, 1977, p. 294). For an explanation of it we return to an analysis of his childhood. At fault was the parenting of neither Alois nor Klara. Rather, from birth to 6 years, Adolf was a particularly narcissistic little boy who was quite unable to develop a loving relationship with his mother (Fromm, 1977, pp. 498–502). In the place of love grew a fantasy world. By the time he was aged between 6 and 11 years this had grown until his prime interest was to escape into games of 'cowboys and indians' (Fromm, 1977, p. 503). Freedom for Hitler did not mean liberty to meet the world in realistic terms, but the avoidance of constraint and reality. Hitler remained narcissistic and his experiences between the ages of 11 to 17, which brought failure at school and confrontation with his father, stengthened his commitment to fantasy. Oddly for a boy of this age, Hitler remained fixated on war games in the fields around his home. With his narcissism unable to bear the risk of failure, and unable to change the reality of poor academic performance, he rejected reality even more significantly (Fromm, 1977, p. 510). He decided to 'drop out' and become an 'artist'.

Then came the First World War. It allowed Hitler's fantasies to be mobilised into reality. He became a hero fighting for his nation. The image was disrupted by defeat and especially Germany's revolution. Hitler understood the latter as an attack on him, his values, hopes and 'grandiosity' (Fromm, 1977, p. 524). Some of the revolutionaries were Jews and the humiliation Hitler felt could only be atoned for by their eradication. This personal crisis at the end of the war created necrophilia in Hitler: the burgeoning desire to annihilate (Fromm, 1977, p. 540). In *Mein Kampf* this was evidenced in extensive talk of tuberculosis, syphilis and poison. Eventually it was made manifest in his desire to kill Poles, Russians and, of course, Jews. Finally Fromm sums Hitler up as 'a withdrawn, extremely narcissistic, unrelated, undisciplined, sado-masochistic, and necrophilous person' (Fromm, 1977, p. 549).

Unfortunately there are serious problems with these psychological inter-pretations. Not least, manifestly they cannot agree about the dynamics of Adolf's family background. Indeed the assertions they all make sooner or later of a genuine malignancy in Hitler's childhood need not be true. In a biography written long ago, Helmut Heiber maintained that Alois was no drunkard, but a respected and generally upstanding man (Heiber, 1961, p. 10). The childhood friend, August Kubizek, said Adolf genuinely respected his father (Kubizek, 1955, p. 38). That there was anything at all wrong in the Hitler family home is doubted by Werner Maser. He says Adolf's childhood was 'exceedingly happy' (Maser, 1974, p. 5). But even if Adolf did contend with a violent father and an over-protective mother (a situation which Ian Kershaw accepts), the effects need not have been so decisive as the psychologists imply. In Hitler's early life there was really 'no hint of what would emerge' later. There are just so many contradictions, grey areas and imponderables in the studies discussed so far in this chapter that they begin to look too much like 'guesswork' (Kershaw, 1998, p. 13). As a result they bring with them the danger of mystifying rather than explaining Hitler's development (Bracher, 1976, p. 207).

Nonetheless, the suspicion remains that the adult Hitler was not strictly normal. This is true even accepting that the distinction between normality and abnormality can be dreadfully 'fuzzy' (Redlich, 1999, p. 336). For example, feelings 'which only caused unease in other people drove him to despair' (Zitelmann, 1993, p. 115). After the suicide of his niece, Geli Raubal, first Hitler had to be restrained from himself committing suicide and then lived in total seclusion for a fortnight. He refused ever to eat meat again (Toland, 1976, pp. 252–6; Payne, 1973, pp. 226–9). What is more, perfectly rational lines of discourse would culminate unexpectedly in anti-Semitic unreason. He was 'almost like the medieval person who sensed the presence of the devil everywhere' (Schramm, 1972, pp. 50–1). If the psychological studies of character cited so far are inconclusive, we are still left with the possibility that Adolf Hitler suffered from a mental illness.

Robert Waite believes Hitler was a 'borderline personality'. The label indicates someone who is mentally ill, existing in the borderland between neurosis and psychosis, but who can still function effectively in many areas of life (Waite, 1993, p. 356). Typically 'borderliners' are paranoid and convinced of their omnipotence. They also have unreconciled Oedipal problems and confused identities. Waite believes Hitler fitted these categories. Lacking treatment for his condition, he projected his 'neuroses' and inner tensions onto the world around him, rationalised them, and established them as ideology and grounds for government policy (Waite, 1993, p. 358). Hitler used hatred of the Jews as the chief defence of his emotional disorder. Combining this point with Oedipalism, Waite contends that 'in attempting to destroy all the Jews, Hitler was attempting to destroy his father' (Waite, 1993, p. 365).

This is one possibility, but not the only one. Psychiatric medical conditions can be hopelessly difficult to diagnose. Over the last twenty years, committees of psychiatrists in America have developed a system of classification of conditions that was published as the *Diagnostic and Statistical Manual of Mental Disorders* (Redlich, 1999, p. 332; Altrocchi, 1980, p. xiii). So many attempts have been made to apply this knowledge to Adolf Hitler that one commentator says, 'I often feel as if I were in a cheap clothing store: Nothing fits, and everything fits' (Redlich, 1999, p. 332). The same author believes that during his life Hitler suffered individual 'grief reactions' (presumably including his responses to the deaths of his mother and Geli), but never an episode of 'severe enduring or psychotic depression' (Redlich, 1999, p. 292). Given the difficulty of defining a clinical mental condition, this unwillingness to recognise some form of psychotic episode during Hitler's life may be too swift.

On 14 October 1918 Hitler suffered a gas attack initiated by the British. It affected his eyes so badly that he could not open them. This event alone must have traumatised a man used to earning a living from a visual art – painting. On 17 October he was sent to the hospital at Pasewalk. Treated with compresses soaked in anti-inflammatory solutions he recovered quickly. On 10 November, however, a regimental chaplain brought the news that Germany had surrendered and the Kaiser had abdicated. The information triggered a spell of hysterical blindness in Hitler (Redlich, 1999, pp. 41–2). In due course the hospital was visited by revolutionaries some of whom happened to be Jews (Hitler, 1985, p. 184). We cannot be certain whether Hitler was treated for a psychiatric condition in Pasewalk since the hospital's records have been lost. In any event individual psychotherapy was extremely rare at this time (Redlich, 1999, p. 42). But during the period in question Hitler certainly did suffer a considerable mental episode. Under conditions which must have generated substantial feelings of stress and depression, it is highly plausible he experienced some kind of breakdown which (for want of treatment) left a lasting mark. The hypothesis fits with evidence that Hitler's character changed in about 1919 (Binion, 1976, p. 2). It would also correspond to Gerald Fleming's identification of the events of November 1918 as absolutely critical to the radicalisation of Hitler from a person who was sympathetic to anti-Semitism to one dedicated to the 'unswerving conviction that the antichrist – Jewry – must be exterminated' (Fleming, 1986, p. 15).

Psychosis is the clinical misapprehension and misinterpretation of reality (Rycroft, 1987, p. 657). Although its precise causes are disputed, it certainly can result from a mixture of stress and depression. It can manifest itself in paranoia, that is to say grandiose persecutory ideas. Many genuinely paranoid casts of mind exist in the population as a whole, but only sometimes do individuals become so disordered as to require hospitalisation (Mechanic, 1981, p. 29). The following is a good description of psychosis.

Document 8.10 Psychosis

Traditionally it has been assumed that psychotic symptoms are unique signs of biological pathology which are discontinuous with normal experience and therefore by definition bizarre and abnormal (Jaspers, 1913/1963). However, there are several observations that indicate it may be more valid to view normal experience and psychosis as existing at two ends of a continuum. If one takes a longitudinal perspective it is clear that psychotic symptoms wax and wane in severity over the course of a disorder. Over time frank hallucinations may become mild abnormalities in the experience of thoughts, and delusional beliefs may become eccentric ideas (Strauss, 1969; Chapman and Chapman, 1988). Conversely, frank symptoms may be preceded by milder experiential anomalies which become apparently less and less understandable as acute psychosis approaches. Surveys have also demonstrated that mild anomalies in experience, thinking and belief which have a resemblance to psychotic symptoms (e.g. experiences of deja vu, beliefs in telepathy and hallucinations) occur in a substantial proportion of people in the normal population (around 15–20%) as well as occurring amongst people with frank psychotic disorder (Claridge, 1985; Chapman and Chapman, 1988; Romme and Escher, 1989). Experimental studies have demonstrated that there are parallels between the performance of people who report schizoidal experiences, and people who meet diagnostic criteria for schizophrenia on a variety of cognitive tasks. There may be commonalities between the processes which give rise to both types of experiences (see Claridge, 1985 for a review). Lastly, hallucinations and other psychotic experiences may be induced in normal people when put under unusual conditions (e.g. conditions of hypnotism, very severe stress, disorientation, etc.) (see Kingdom and Turkington, 1994 for a review).

Collectively these findings suggest that it may be useful to think of frank psychosis as a more severe manifestation of some of the anomalies in belief, thought and experience that may affect many normal people at some time or another. The assumption of a continuity between normality and psychosis has important clinical implications. It opens the way for a group of therapeutic techniques that focus on reducing the stigma and anxiety often associated with the experience of psychotic symptoms and with diagnostic labelling. Kingdom and Turkington (1991; 1994) have described such approaches as normalising strategies, which involve explaining and demystifying the psychotic experience. They may involve suggesting to patients that their experiences are not strange and un-understandable, but are common to many people, and even found amongst people who are relatively normal and healthy. Normalising strategies can help instil hope and decrease the stigma and anxiety which may be associated with the experience of psychotic symptoms. The reassuring benefits of these relatively subtle clinical interventions can be striking.

Source: D. Fowler, P. Garety and E. Kuipers, Cognitive Behaviour Therapy for Psychosis, *1995, pp. 38–9*

Psychosis should not be understood only as a discrete biological condition reflecting physiological dysfunction; it is somehow on a continuum with normality. Its symptoms wax and wane over the course of an illness and reflect the way individuals adapt to the world (Fowler *et al.*, 1995, p. 42). The condition does not simply lead to the disablement of the sufferer. Symptoms exist in 15 to 20% of the population and impact upon thoroughly normal people from time to time. There are in-built tendencies in the thinking of some individuals which lead to psychotic tendencies even in normal circumstances. Fowler *et al.* add that character traits associated with individuals who are particularly susceptible to psychosis include a tendency to jump to conclusions, anxiety, social withdrawal, distrust and an inability to understand the motives of others (Fowler *et al.*, 1995, p. 57).

This discussion can be applied to Hitler. On the one hand, paranoia was certainly a central characteristic of his personality (Redlich, 1999, p. 335). On the other hand, his personality overlaps with the psychotic criteria. He had a tendency to jump to conclusions. He could 'build enormous hypotheses on a most limited selection of facts' (Cross, 1973, p. 45). Aged 17, he bought a lottery ticket, and proceeded to jump to the conclusion of what he would do when he won. His speculations went on at abnormal length.

Document 8.11 Lottery

Although the first prize represented a lot of money, my friend [Hitler] was by no means tempted to spend it thoughtlessly. On the contrary. He went about it in the most calculating and economical way. It would have been senseless to invest the whole sum in one of the projects, say the rebuilding of the museum, for this would only have been a small part within the framework of the great town-planning scheme. It was more reasonable to use the money for our own benefit, to help us to a standing in public life which would enable us to progress further towards our ultimate aims.

It would have been too expensive to build a villa for ourselves; it would have swallowed up so much of our fortune that we would have moved into this splendour quite penniless. Adolf suggested a compromise: we should rent a flat, he said, and adapt it to our purpose. After long and careful examination of the various possibilities, we selected the second floor of No. 2 Kirchengasse in Urfahr; for this house was in a quite exceptional position. Near the bank of the Danube, it had a view over the pleasant green fields which culminated in the Pöstlingberg. We crept into the house secretly, looked at the view from the staircase window, and Adolf made a sketch of the ground plan.

Then we moved in, so to speak. The larger wing of the flat should be for my friend, the smaller one was reserved for me. Adolf arranged the rooms so that his study was as far removed as possible from mine, so that he, at his drawing board, would not be disturbed by my practising.

My friend also saw to the furnishing of the rooms, drawing each single piece of furniture to scale on the ground plan. The furniture was of the most beautiful and superior quality, made by the town's leading craftsmen, by no means cheap, mass-produced stuff. Even the decorations for the walls of each single room were designed by Adolf. I was only allowed to have a say about the curtains and draperies, and I had to show him how I suggested dealing with the rooms he had given me. He was certainly pleased with the self-assured manner in which I co-operated with the arrangement of the flat. We had no doubt that the first prize was ours. Adolf's own faith had bewitched me into believing as he did. I, too, expected to move into No. 2 Kirchengasse very soon.

Although simplicity was to be the keynote of our home, it was nevertheless imbued with a refined, personal taste. Adolf proposed to make our home the centre of a circle of art lovers. I would provide the musical entertainment. He would recite something, or read aloud, or expound his latest work. We would make regular trips to Vienna to attend lectures and concerts, and to go to the theatre. . . .

Adolf thought of everything, even the running of the household, which was necessary as the day of the draw was approaching. A refined lady should preside over our home and run it. It had to be an elderly lady, to rule out any expectations or intentions which might interfere with our artistic vocation. We also agreed on the staff that this big household would need. Thus, everything was prepared. The image remained with me for a long time to come; an elderly lady, with greying hair, but incredibly distinguished, standing in the brilliantly lit hall, welcoming, on behalf of her two young, gifted gentlemen of seventeen and eighteen years, the guests who formed their circle of select, lofty-minded friends.

Source: August Kubizek, The Young Hitler I Knew, *1955, pp. 93–5*

Hitler was socially withdrawn and did not form close relationships with those around him. The point was noted at the start of this chapter in the context of Hitler's relationship to Speer, Hess and Jodl, but it was also reflected in his early sex life – or the lack of it. While in Linz, he became completely besotted with a girl called Stefanie. Hitler wrote poetry about her, fantasised about her for four years, and yet he never once approached her directly. Once again, Kubizek related the story.

Document 8.12 Stefanie

To be sure, Stefanie had no idea how deeply Adolf was in love with her; she regarded him as a somewhat shy but, nevertheless remarkably tenacious and faithful admirer. When she responded with a smile to his inquiring glance, he was happy, and his mood became unlike anything I had ever observed in him; everything in the world was good and beautiful and well ordered, and he was content. When Stefanie, as happened just as often, coldly ignored his gaze, he was crushed and ready to destroy himself and the whole world.

Certainly such phenomena are typical of every first great love, and one might perhaps be tempted to dismiss Adolf's feelings for Stefanie as calf love. This may have been true as far as Stefanie's own conception of them was concerned, but for Adolf himself, his relation to Stefanie was more than calf love. The mere fact that it lasted more than four years, and even cast its splendour over the subsequent years of misery in Vienna, shows that Adolf's feelings were deep and true, and real love. Proof of the depth of his feelings is that for Adolf, throughout these years, no other woman but Stefanie existed – how unlike the usual boy's love, which is always changing its object. I cannot remember that Adolf ever gave any thought to another girl. Later in Vienna, when Lucie Weidt roused his enthusiasm in the part of Elsa in Lohengrin, the highest praise he could give her was that she reminded him of Stefanie. In appearance, Stefanie was ideally suited for the part of Elsa, and other female roles of Wagner's operas, and we spent much time wondering whether she had the necessary voice and musical talent. Adolf was inclined to take it for granted. Just as her Valkyrie-like appearance never failed to attract him and could fire him with unbounded enthusiasm. He wrote countless love poems to Stefanie. 'Hymn to the Beloved' was the title of one of them, which he read to me from his little black notebook. Stefanie, a high-born damsel, in a dark blue, flowing velvet gown, rode on a white steed over the flowering meadows, her loose hair fell in golden waves on her shoulders. A clear spring sky was above. Everything was pure, radiant joy. I can still see Adolf's face glowing with fervent ecstasy and hear his voice reciting these verses. Stefanie filled his thoughts so completely that everything he said, or did, or planned for the future, was centred around her. With his growing estrangement from his home, Stefanie gained more and more influence over my friend, although he never spoke a word to her.

Source: August Kubizek, The Young Hitler I Knew, *1955, pp. 58–9*

Fowler *et al.* also say that the construction of grand psychotic delusions may be tied up with attitudes to work. Among those driven to succeed, a grand delusional fantasy is a means to compensate for failure (Fowler *et al.*, 1995, p. 66). For all the uncertainties about his early life, it seems Hitler did react to his failures badly. Difficulties at secondary school caused a retreat to fantastic play about 'cowboys and indians'. Failure to achieve a place at either art or architecture school led him to retreat into his own fantastic schemes of study (see Chapter 7). It is also significant that Hitler did not tell his family of his failure to become a student, and after his second rejection by the Academy broke contact with his friend Kubizek. He could not face anyone on the basis of rejection (Kershaw, 1998, pp. 38–9 and 48). We also know that the loss of the First World War and revolution were associated with a major reaction in him.

And so we come back to the basic plausibility of the proposal that, subject to profound feelings of stress and depression, while he was in Pasewalk hospital Hitler suffered a breakdown which engendered paranoid psychosis. This would have reflected his wider experiences of the world (Fowler *et al.*, 1995, p. 42). Hitler was aware of anti-Semitism. Its doctrine of conspiracy, exploitation and threat made it a highly suitable vehicle for paranoia. The net effect would have imbued the belief with a whole new vividness.

Related to this point is Hitler's conviction that the world functions according to principles of struggle. The idea is harmonious with psychotic paranoia because it implies that all other inhabitants of the world are struggling mercilessly against oneself. The idea expressed the course of Hitler's life and must have represented a further haven for psychological retreat. During his time in Vienna Hitler struggled hard to stay alive. He had been rootless and alone in a great city. He lacked the support of his formerly affluent family (Carr, 1978, p. 120). His life became one of misery and a desperate fight to get from day to day (Hoffmann, 1955, p. 174). There are descriptions of him turning up at hostels for the homeless in a terrible state, begging money from drunks and carrying luggage at the station to earn a few coppers (Hanisch, 1939a, pp. 239–40). During this time he painted small watercolours which Reinhold Hanisch sold to dealers. It was an ill-starred relationship which ended in a legal confrontation in an environment in which everyone had to look out for himself.

Document 8.13 Reinhold Hanisch

As I have said, Hitler had noticed that I was trying to get rid of him, because of his laziness, and had asked for the list of customers. I knew that Hitler was an irascible person; and I had been afraid that he would find me anywhere I went. If he lost his shelter in the Night Asylum because of his laziness I was afraid he would descend on me and be a burden to me. So for these reasons I had been living for several weeks under an assumed name. But at the police station, of course, they immediately discovered this, to my disaster. For at that time living under a false name in Vienna was a criminal offense.

But I still hoped that Hitler would clear up this error and that then the whole affair would turn out satisfactorily. I was taken to the Brigittenau Police Commissariat and confronted with Hitler. How great was my disappointment! Hitler, of whom I had thought so highly, whom I had helped so often, whose errands I had done, declared that I had misappropriated a watercolor of his worth fifty kronen. When I objected that I had given him his share of the twelve kronen paid for it he denied this. He denied, too, that he had told me to sell the picture as best I could. I testified that I had sold the picture to a dealer in the IXth District, but I didn't tell the dealer's name because I thought that if the bank director found out that it had not been I who had painted the Parliament he might withdraw the order he had given me.

At the trial two days later I had regained better spirits. I was asked again where I had sold the picture and I withheld the name of the dealer as before. My prison mates had already told me that I would certainly be sentenced for living under a false name, so I didn't take much pains with my defense. Perhaps I could have pointed out that Hitler couldn't possibly paint a picture worth fifty kronen. I don't know whether this would have shattered Hitler's testimony immediately. The only desire I had was to get out of it as soon as possible, and I hadn't much confidence in the justice of my case. After all, I was a poor devil and I had lived under a false name. Appearances were against me. I was sure I'd be sentenced, so it all made no difference to me. Hitler persisted in his false accusation, and as the payment and other things had all been arranged orally, I couldn't furnish any proof of my denials. I was sentenced to a short term. After the sentence had been passed I called to Hitler, 'When and where will we see each other again to make a settlement?'

Source: R. Hanisch, 'I Was Hitler's Buddy. III', p. 299

Hitler experienced another scene characterised by struggle. As a soldier, he was 'comradely, level-headed and unusually brave' (Maser, 1973, p. 83). Having already won the Iron Cross Second Class in December 1914, on 31 July 1918 he was recommended for the Iron Cross First Class by Colonel Freiherr von Godin (Maser, 1973, p. 88). But war is about loss. Hitler was a member of the List regiment which contained about 3,500 men at any one time. During the four years of war, it lost a total of 3,754 souls (Cross, 1973, p. 48). Hitler himself was injured by shrapnel in 1916 and by gas in October 1918. This life really was a desperate struggle liable to strike down anyone at any time. The full quality of this experience is shown in the letters Hitler sent from the Front. Such powerful personal experiences could well have formed the raw material for a paranoid fixation.

Document 8.14 Like Ninepins

Four guns had been dug in just in front of us. We took up position behind them in some large craters and waited. By now the first shrapnel was coming over and bursting at the edge of the wood, shredding the trees as though they were wisps of straw. We watched curiously without any real idea of the danger. None of us was afraid. We were all waiting impatiently for the order to advance. The racket was getting worse and worse. We heard that some of our people had already been wounded. Suddenly everyone cheered at the sight of five or six chaps in dun-coloured uniforms approaching on our left. Six Englishmen and a machine-gun. We looked at their escorts who were marching proudly behind their quarry. And for us, we had to go on waiting, hardly able to see through the fog and smoke of the witches' cauldron ahead of us. At long last came the order 'Advance!' We swarmed out of our craters, came to some fields and raced across them towards a small farmhouse.

Shrapnel was bursting to right and left of us and English bullets went singing in between but we took no notice of them. We lay there for ten minutes after which we were again ordered to advance. I was right out in front and no longer with our platoon. Suddenly the word went round that Stöwer, our platoon commander, had been hit. Crikey, I thought, that's a fine beginning. But we were out in the open and it was best to get a move-on. The captain was leading us. Now we had our first losses. The English had brought their machine-guns to bear on us. So we threw ourselves down and crawled slowly along a furrow. . . .

Again we advanced. Running and jumping as best I could, I crossed meadows and beet-fields, leapt over ditches, struggled over wire and through hedges and then ahead of me I heard someone shouting: 'In here! Everyone in here!' There was a long trench just in front of me. A moment later, with countless others ahead of me, behind me and to my left and right, I leapt down into it. Alongside me were Württembergers, under my feet dead and wounded English soldiers. The Württembergers had stormed the trench before we arrived. And now I knew why I had landed so softly. 250–290 yards away on our left front the English were still entrenched and on our right they still held the road to [illegible]. An uninterrupted hail of metal went hurtling over our heads. At last, at ten o'clock, our own artillery began to join in. 1–2–3–5 etc. continuously. Shell after shell began to strike the English trenches in front of us. The blokes began swarming out like ants out of an ant-heap and then we charged.

We were across the fields in a flash and after some bloody hand-to-hand fighting we cleared one trench after another. A lot of the enemy put their hands up. Those that didn't surrender were slaughtered. So it went on from trench to trench. At last we reached the main road, coppices on either hand. In we went and herded the English out in droves. In this way we came to the edge of the wood where the road ran out into open country. Some farm buildings to the left of us were still in enemy hands and came under ferocious fire. We started going down like ninepins.

Source: W. Maser, Hitler, *1973, pp. 80–2*

The psychiatric evidence can be summarised as follows. Psychotic disturbance is on a continuum with normality, can be found in 15 to 20% of the population and waxes and wanes through time. Hitler's personality contained a variety of traits which overlapped with those of individuals deemed susceptible to psychosis. It is plausible that he experienced a psychotic trauma. The key crisis in his life occurred when he was in hospital at Pasewalk. The resulting disturbances were left untreated and resulted in susceptibilities which followed paths already established in his lifetime experiences. These paths included a propensity towards anti-Semitism (including a belief in a Jewish world conspiracy) and the notion that life is a mortal struggle threatening all individuals. The interpretation fits well with the proposition that Hitler's race hatred only really burgeoned after 1918. When all of the pieces are put together, the idea of a mentally flawed Führer looks exactly what we need to render his personality comprehensible.

So did Hitler have a revolutionary personality, namely one stamped by an Oedipal complex or some other form of significant disturbance? Half-education, fear of his own mortality and amphetamine abuse all played a part in pushing Hitler along his chosen path. The latter two especially contribute to a complete understanding of the increasing haste and radicalisation of political and military choices he made after about 1937. Drug abuse in particular must have increased his *confidence* and readiness to be *ruthless*. Although Waite and others favour the idea of an *Oedipal complex*, perhaps this is best left to one side. It is unclear whether Hitler's relationship with his father was really so bad as such a diagnosis suggests. More likely is that, following his experiences at the end of the war, Hitler suffered a psychotic event which mobilised his mind along the lines of anti-Semitism and more general Darwinism. Hitler's political ideology and personal psychological needs gelled with profound results (see Chapter 9, thesis 4). The mental imbalance must have provided a profound dynamism, an additional revolutionary élan, to his career as a politician. Of course the observation that Hitler experienced *psychological instability* implies that he may not entirely have been responsible for the crimes which he brought his government to commit (see Chapter 9, thesis 5). But all notions of responsibility are relative and Hitler certainly led his state with 'pride and enthusiasm' (Redlich, 1999, p. 339). His revolutionary mind provided the impetus behind the manifold crimes which were committed between 1933 and 1945, and whatever the status of his mental health there is little option but to leave him carrying the can.

Conclusion – study of a revolutionary? 9

Finally we are in a position to synthesise an answer to the question posed in the title: has the analysis of the life of Adolf Hitler been 'the study of a revolutionary'? Each of the chapters has contributed substantively to a conclusion which grows organically from the main body of the text.

The nature of revolution was defined at the outset of the book. It involves people seizing the initiative in illegal ways to apply violence to precipitate change to the constitution of a society's political power. The actions reformulate the basis of political legitimation together with the popular myths associated with it. At stake also is the rooting out of perceived social ills in such a way that the structure of the community is transformed. Revolutions are pursued in the belief that they will modernise or improve the world. Clearly a revolutionary is anyone who embarks on such a course of action. These people tend to be idealists who are driven by what they perceive as injustices. They have the ability to motivate a substantial popular following. Revolutionaries are bold, confident individuals capable of ruthless action who understand society in 'black and white' ways. Their personalities can be off-putting and they may suffer from psychological instability. Certainly Hitler portrayed himself as a revolutionary (see documents 1.2 and 1.4), but was he justified in doing so? The evidence has been pretty much overwhelming.

'Ideologue' discussed whether Hitler's aims were revolutionary. He was depicted as an idealist decisively at odds with prevailing society and the structures of political power which predominated in Germany, not to say Europe, in the 1920s. He wanted Germany's political system, state and economy to be transformed until they would be legitimated by his racial myth. The cornerstone of his project was defined as an extreme type of anti-Semitism which betrayed a profoundly 'black and white' way of thinking in which Jews came to stand for everything that was evil and unjust in the world. For Hitler they were a profound social ill which he would have to deal with in order to renew the country. Hitler's ideology also dictated a new order of foreign policy which implied the revolutionising of the existing international community. Germany was to capture massive areas of central Europe and Russia, and to remove whole populations. Obviously his aims implied the deep-seated alteration of political and social structures of the nations which lay beyond Germany's borders.

The chapter 'Agitator' asked whether Hitler applied revolutionary means against the Weimar Republic. Operating in a violent milieu, he was a bold, tough-minded orator who knew how to motivate a dynamic following. Initially he grasped the political initiative to pursue violent, illegal action which in 1923 culminated in a direct revolt against the state. Failure at this point led to imprisonment and (despite his enduring revolutionary instincts) compelled him to seek power not through direct action, but through the parliamentary process. As a result Hitler changed to a position of pseudo-legality from which he still managed to threaten and glorify violence against both the republican state and his enemies.

'Dictator' discussed whether Hitler led National Socialism as a revolutionary movement and the Third Reich as a revolutionary state. Through the abolition of civil rights in Germany and the supersession of rule by multi-party democracy, he brought about a fundamental change to the constitution of the nation's political power. He presided over institutions which meted out violence against perceived opponents and attempted to root them out as social ills. This was done to left-wing activists and Jews in particular. By necessity the actions implied changes to Germany's social structure. The sort of violence Hitler unleashed across the country was illegal by any reasonable standards. From this chapter Hitler emerged as a ruthless manipulator of everything around him – people and political organisations alike. It was a style of leadership which enabled him to motivate followers to implement his desires. As Reich Chancellor he embarked on a significant effort to mobilise behind him as much of the nation as possible. Even when possible limitations to Hitler's revolutionary credentials were identified (e.g. the facts that he came to power in a coalition cabinet with traditional conservatives and that he refused to try to Nazify the army at an early point), these were explained as short-term measures to improve the prospects for bringing about subsequent lasting change.

The chapter 'Deceiver' asked if there can be a revolutionary foreign policy and whether Hitler implemented one. Certainly it reiterated the image of the man as a motivator. Foreign policy triumphs rallied the German people behind him. He displayed substantial initiative, toughness of mind, self-confidence and ruthlessness as he lied to and bullied Europe's statesmen to achieve his objectives. Transcending the reasonable approaches of his predecessors such as Stresemann and Rathenau, Hitler showed a readiness for violence in dealing with Austria and Czechoslovakia. Illegally he supported fifth columns abroad. As first came to light in the chapter 'Ideologue', Hitler championed completely new legitimating principles and myths for the implementation of foreign policy. Through a programme of the most radical imperialist expansion he hoped to rectify perceived social ills facing Germany, such as the danger of over-population. By early 1939 he had taken the initiative to pursue aggressively expansionist ends. He overturned the Versailles system (which he had always despised as unjust) and transformed the constitution of political power in the international arena. If anything ever constituted a revolutionary foreign policy, this was it.

'Warlord' raised the possibility that the Second World War was led as a revolutionary conflict. From 1939 on, Hitler applied political violence across Europe to alter the constitution of international and national power structures in the most direct and radical of ways. The single-party nation gave way to the single-party continent as country after country toppled before Hitler's armies. In the process, Europe was edged along the road to becoming a function of Germany's needs as Hitler defined them. From the outset Hitler embarked on a project to transform the social structures of the nations his forces occupied. This was evident in plans to eradicate Polish intellectuals and to resettle Polish lands with ethnic Germans. He took the initiative in 1941 and escalated the conflict with an assault on the Soviet Union. The nature of warfare was redefined by a series of orders sponsored by Hitler which must be defined as illegal by any reasonable standards. Massive plans for extermination (of Communists, Jews and Slavs) became part and parcel of the war in the East such that Hitler championed the most radical political and social transformation of the whole continent. There is no doubt that he used war as a means to export his revolutionary principles (both in the way it was fought and in the occupation policies which followed his victories) and used the period 1939–45 as an opportunity to realise his ideas in their most murderous form. The extremity of the exterminatory actions expressed thought that was 'black and white', violent and idealistic in equal measure. In Hitler's mind the bases of evil were being destroyed as a means to eradicating social ills (e.g. Jewry and Communism) which were perceived as threatening Germany. The seizure of land was a means to solving the perceived social ill of over-population.

The chapter 'Artist and architect' explored how Hitler's artistic conceptions related to his revolutionary credentials. Here the most significant potential flaw in his revolutionary character came to light. Hitler's tastes, which revolved around grandeur, classicism and insipid pastoralism, were hardly a break with tradition. They were a reaction against the way the contemporary arts had been developing since about 1910. Hitler was no supporter of the cultural modernisation which Germany experienced after the First World War. But this does not mean that his approach to the arts lacked everything revolutionary. On the one hand, he introduced racism as a new source of legitimation defining the type of artistic expression he expected in Germany. On the other hand, he wanted to use 'racially sound' construction projects to establish a national myth supporting principles of community, national greatness and the permanence of his political values. If we interpret Hitler's approach to the arts as a propagandistic device to reinforce the wider changes to political systems and social structures which he brought about across Europe, even this aspect of his life becomes revolutionary.

Finally 'Mind' addressed whether Hitler had a revolutionary personality. Worries about his mortality and drug abuse encouraged him to accelerate and radicalise his policies from the late 1930s. The latter must have boosted his self-confidence and ruthlessness. In terms of Hitler's experiencing a personality disorder, it has been proposed that he suffered from an Oedipal complex. This possibility was left to one side for lack of evidence. Instead it was proposed that at the end of the First World War, while stressed and depressed in Pasewalk hospital, Hitler suffered a paranoid psychotic episode which mobilised his mind against Jews and encouraged him to understand the world in terms of a Darwinian struggle of each against the other.

This experience, which was never treated properly, added a significant dynamism to his subsequent political career.

A careful tracing of these comments shows that Hitler's life covered all of the definitional characteristics of what it is to undertake a 'revolution' and to be a 'revolutionary'. The main points are summarised in the table here.

Summary of Adolf Hitler's revolutionary credentials

Revolutionary characteristic	*Evidence of expression*
Transformation of society's political power	– abolition of parliamentary democracy – abolition of civil rights – overturning of the Treaty of Versailles – destruction of the European international order through war – transformation of the political systems of the states occupied 1939–45
Transformation of society's social structure	– removal of Communists – removal of Jews – population policies pursued in eastern European states occupied 1939–45
Reformulation of society's legitimating myths and legends	– general application of anti-Semitic and racialist theories – war seen as the ultimate rationale of foreign policy and an inevitable part of life – use of art and architecture to bolster the place of National Socialism in the world
Root out perceived social ills	– actions versus Communism – actions versus Jews – attempt to provide 'living space' to solve Germany's perceived problem of over-population
React against injustice	– denouncing of 'Jewish' activity in the economy – attitude to the Treaty of Versailles
Take the initiative	– precipitation of 1923 putsch – expansionist foreign policy projects 1933–39 – precipitation of war in 1939 – invasion of the USSR in 1941

Revolutionary characteristic	*Evidence of expression*
Act illegally and violently	– direct application and glorification of political violence against opponents in the Weimar Republic – revolt of 1923 – persecution of Communists and Jews in the Third Reich – Röhm putsch – use of 'fifth columns' to subvert neighbouring states – ready resort to war – criminal orders and initiatives of Second World War
Modernisation of society	See following discussion in the text
Ability to motivate a following	– oratory, especially during the Weimar years – techniques of political organisation – use of foreign policy successes 1933–9
Idealism	– all-embracing nature of racial convictions – readiness to apply ultimate solutions to perceived problems: e.g. the pursuit of goals through war and exterminationism
'Black and white' views	– division of the world into 'Good and Evil', Germans versus Jews – application of eliminationism to solve perceived political problems indicative of an 'All or Nothing' mentality
Boldness and confidence	– beer-hall politics during Weimar – bullying of Europe's statesmen 1933–9
Ruthlessness	– Röhm putsch – readiness to apply military force against Austria and Czechoslovakia
Psychological instability	– possibility that he was energised by drugs and experienced a paranoid psychosis

Just one important issue has been left largely to one side (as indicated in the table): the aim of modernising or improving the world. Strong cases have been made by a number of historians that fascists, Hitler along with them, were fundamentally reactionary. The nature of Hitler's artistic tastes supports the proposition. Famously, in the 1960s Ernst Nolte argued that Hitler's National Socialism was a rejection of historical progress (Nolte, 1969, p. 529). Recent interpretations have maintained the image of a strongly conservative strain in the movement. Jeffrey Herf has coined the phrase 'reactionary modernism' to describe Hitler's politics. It applied modern techniques to promote ends which were still fundamentally reactionary (Herf, 1984, pp. 1–2).

It is easy to see Hitler's central fixation on racism as a kind of throwback. Anti-Semitism has existed for millennia and there was certainly nothing new about anti-Slavic prejudice in either Germany or Austria (Herbert, 1997, chapter 2; Mason, 1988, p. 11). It is impossible to deny there was something atavistic about the passion and intensity Hitler brought to his prejudice. This should be no surprise if we are right that it was energised significantly by a bout of mental ill-health experienced at the end of the First World War (see Chapter 8). But there was more to his hatred than just this. Its expression was actually quite complex, as were the initiatives it spawned. As early as his first anti-Semitic tract (see document 2.2), Hitler said his aim was to transcend the traditional 'pogrom' mentality (which characterised established anti-Semitism) in favour of something else, by implication something new. Hitler was not interested in just expressing hatred of Jews. He expected their removal from society to herald the creation of a different society, by implication a better one (Baumann, 1989, p. 91). It is also quite correct that, once Reich Chancellor, Hitler's practical objective of trying to create a community without 'lesser races' was not 'a form of regression to past times'. No comparable project had ever been attempted before in German history (Burleigh and Wippermann, 1991, p. 301).

This was an initiative whose time had come. Debates about biological and social engineering were well-established in circles of German life beyond National Socialism. Since at least 1895 they had involved some established intellectuals. As a result one historian has concluded that the morality of biological engineering is not so much a problem of fascism, but one of modernity (Schwartz, 1998, p. 619). Not even Hitler's wartime efforts to restructure Europe's populations can be divorced from modern trends of thought. During the 1920s and 1930s German scientists embarked on significant projects to assess objectively the extent to which eastern European states were over-populated (Aly and Heim, 1993, pp. 72–82 and 104–19). The implication was that *something* had to be done to improve the economic efficiency of eastern European societies. In this light, Hitler's plans to depopulate the East through genocide can be linked to *ideas that were current* at the time among progressive economists and demographers (Aly and Heim, 1993; Housden, 1995, p. 479). Even his eliminationism cannot be divorced entirely from notions of purposeful, progressive change (Baumann, 1989, pp. 91–2).

Wider perspectives add more to the understanding of Hitler's career. While National Socialism was the most obvious political movement to promote racial hygiene this century, it was far from the only one. Increasingly today the measures pursued in Germany are being understood as encapsulating 'merely one offshoot of an international movement with many national variations' (Quine, 1996, p. 134). Even admitting that the fixation on excluding Jews from the community was singular to Hitler's politics, legislating about what constituted acceptable sexuality (as he outlined it in the Nuremberg Laws, document 4.18) was not. At about the same time Hitler was pursuing his ends in the Third Reich, democracies such as the USA 'implemented aggressive and activist policies aimed at biological engineering and social regimentation' (Quine, 1996, p. 136). In the end, it is inescapable that during the early half of the twentieth century, biological and social engineering were widely *believed* to be valid components of strategies to improve and modernise society.

So even if it is accepted that, objectively speaking, *something* about Hitler's prejudice spoke of a primeval force at work, there are still compelling grounds for maintaining that when he peddled his racism, in the 'rational' part of his mind Hitler *believed* he was pursuing a radical new policy, fit for the times, which was tailored to bringing about the improvement and modernisation of Germany. In terms of what was accepted as valid during his lifetime, Hitler's application of prejudice (not to mention the fact that he found people ready to go along with it) cannot be divorced from the context of the modern world and modern ideas (Baumann, 1989, p. xiii). The way his racism was expressed and applied was only conceivable in the early twentieth century (Payne, 1995, pp. 483–4). It may have offered an alternative view to that which is generally held about progress today, but it was not a rejection of that which *at the time* in the minds of many people constituted *bona fide* elements of modernity and the process of modernisation (Griffin, 1993, p. 47). In the last analysis (and whatever the exact nature of the forces which generated it) Hitler's racism cannot simply be used to define him as a reactionary. It spoke of a revolutionary whom history subsequently showed to have got things wrong.

This is indeed the study of a revolutionary. The proposition is true regardless of the limiting points touched on here, for example, Hitler's participation in Germany's electoral process, his coming to power in a coalition government, his reluctance to Nazify the armed forces quickly and his reactionary artistic tastes. With this said, even if, like Karl Dietrich Bracher, we want to maintain that Hitler was an inferior individual (for instance intellectually) in comparison to other revolutionary figures such as Rousseau, Robespierre, Napoleon, Marx, Lenin, Trotsky and Stalin, still it has to be recognised that he actually fulfilled the roles of all of them put together. He compiled a most extensive set of revolutionary goals (calling for radical social and political change); he mobilised a revolutionary following so extensive and powerful that many of his aims were achieved; he established and ran a dictatorial revolutionary state; and he disseminated his ideals abroad through a revolutionary foreign policy and war. In short, he defined and controlled the National Socialist revolution in all its phases (Bracher, 1976, p. 206). Even taking his shortcomings into account, a good case remains for saying that Hitler approximated to 'the prototype of a revolutionary' (Bracher, 1976, p. 206). With this established, we can provide five final theses about the nature of Adolf Hitler. These grow out of a series of central observations highlighted during the course of the study.

Thesis 1: In Adolf Hitler's revolutionary life, ideas provided a continuity which determined actions.

Of course not everything Hitler said and wrote before 1933 was realised thereafter, but enough did come to pass to underline the validity of the proposition. He denounced Marxist Socialism in the pages of *Mein Kampf* and as soon as he was dictator took decisive steps against its appearance in Germany. He spoke and wrote about anti-Semitism at length in the 1920s and from 1933 pursued an ever more radically anti-Semitic path. He first wrote about the need to establish a sizeable core of Germandom in central Europe and subsequently set out to achieve this. He wrote about a *Lebensraum* empire and then pursued it through war. As both a teenager and during the 1920s he created architectural plans which he set about realising once he was in charge of Germany. Adolf Hitler shaped the world as he did because he believed consistently that to do so was correct.

This position looks at variance with that championed by Hans Mommsen. He has argued that Nazi ideology and Hitler's personality are not enough to explain policy formulation in the Third Reich (Mommsen, 1976, p. 156). He believes Hitler only became involved in formulating Germany's domestic policy rarely and, like Karl Schleunes, does not accept for a minute that Hitler ever had a systematic plan of how to approach the Jewish Question (Schleunes, 1970, p. 257; Mommsen, 1976, p. 227 1991, p. 233). Only hindsight gives a sense of consistency and ideological pre-determination to events as they unfolded. Policy in the Third Reich came into effect largely through a process called 'cumulative radicalisation' (Mommsen, 1976, p. 156). This involved government functionaries losing their sense of reality and radicalising their actions as they struggled to function in a state system that was corrupt, which could be self-contradictory and which engendered dramatic competition between operatives. Amidst the organisational chaos, policy developments took on a dynamism all of their own. Only such a train of events could ever have brought into sight, as actual goals of policy, the sort of metaphorical statements (including extreme racialist pronouncements) Hitler made in keynote speeches (Mommsen, 1991, pp. 236–7).

Mommsen's analysis is intellectually challenging and does reflect the administrative complexity which characterised the Hitler state. But just because a state system was terribly ill-defined and 'irrational' does not actually mean it failed to do exactly what the person leading it always wanted. Mommsen himself accepts that Hitler's personal ideas certainly did involve the destruction of the Jews and other entire populations (Mommsen, 1976, p. 234). There is no sign that the Third Reich brought about initiatives Hitler did not want to see happen, and there is no question that he ever considered preventing the steady radicalisation of the treatment of Jews (Schleunes, 1970, p. 259). All the signs are that for the key areas of his government, Hitler's beliefs were absolutely central (Dülffer, 1996, p. 293).

In other words, even if some process of 'cumulative radicalisation' did operate within the Hitler state, pushing its functionaries down particular avenues of policy, the impression remains that the system was only achieving exactly the sort of 'ideological drive' Hitler wanted anyway (Kershaw, 1995, p. 336). In the last analysis, Hitler established the state and was responsible for the way it worked. The system he presided over was orientated decisively towards important goals he believed in personally. No matter how exactly it functioned, it is inescapable that when it really mattered the Third Reich provided a pretty effective platform for its dictator and his ideas. Notwithstanding Mommsen's analyses, the truth of this thesis stands.

Thesis 2: Adolf Hitler was a racial revolutionary.
In establishing his project for the internal constitution of Germany, and especially in his planning for her external expansion, Hitler was prepared to give pride of place to what he deemed racial necessities. In this light Hermann Rauschning's idea, expressed long ago, that Hitler led a 'revolution of nihilism', which lacked any fixed aims, is wrong (Rauschning, 1939a, pp. xii and 23). National Socialism did stand for something: the radical denial of universal values to mankind (Sternhell, 1994, p. 251).

Under Hitler, Germany saw a completely new kind of racial revolution (Hauner, 1984, p. 670). He spoke to audiences in Munich's beer halls as a convinced anti-Semite; he led the nation as an anti-Semitic dictator; he fought the Second World War as a convinced racist; he theorised about art in the same way he theorised about politics, economics and history, namely in the manner of a prejudiced zealot. Hitler breathed a bigotry which found the most profound form of expression in everything he did. Daniel Goldhagen has taken the analysis of this reality to its logical conclusion. He says that radical racial convictions and an appropriate agenda made Hitler and his followers the 'most profound revolutionaries of modern times'. They brought about a revolution that was the 'most extreme and thoroughgoing in the annals of western civlization' (Goldhagen, 1996, p. 456). It is hard to quibble with the point.

With this said, Rainer Zitelmann's equating of Hitler's movement with Communism (see Chapter 1) runs the risk of becoming misleading. This is so despite the very well-documented cross-over of party memberships which occurred during the later 1920s and early 1930s between followers of the German Communist Party and the NSDAP, and also despite the fact that the two movements certainly did compete for the same votes (Fischer, 1991, p. 117 and chapter 8; Housden, 1993, pp. 478–9). Document 3.12, which advertises a Nazi meeting, actually specified that Communists and Socialists could attend the event free of charge. But Hitler was not just anti-Communist because the two movements sometimes competed for the same supporters and tended to use comparable political techniques. These points are superficial and do not get to the heart of Hitler's attitude towards Communism. Before he was even a *V-Mann* (see Chapter 3), Hitler hated Marxism enough to denounce soldiers who had sympathised with the Munich uprising. As his thinking grew, he equated Communism with Judaism and allocated it to the ranks of all that was truly evil in the world. As with his stance on the Jewish Question (and appropriately since he understood the two as overlapping categories), there was never really any way back from this position. It was logical that the invasion of the Soviet Union was conceived in a particularly bloody way and became enmeshed with the implementation of the Holocaust. The ultimate 'land grab' was at the same time the ultimate racial action. Hitler and Communists may both be classified as revolutionaries, but Hitler was certainly not a closet Bolshevik. He was something else: a racial revolutionary who understood Communism as a racial phenomenon that required eradication.

Thesis 3: Adolf Hitler was a turn-of-the-century revolutionary.
We have accepted that Hitler wanted to solve society's ills by the application of his own ideas and that he wanted to see social improvement and modernisation according to his understanding of the terms. The irony is that much of his thinking for the future was rooted in the past. The primitive side of his prejudice has been mentioned in this chapter already. More specifically, he took intellectual inspiration from the world as it was particularly before 1914. In the field of politics he looked to the turn-of-the-century anti-Semites, Schönerer and Lueger. As regards ideology, he was inspired by the racial fantasies which were abroad in pre-war Austria. Hitler's ideas about foreign policy built on paradigms that had been well-established in right-wing circles before 1914 and which could be found among the members of the General Staff during the First World War. As an artist he rejected all developments since about 1910; in music he was enthralled by Richard Wagner (who lived from 1813 to 1883); in architecture he revelled in the classicism of the late nineteenth century.

That Hitler owed much to the past does not at all invalidate his revolutionary status. It should be expected. All revolutions draw on references from history (Weber, 1976, p. 514). The bible of revolutionary Marxism, *The Communist Manifesto*, was written in 1847–8. That twentieth-century figures from Lenin to Che Guevara drew on it hardly lessens their revolutionary status. The point only serves to support the truth of Billington's argument that the revolutionary fervour of the twentieth century grew out of that previous one (Billington, 1999, p. vii). The nineteenth-century cultural movements experienced in Germany, as exemplified especially by Wagner's artistic projects, were revolutionary in the widest sense (Rose, 1990, p. 16). The nationalist anti-Semitism of that period was similar. It promised the 'moral regeneration of the German people' through the removal of Jews (Rose, 1990, p. 18). It is just an empirical fact that the revolutionism begun during this earlier time provided the inspiration for, and found its ultimate expression in, the minds of men like Adolf Hitler in the wake of the First World War. Even if there were few completely new principles in his thinking, he did build upon the pre-existing foundations with the important characteristics of rigour, scale, passion and total want of moral restraint. Colossal classical building projects and colossal exterminationism: the traits were intimately related and spoke of an intensity of belief, commitment and idealism which was nothing if not revolutionary (Billington, 1999, p. 3).

Thesis 4: The normal and pathological mental worlds of Adolf Hitler corresponded closely. This proximity helped render him particularly energetic and at times precipitative. It predisposed him to revolutionary action.

The key ideological tenets of Hitler's life, namely anti-Semitism (linked to the fear of global Jewish conspiracy) and a belief that life is a struggle for existence, fitted together well, and expressed the paranoia associated with a psychotic delusional experience. The result of this overlap could only be a flowing together of motivation stemming from the 'rational' thoughts of the individual (i.e. that a course of action should be pursued because it seems intellectually supportable) and from the pathological (i.e. that a course of action should be pursued because paranoia dictates as much). The result helps account for the profound energy Hitler showed throughout much of his life, as well as his capacity to dash towards showdowns. If he wanted, he could always find reasons to act today, rather than wait until tomorrow. For example, in 1939 economic problems became grounds to invade Poland, not reasons to defer action. In 1940/41 the need to defeat Britain militarily became (after an initial hesitation) a justification to race eastwards against the USSR; it was not a reason to bide one's time. Likewise in 1941 Hitler's belief that the Soviet armed forces had to be weak held sway over his understanding that, once war was declared, anything could happen. This perspective on the causal mechanism which lay behind Hitler's actions is supplementary to what we know of other issues, such as drug abuse, fears for his health and the concrete circumstances in which given political decisions were taken. It goes without saying that the coalescence of drives predisposed Hitler to take revolutionary measures. The intensity of belief and fixity of purpose this coalescence must have engendered also helps explain why he never wavered in his determination to realise a set of 'visions of forceful change and domination' (Bracher, 1976, pp. 205–6). Without such singlemindedness, the history of Germany and Europe would have been very different.

Thesis 5: Adolf Hitler was a criminal revolutionary.

According to our definition, all revolutionaries act outside the law. But Adolf Hitler was not just interested in petty crime. He did not infringe the law only here and there as a short-cut to the creation of a better world for the vast majority of its inhabitants. He was a criminal in the first degree. His politics became the premeditated mass murder of vast swathes of Communists, Slavs and Jews. Even his hope that the aim of civilisation should be the production of great works of art was fatally compromised by the conviction that race determines artistic sensitivity. Had he survived 1945, his only hope at a war crimes trial would have been to plead insanity. At the time no one would have listened. He had been the initiator of far too much. The extent of his criminality underlines the fact that Hitler's revolution was only ever *perceived* to be modernising. There was a terrific gulf between conception and reality. Principles of division, hatred and murder are hardly the lasting values of mankind. The actuality of the revolution which shook Europe between 1933 and 1945 was hopelessness: it led nowhere worth going. So although his figure undeniably exerts a voyeuristic fascination even today, and notwithstanding so much being written about him, Adolf Hitler represents the ultimate in historical dead-ends. His biography is very much a warning; certainly it is not an inspiration.

An interesting point remains that once this is accepted firmly, it becomes clear that Hitler did contribute something to the modernisation of the world, albeit unintentionally and at a terrible cost. After the Second World War, with Hitler having shot himself in the ruins of Berlin on 30 April 1945, his henchmen were left to stand trial before Allied judges in a specially convened court held in Nuremberg. They were accused of crimes against peace (the planning of a war of aggression), war crimes (including the mistreatment and murder of prisoners of war) and crimes against humanity (which included murder, annihilation and slavery) (Friedrich, 1996, p. 21). The world looked on aghast as the prosecuting lawyers detailed the horrors which Hitler's regime had unleashed. Of the 22 accused, 19 were found guilty on 30 September 1946 and 12 of them were sentenced to death (Friedrich, 1996, p. 299). In this way Hitler's style of politics was invalidated and put beyond the pale once and for all. By criminalising aggression in the international area, and by outlawing persecution and racial intolerance, the court highlighted the more worthy principles for the development of the modern world: the preservation of peace, respect for others and the recognition of racial equality. Because Hitler showed so dreadfully where alternative ways of thinking can lead, this lesson should never be forgotten.

Timeline

20 April 1889	birth of Adolf Hitler
1903	father dies
1905	leaves school
1907–13	lives in Vienna
December 1907	mother dies
May 1913	moves to Munich
August 1914	joins the Bavarian army
December 1914	awarded the Iron Cross Second Class
August 1918	awarded the Iron Cross First Class
October 1918	gassed and sent to Pasewalk hospital to recover
November 1918	revolution in Germany
June 1919	attends army political education course in Munich
12 September 1919	attends meeting of the German Workers' Party
24 February 1920	proclamation of the Party Programme of the German Workers' Party
31 March 1920	leaves the army
29 July 1921	becomes leader of the Nazi Party
8–9 November 1923	beer hall putsch
April–December 1924	in Landsberg prison
26 February 1925	refounding of the Nazi Party
14 February 1926	Bamberg conference
14 September 1930	Nazi Party wins 107 Reichstag seats (18.3% of the vote)
31 July 1932	Nazi Party wins 230 Reichstag seats (37.4% of the vote)
6 November 1932	Nazi Party wins 197 Reichstag seats (33.1% of the vote)
30 January 1933	becomes Reich Chancellor
28 February 1933	Reichstag Fire Decree
5 March 1933	Nazi Party wins 288 Reichstag seats (43.9% of the vote)
30 June 1934	start of 'Night of the Long Knives'
2 August 1934	death of von Hindenburg: Hitler becomes Reich President as well as Reich Chancellor

15 September 1935	promulgation of the Nuremberg Laws
7 March 1936	remilitarisation of the Rhineland
12 March 1938	invasion of Austria
29–30 September 1938	Munich conference
9 November 1938	'Crystal Night'
14–15 March 1939	invasion of Bohemia and Moravia
1 September 1939	invasion of Poland
9 April 1940	invasion of Denmark and Norway
10 May 1940	Western offensive begins
March 1941	order to establish Special Action groups
6 April 1941	invasion of Yugoslavia and Greece
22 June 1941	Operation Barbarossa launched
16 July 1941	'Garden of Eden' speech
September 1941	German Jews ordered East
11 December 1941	declaration of war on USA
20 July 1944	assassination attempt
30 April 1945	commits suicide

Further reading

I have assumed that most of my readers do not have the German language, but for those who do, three overviews of Hitler's life should be of particular interest. The latest edition of Rainer Zitelmann's study, *Hitler. Selbstverständnis eines Revolutionärs* (1998) offers controversial approaches to most aspects of his life and ideas. Equally full of thought-provoking material is Hans-Jurgen Eitner's *Hitler. Das Psychogramm* (1994). This has the advantage of being much briefer and written in a more economical style. Also worth looking at is *Hitler. Eine Bilanz* (1995) by Guido Knopp. This comes complete with an interesting array of illustrations. Of course English language readers should not feel too left out. Joachim Fest's *Hitler* (1973) remains well worth reading. Its primacy among Hitler biographies is threatened only by Ian Kershaw's massive two-volume investigation, *Hitler. 1889–1936. Hubris* (1998) and *Hitler. 1935–1945. Nemesis* (in press). For a much more concise overview of the key themes in Hitler's career, see David Welch's *Hitler* (1998). Werner Maser's *Hitler* (1973), Bradley Smith's *Adolf Hitler. His Family, Childhood and Youth* (1979) and August Kubizek's *The Young Hitler I Knew* (1955) are all good on Hitler's earlier years. Brand new in English is Brigitte Hamann's *Hitler's Vienna* (1999). Two further studies, which are constructed thematically rather than chronologically, also merit mention. Ronald Lewin's book, *Hitler's Mistakes* (1984), contains a great many insights into the way the Führer worked. William Carr's *Hitler. A Study in Personality and Politics* (1978) is of value for the chapter on Hitler's health alone.

Regarding Hitler's ideology, no one can miss *Mein Kampf* (1985 ed.). Just as interesting, more clearly expressed and less frequently referred to is *Hitler's Secret Book* (1961). For Hitler's speeches, a person can turn to either N.H. Baynes, *The Speeches of Adolf Hitler*, in two volumes (1942) or Max Domarus, *Hitler. Speeches and Proclamations 1932–1945* (1990). The latter is the more comprehensive and unwieldy. For Hitler expressing himself in more confidential mode to smaller circles of acquaintances, do not overlook either *Hitler – Memoirs of a Confidant* (1985), edited by H.A. Turner, or *Hitler Speaks* (1939) by Hermann Rauschning. The latter is an absolute classic. From the war years, *Hitler's Secret Conversations. 1941–1944* (1961), edited by Hugh Trevor-Roper, gives a remarkable insight into the workings of Hitler's mind. From his very last months, *The Testament of Adolf Hitler*

(1959), edited by F. Genoud, displays a personality pitching towards full-blown insanity. For discussions of how to interpret Hitler's ideology see Eberhard Jäckel, *Hitler's World View* (1981) and Martin Broszat, *German National Socialism, 1919–1945* (1966). They give completely different views.

Regarding Hitler's early political career, those who can read German are particularly lucky. Albrecht Tyrell has edited a collection of documents called *Führer befiehl* . . . (1969) and has written the study *Vom 'Trommler' zum 'Führer'* (1975). Both offer sensitive approaches to the topic. *Der Aufstieg der NSDAP* (1974) is a collection of documents compiled by Ernst Deuerlein. In English, C.B. Flood's *Hitler. The Path to Power* (1989) is a comprehensive study of the period. More anecdotal, not to say rare, is *Germany's Hitler* (1934) by someone supposedly called Heinz A. Heinz (although the initials also stand for *'Heil Adolf Hitler!'*). It is a collection of interviews with Nazi Party loyalists compiled in the late 1920s and early 1930s.

There is no shortage of studies dealing with Hitler's dictatorship of Germany. Thoughtful scholarly contributions to the literature include Ian Kershaw's *The Nazi Dictatorship* (1993 ed.) (especially chapter 4), the essays by Hans Mommsen, 'Hitler's Position in the Nazi System' and 'National Socialism: Continuity and Change', and Martin Broszat's *The Hitler State* (1981). There is a worthwhile memoir literature too. Not to be missed is *Inside the Third Reich* (1971) by Hitler's pet architect and war criminal, Albert Speer. Gitta Sereny's study *Albert Speer: His Battle with Truth* (1995) says much about Hitler and the Third Reich. Leni Riefenstahl's *The Sieve of Time* (1992) contains some interesting passages which really give you the impression of what Hitler was like when he 'let his guard drop'.

Equally voluminous is the number of studies dealing with Hitler's foreign policy. T.L. Jarman's *The Rise and Fall of Nazi Germany* (1955) is clearly very old, but it has got things right. More up to date is N. Rich's *Hitler's War Aims* (1992). For a good series of essays about very many aspects of Hitler's foreign policy, look no further than *Germany, Hitler and World War II* (1995) by Gerhard Weinberg. John Hiden's work on German foreign policy always offers sound advice. His studies include *Explaining Hitler's Germany* (1989) (with John Farquharson – see especially chapter 5), *Germany and Europe 1919–1939* (1993) and *Republican and Fascist Germany* (1996) (see especially chapter 12). There are a number of fine sources for documents relating to German foreign policy of 1933–9. English language readers should look at *Documents on German Foreign Policy 1918–1945* (1956). Germanists can try *Akten zur auswärtigen Politik 1918–45* (1964) and *Ursachen und Folgen* (1965–8). The latter is edited by H. Michaelis and E. Schraepler.

When it comes to Hitler's leadership of the war, there are a variety of excellent sources available to people with German. There is the *Kriegstagebuch des Oberkommandos der Wehrmacht* (1965) edited by H.-A. Jacobsen, *Generaloberst Halder. Kriegstagebuch* (1963) also edited by H.-A. Jacobsen, and *Lagebesprechungen im Führerhauptquartier* (1963) edited by Helmut Heiber. For the English language audience, *Hitler's War Directives* (1966) edited by Hugh Trevor-Roper is useful. Walter Warlimont's *Inside Hitler's Headquarters 1939–1945* (1964) gives a really good insight into how the war effort developed. For an interpretation of the way Hitler led Germany from the point of view of a general who had close contact with him, see Franz Halder, *Hitler as War Lord* (1950). Also interesting is Percy Schramm's *Hitler. The Man and the Military Leader* (1973). Schramm was a historian attached to the High Command during World War II and met Hitler on a number of occasions. For an Anglo-Saxon interpretation, J. Strawson's *Hitler as Military Commander* (1971) is as good a starting point as any. There are not that many sources in English dealing with the relationships between Slavic and Jewish policies as they developed during the war years. One of the few is M. Housden, 'Population, Economics and Genocide: Aly and Heim versus All-Comers in the Interpretation of the Holocaust', *Historical Journal*, 38 (1995), pp. 479–86.

The classic study of Hitler as architect and artist is only available in the German language. It is Jochen Thies, *Architekt der Weltherrschaft* (1976). As the title suggests, this analyses Hitler's architectural aspirations and draws conclusions about the nature of his world politics. Also of interest in German is *Architektur im Dritten Reich. 1933–1945* (1967) by Anna Teut. For readers of English only, reference can be made to either R.R. Taylor's *The Word in Stone. The Role of Architecture in the National Socialist Ideology* (1974) or Barbara Lane's *Architecture and Politics in Germany 1918–1945* (1985). Absolutely not to be missed in this connection is, however, one book referred to already – *Inside the Third Reich* (1971) by Albert Speer. There is no substitute for it.

Attempts to analyse Hitler's mind are numerous and varied. For a study which focuses on the role of the father see G.M. Gilbert, *The Psychology of Dictatorship* (1950); for the importance of his mother see R. Binion, *Hitler among the Germans* (1976); and for a more general treatment see Erich Fromm, *The Fear of Freedom* (1960). For an approach to Hitler as a 'borderline' personality, a comprehensive study has been completed by R.G.L. Waite, namely *The Psychopathic God. Adolf Hitler* (1993). For a brand new approach see Fritz Redlich, *Hitler. Diagnosis of a Destructive Prophet* (1999).

The list of recommended reading for those interested in Hitler is, frankly, almost limitless. A final useful guide to his period of German history can be found in the encyclopedia edited by D.K. Buse and J.C. Doerr, *Modern Germany* (1998). It contains references and recommendations for further reading relating to most of the personalities and topics touched on in this book. For those who want more still, all of the works cited in the bibliography have something to commend them.

Bibliography

Akten zur auswärtigen Politik 1918–45. Bonn: Gebr. Hermes KG. 1964.

Altrocchi, J., *Abnormal Behavior*. New York: Harcourt Brace Jovanovich. 1980.

Aly, G. and Heim, S., *Vordenker der Vernichtung. Auschwitz und die deutschen Pläne für eine neue europaische Ordnung*. Frankfurt am Main: Fischer. 1993.

Anderson, J.L., *Che Guevara. A Revolutionary Life*. London: Bantam. 1997.

Arendt, H., *On Revolution*. London: Faber and Faber. 1963.

Arendt, H., *The Origins of Totalitarianism*. London: Allen and Unwin. 1966.

Asmuss, B., *Republik ohne Chance? Akzeptanz und Legitimation der Weimarer Republik in der deutschen Tagespresse zwischen 1918 und 1923*. Berlin: de Gruyter. 1994.

Barkai, A., *Nazi Economics: Ideology, Theory and Policy*. Oxford: Oxford University Press. 1990.

Batowski, H., 'Nazi Germany and Jagiellonian University', *Polish Western Affairs*, 19–20 (1978–79), 113–20.

Baumann, Z., *Modernity and the Holocaust*. Oxford: Polity Press. 1989.

Baynes, N.H. (ed.), *The Speeches of Adolf Hitler*. Vols 1 and 2. London: Oxford University Press. 1942.

Beevor, A., *Stalingrad*. London: Penguin. 1999.

Benz, W., 'Der Generalplan Ost. Germanisierungspolitik in den besetzten Ostgebieten' in W. Benz (ed.), *Herrschaft und Gesellschaft in national-sozialistischen Staat*. Frankfurt am Main: Fischer. 1990.

Benz, W., *Der Holocaust*. Munich: Beck. 1995.

Berghahn, V.R. and Kitchen, M. (eds), *Germany in the Age of Total War*. London: Croom Helm. 1981.

Bessel, R., 'The Potempa Murder', *Central European History* 10 (1977), 241–55.

Billington, J.H., *Fire in the Minds of Men. Origins of the Revolutionary Faith*. New Brunswick, NJ: Transaction. 1999.

Binion, R., 'Hitler Looks East', *History of Childhood Quarterly* 3 (1975), 85–102.

Binion, R., *Hitler among the Germans*. New York: Elsevier. 1976.

Bloch, M., *Ribbentrop*. London: Bantam Press. 1992.

Bracher, K.D., 'The Role of Hitler: Perspectives of Interpretation' in Laqueur (1976).

Breitling, R., *Die nationalsozialistische Rassenlehre*. Frankfurt am Main: Anton Hain. 1971.

Breitman, R., 'Hitler and Genghis Khan', *Journal of Contemporary History*, 25 (1990), 337–52.

Breitman R., *The Architect of Genocide. Himmler and the Final Solution*. London: Bodley Head. 1991.

Brinton, C., *The Anatomy of Revolution*. New York: Random House. 1952.

Broszat, M., 'Die völkische Ideologie und der Nationalsozialismus', *Deutsche Rundschau* 84 (1958), 53 ff.

Broszat, M., *Nationalsozialistische Polenpolitik, 1939–1945*. Stuttgart: Deutsche Verlags-Anstalt. 1961.

Broszat, M., *German National Socialism 1919–1945*. Santa Barbara, Calif.: Clio Press. 1966.

Broszat, M., 'Soziale Motivation und Führer-Bindung des National-sozialismus', *Vierteljahrshefte für Zeitgeschichte*, 18 (1970), 392–409.

Broszat, M., *The Hitler State*. London: Longman. 1981.

Broszat, M., 'Hitler and the Genesis of the Final Solution' in Koch (1985).

Broszat, M., *Hitler and the Collapse of Weimar Germany*. Oxford: Berg. 1987.

Broszat, M. and Frei, N. (eds), *Das Dritte Reich im Überblick*. Munich: Piper. 1996 ed.

Browder, G.C., *Hitler's Enforcers. The Gestapo and the SS Security Service in the Nazi Revolution*. Oxford: Oxford University Press. 1996.

Browning, C.R., 'Beyond Intentionalism and Functionalism: The Decisions for the Final Solution Reconsidered' in C.R. Browning, *The Path to Genocide. Essays on the Launching of the Final Solution*. Cambridge: Cambridge University Press. 1992.

Bucher, P., *Der Reichswehrprozess. Der Hochverrat der Ulmer Reichswehroffiziere 1929/30*. Boppard am Rhein: Harald Boldt Verlag. 1967.

Bullock, A., *Hitler: A Study in Tyranny*. London: Penguin. 1952, 1981 edition.

Bullock, A., *Hitler and Stalin. Parallel Lives*. London: HarperCollins. 1991.

Burckhardt, C.J., *Meine Danziger Mission 1937–1939*. Munich: DTV. 1967.

Burleigh, M. and Wippermann, W., *The Racial State. Germany 1933–1945*. Cambridge: Cambridge University Press. 1991.

Buse, D.K. and Doerr, J.C. (eds), *Modern Germany. An Encyclopedia of History, People and Culture, 1871–1990*. New York: Garland. 1998.

Calic, E., *Hitler ohne Maske. Hitler-Breitling Geheimgespräche 1931*. Frankfurt am Main: Fischer. 1968.

Calvert, P., *A Study of Revolution*. Oxford: Clarendon. 1970.

Campbell, B.B., 'The SA after the Röhm Purge', *Journal of Contemporary History*, 28 (1993), 659–74.

Carr, W., *Hitler. A Study in Personality and Politics*. London: Edward Arnold. 1978.

Cecil, R., *Hitler's Decision to Invade Russia 1941*. London: Davis-Poynter. 1972.

Chodorowski, J., *Niemiecka Doktryna Gospodarki Wielkiego Obszaru. Grossraumwirschaft 1800–1945*. Wroclaw: Zaklad Narodowy. 1972.

Close, D., 'The Meaning of Revolution' in Close and Bridge (1985).

Close, D. and Bridge, C. (eds), *Revolution. A History of the Idea*. London: Croom Helm. 1985.

Cohn, N., *Warrant for Genocide: The Myth of the Jewish World Conspiracy and the Protocols of the Elders of Zion*. London: Eyre and Spottiswoode. 1967.

Conze, W. (ed.), *Der Nationalsozialismus 1919–1933. Die Krise der Weimarer Republik und die nationalsozialistische Machtergreifung*. Stuttgart: Tempra. 1983.

Craig, G.A., *Germany 1866–1945*. Oxford: Oxford University Press. 1981.

Crew, D.F. (ed.), *Nazism and German Society, 1933–45*. London: Routledge. 1994.

Cross, C., *Adolf Hitler*. London: Hodder and Stoughton. 1973.

Dahrendorf, R., *Society and Democracy in Germany*. New York: Norton. 1979.

Davidson, E., *The Making of Adolf Hitler*. London: Macdonald and Jane's. 1977.

Der Hitler Prozeß vor dem Volksgericht in München. Glashütten im Taunus: Verlag Detlev Auvermann KG. 1973.

Deuerlein, E., 'Hitlers Eintritt in die Politik und die Reichswehr', *Vierteljahrshefte für Zeitgeschichte* (1959), 177–227.

Deuerlein, E., *Der Aufstieg der NSDAP in Augenzeugenberichten*. Munich: DTV. 1974.

Diner, D., *Kreisläufe. Nationalsozialismus und Gedächtnis*. Berlin: Berlin Verlag. 1995.

Documents on German Foreign Policy 1918–1945. London: HMSO. Various volumes and dates.

Dodd, W.E. and Dodd, M., *Ambassador Dodd's Diary 1933–1938*. London: Victor Gollancz. 1941.

Domarus, M., *Hitler. Speeches and Proclamations 1932–1945. The Chronicle of a Dictatorship. Vol. 1. The Years 1932 to 1934*. London: I.B. Tauris. 1990.

Domarus, M., *Hitler. Speeches and Proclamations. 1932–1945. Vol. 2, The Years 1935 to 1938*. London: I.B. Tauris. 1992.

Dukes, P. and Hiden, J., 'Towards an Historical Comparison of Nazi Germany and Soviet Russia in the 1930s', *New Zealand Slavonic Journal*, (1979), 45–79.

Dülffer, J., *Nazi Germany 1933–1945. Faith and Annihilation.* London: Arnold. 1996 ed.

Eichholz, D., 'Der Generalplan Ost', *Jahrbuch für Geschichte*, 26 (1982), 217–74.

Eitner, H.-J., *Hitler. Das Psychogramm.* Frankfurt am Main: Ullstein. 1994.

Ensor, R.C.K., *Who Hitler Is.* Oxford: Clarendon. 1939

Fest, J., *Hitler.* London: Weidenfeld and Nicolson. 1973.

Fischer, C., *The German Communists and the Rise of Nazism.* London: Macmillan. 1991.

Fleming, G., *Hitler and the Final Solution.* Oxford: Oxford University Press. 1986.

Flood, C.B., *Hitler. The Path to Power.* Boston: Houghton Mifflin. 1989.

Fowler, D., Garety, P. and Kuipers, E., *Cognitive Behaviour Therapy for Psychosis. Theory and Practice.* Chichester: Wiley. 1995.

François-Poncet, A., *The Fateful Years: Memoirs of a French Ambassador in Berlin 1931–1938.* New York. 1949.

Frank, H., *Im angesicht des Galgens. Deutung Hitlers und seiner Zeit auf Grund eigener Erlebnisse und Erkenntnisse.* Munich: Friedrich Alfred Beck. 1953.

Frank, N., *Der Vater. Eine Abrechnung.* Munich: Goldmann. 1993.

The French Yellow Book. Diplomatic Documents 1938–1939. London: Hutchinson. 1939.

Friedrich, J., *Das Urteil von Nürnberg 1946.* Munich: DTV. 1996.

Fromm, E., *The Fear of Freedom.* London: Routledge and Kegan Paul. 1960.

Fromm, E., *The Anatomy of Human Destructiveness.* London: Penguin. 1977.

Funke, M., 'Großmachtpolitik und Weltmachtstreben' in Broszat and Frei (1996).

Garlinski, J., *Poland in the Second World War.* London: Macmillan. 1985.

Geiss, I., 'Die Totalitarismen unseres Jahrhunderts' in Jesse (1996).

Genoud, F. (ed.), *The Testament of Adolf Hitler.* London: Cassell. 1959.

Gerlach, C., 'Deutsche Wirtschaftsinteressen, Besatzungspolitik und der Mord an den Juden in Weißrußland, 1941–1943' in Herbert (1998). [a].

Gerlach, C., 'The Wannsee Conference, the Fate of German Jews, and Hitler's Decision in Principle to Exterminate All European Jews', *Journal of Modern History*, 70 (1998), 759–812. [b].

Gilbert, G.M., *The Psychology of Dictatorship.* New York: Ronald Press. 1950.

Giordano, R., *Wenn Hitler den Krieg gewonnen hätte. Die Pläne der Nazis nach dem Endsieg.* Hamburg: Rasch und Röhring. 1991.

Goldhagen, D., *Hitler's Willing Executioners. Ordinary Germans and the Holocaust.* London: Little, Brown. 1996.

Goodrick-Clarke, N., *The Occult Roots of Nazism.* London: I. B. Tauris. 1992.

Graml, H., *Antisemitism in the Third Reich.* Oxford: Blackwell. 1992.

Graml, H., 'Die "Eroberung von Lebensraum" als Leitmotiv der NS-Außenpolitik' in Studt (1995).

Graml, H., 'Die Wehrmacht im Dritten Reich', *Vierteljahrshefte für Zeitgeschichte*, 45 (1997), 365–85.

Greene, T.H., *Comparative Revolutionary Movements.* Englewood Cliffs, NJ: Prentice-Hall. 1974.

Gregory, R.L., *The Oxford Companion to the Mind.* Oxford: Oxford University Press. 1987.

Griffin, R., *The Nature of Fascism.* London: Routledge. 1993

Griffin, R. (ed.), *International Fascism. Theories, Causes and the New Consensus.* London: Arnold. 1998.

Gross, J.T., *Polish Society under German Occupation.* Princeton, NJ: Princeton University Press. 1979.

Grosser, A., *Verbrechen und Erinnerung. Der Genozid im Gedächtnis der Völker.* Munich: DTV. 1993.

Gruchmann, L., *Nationalsozialistische Grossraumordnung. Die Konstruktion einer deutschen Monroe-Doktrin.* Stuttgart: Deutsche Verlags-Anstalt. 1962.

Grusky, O. and Pollner, M. (eds), *The Sociology of Mental Illness. Basic Studies.* New York: Holt, Rinehart and Winston. 1981.

Haffner, S., *The Meaning of Hitler.* London: Weidenfeld and Nicolson. 1988.

Halder, F., *Hitler as War Lord.* London: Putnam. 1950.

Hamann, B., *Hitler's Vienna. A Dictator's Apprenticeship.* Oxford: Oxford University Press. 1999.

Hanfstaengl, E., *Unheard Witness.* Philadelphia: J.B. Lippincott. 1957.

Hanisch, R., 'I Was Hitler's Buddy. I', *New Republic*, 5 April 1939. [a].

Hanisch, R., 'I Was Hitler's Buddy. II', *The New Republic*, 12 April 1939. [b].

Hanisch, R. 'I Was Hitler's Buddy. III', *The New Republic*, 19 April 1939. [c].

Hartmann, C. and Slutsch, S., 'Franz Halder und die Kriegsvorbereitungen im Frühjahr 1939', *Vierteljahrshefte für Zeitgeschichte*, 45 (1997), 467–95.

Hassell, U. von, *The von Hassell Diaries 1938–1944.* London: Hamish Hamilton. 1948.

Hatheway, J., 'The Pre-1920 Origins of the National Socialist German Workers' Party', *Journal of Contemporary History*, 29 (1994), 443–62.

Hauner, M., 'A German Racial Revolution?', *Journal of Contemporary History*, 19 (1984), 669–87.

Heiber, H., 'Der Generalplan Ost', *Vierteljahrshefte für Zeitgeschichte*, 6 (1958), 319–20.

Heiber, H., *Adolf Hitler. A Short Biography.* London: Oswald Wolff. 1961.

Heiber, H. (ed.), *Lagebesprechungen im Führerhauptquartier. Protokoll-fragmente aus Hitlers militärischen Konferenzen 1942–1945.* Munich: DTV. 1963.

Heinz, H.A., *Germany's Hitler*. London: Hurst and Blackett. 1934.

Herbert, U., *Best. Biographische Studien über Radikalismus, Weltanschauung und Vernuft. 1903–1989*. Bonn: Dietz. 1996.

Herbert, U., *Hitler's Foreign Workers. Enforced Foreign Labour in Germany under the Third Reich*. Cambridge: Cambridge University Press. 1997.

Herbert, U. (ed.), *Nationalsozialistische Vernichtungspolitik 1939–1945. Neue Forschungen und Kontroversen*. Frankfurt am Main: Fischer. 1998.

Herf, J., *Reactionary Modernism. Technology, Culture, and Politics in Weimar and the Third Reich*. Cambridge: Cambridge University Press. 1984.

Herrmann, J. *et al.* (eds), *Deutsche Geschichte in 10 Kapiteln*. Berlin, DDR: Akademie-Verlag. 1988.

Hiden, J., *Germany and Europe 1919–1939*. London: Longman. 1993 ed.

Hiden, J., *Republican and Fascist Germany*. London: Longman. 1996.

Hiden, J. and Farquharson, J., *Explaining Hitler's Germany*. London: Batsford. 1989.

Hirsch, M., Majer, D. and Meinck, J., *Recht, Verwaltung und Justiz im Nationalsozialismus*. Cologne: Bund. 1984.

Hitler, A., *Second Book* – see Hitler, A., *Hitler's Secret Book*.

Hitler, A., 'Blut und Kultur', *Odal*, October 1934, 233–4.

Hitler, A., *Hitler's Secret Book*. Introduction by Telford Taylor. New York: Grove Press. 1961.

Hitler, A., *Mein Kampf*. London: Hutchinson. 1985.

Hofer, W., *Der Nationalsozialismus Dokumente 1933–1945*. Frankfurt am Main: Fischer. 1989.

Hoffmann, H., *Hitler was my Friend*. London: Burke. 1955.

Hohlfeld, K. (ed.), *Dokumente der Deutschen Politik und Geschichte von 1848 bis zur Gegenwart*. 1953.

Höhne, H., *The Order of the Death's Head*. London: Pan. 1969.

Holborn, H., 'Origins and Political Character of Nazi Ideology', *Political Science Quarterly*, LXXIX (1952), 542ff.

Housden, M., *Helmut Nicolai and Nazi Ideology*. London: Macmillan. 1992.

Housden, M., 'Opposition to National Socialism – An Anatomy of Failure?', *Historical Journal*, 36 (1993), 477–85.

Housden, M., 'Population, Economics and Genocide: Aly and Heim versus All-Comers in the Interpretation of the Holocaust', *Historical Journal*, 38 (1995), 479–86.

Housden, M., *Resistance and Conformity in the Third Reich*. London: Routledge. 1997.

Hubatsch, W., *Hitlers Weisungen für die Kriegführung 1939–1945*. Frankfurt am Main. 1962.

Ingrim, R., *Der Griff nach Oesterreich*. Zurich. 1938.

Jäckel, E., *Hitler's World View. A Blueprint for Power*. Cambridge, Mass.: Harvard University Press. 1981.

Jäckel, E., *Hitler in History.* Hanover: University of New England Press. 1984.

Jäckel, E., 'Die Eroberung von Raum in Hitlers Weltanschauung' in Wippermann (1986).

Jacobsen, H.-A. (ed.), *Generaloberst Halder. Kriegstagebuch. Band II. Von der geplanten Landung in England bis zum Beginn des Ostfeldzuges. (1.7.1940 – 21.6.1941).* Stuttgart: W. Kohlhammer Verlag. 1963.

Jacobsen, H.-A. (ed.), *Kriegstagebuch des Oberkommandos der Wehrmacht. Band 1: 1 August 1940 – 31 Dezember 1941.* Frankfurt am Main: Bernard and Graefe. 1965.

Jansen, C., Niethammer, L. and Weisbrod, B. (eds), *Von der Aufgabe der Freiheit. Festschrift für Hans Mommsen.* Berlin: Akademie Verlag. 1995.

Jarausch, K.H., 'The Crisis of German Professions 1918–33', *Journal of Contemporary History*, 20 (1985), 379–98.

Jarausch, K.H., 'The Decline of Liberal Professionalism: Reflections on the Social Erosion of German Liberalism, 1867–1933' in Jarausch and Jones (1990). [a].

Jarausch, K.H., *The Unfree Professions. German Lawyers, Teachers and Engineers, 1900–1950.* Oxford: Oxford University Press. 1990. [b].

Jarausch, K.H. and Jones, L.E. (eds), *In Search of a Liberal Germany. Studies in the History of German Liberalism from 1789 to the Present.* Oxford: Berg. 1990.

Jarman, T.L., *The Rise and Fall of Nazi Germany.* London: The Cresset Press. 1955.

Jesse, E. (ed.), *Totalitarismus im 20. Jahrhundert. Eine Bilanz der internationalen Forschung.* Baden-Baden: Nomos. 1996.

Johnson, C., *Revolutionary Change.* Boston: Little, Brown. 1966.

Jones, L.E., '"The Greatest Stupidity of My Life": Alfred Hugenberg and the Formation of the Hitler Cabinet, January 1933', *Journal of Contemporary History*, 27 (1992), 63–87.

Kamenetsky, I., 'German Colonization Plans during World Wars I and II' in Torke and Himka (1994).

Kenrick, D. and Puxon, G., *Gypsies under the Swastika.* London: University of Hertfordshire Press. 1995.

Kershaw, I., 'Ideology, Propaganda and the Rise of the Nazi Party' in Stachura (1983).

Kershaw, I., *The Hitler Myth.* Oxford: Clarendon Press. 1987.

Kershaw, I., *Hitler.* London: Longman. 1991.

Kershaw, I., 'Ideologue und Propagandist. Hitler im Lichte seiner Reden, Schriften und Anordnungen 1925–1928', *Vierteljahrshefte für Zeitgeschichte*, (1992), 264–71.

Kershaw, I., *The Nazi Dictatorship. Problems and Perspectives of Interpretation.* London: Arnold. 1993.

Kershaw, I., 'The "Hitler Myth". Image and Reality in the Third Reich' in Crew (1994).

Kershaw, I., 'Cumulative Radicalisation and the Uniqueness of National Socialism' in Jansen *et al.* (1995).

Kershaw, I., 'Nazisme et Stalinisme', *Extrait du Débat*, (1996), 177–89. [a].

Kershaw, I., 'Nationalsozialistische und stalinistische Herrschaft. Möglichkeiten und Grenzen des Vergleichs' in Jesse (1996). [b].

Kershaw, I., *Hitler. 1889–1936. Hubris.* London: Allen Lane. 1998.

Kershaw, I., *Hitler. 1935–1945. Nemesis.* London: Allen Lane. In press.

Kimmel, M.S., *Revolution. A Sociological Interpretation.* Oxford: Polity Press. 1990.

Knopp, G., *Hitler. Eine Bilanz.* Berlin: Siedler. 1995.

Knopp, G., *Hitlers Helfer.* Munich: Goldmann. 1998.

Koch H.W. (ed.), *Aspects of the Third Reich.* London: Macmillan. 1985

Koch, H.W. 'Operation Barbarossa – The Current State of the Debate', *Historical Journal*, 31 (1988), 377–90.

Koebner, T. (ed.), *'Bruder Hitler'.* Munich: Wilhelm Heyne Verlag. 1989.

Koehl, R.L., *RKFVD: German Resettlement and Population Policy 1939–1945. A History of the Reich Commission for the Strengthening of Germandom.* Cambridge, Mass.: Harvard University Press. 1957.

Kohl, P., *Der Krieg der deutschen Wehrmacht und der Polizei 1941–1944.* Frankfurt am Main: Fischer. 1995.

Krausnick, H., 'Denkschrift Himmlers über die Behandlung der Fremdvölkischen im Osten (Mai 1940)', *Vierteljahrshefte für Zeitgeschichte*, (1957), 195–8.

Krausnick, H. and Broszat, M., *Anatomy of the SS State.* London: Paladin. 1982.

Kroeger, E., *Der Auszug aus der alten Heimat.* Tübingen: Verlag Deutschen Hochschullehrer-Zeitung. 1967.

Kroll, F.-J., 'Geschichte und Politik im Weltbild Hitlers', *Vierteljahrshefte für Zeitgeschichte*, 44 (1996), 327–55.

Kubizek, A., *The Young Hitler I Knew.* Westport, Conn.: Greenwood Press. 1955.

Lane, B.M., *Architecture and Politics in Germany 1918–1945.* Cambridge, Mass.: Harvard University Press. 1985.

Langer, W.C., *The Mind of Adolf Hitler.* London: Secker and Warburg. 1973.

Laqueur, W. (ed.), *Fascism. A Reader's Guide.* London: Penguin. 1976.

Laschitza, H. and Vietzke, S., *Geschichte Deutschlands und der deutschen Arbeiterbewegung 1933–1945.* Berlin. 1964.

Lauber and Rothstein, *Der 1.Mai unter dem Hakenkreuz. Hitlers 'Machtergreifung' in Arbeiterschaft und in Betrieben.* Stuttgart: Bleicher Taschenbuch. 1983.

Lewin, R., *Hitler's Mistakes.* London: Leo Cooper. 1984.

Loiperdinger, M., Herz, R. and Pohlmann, U. (eds), *Führerbilder. Hitler, Mussolini, Roosevelt, Stalin in Fotografie und Film.* Munich: Piper. 1995.

Longerich, P. (ed.), *Die Erste Republik. Dokumente zur Geschichte des Weimarer Staates*. Munich: Piper. 1992.

Löwenthal, R., 'The Missing Revolution in Industrial Societies: Comparative Reflections on a German Problem' in Berghahn and Kitchen (1981).

Ludecke, K.G.W., *I Knew Hitler. The Story of a Nazi who Escaped the Blood Purge*. London: Jarrolds. 1938.

Lukács, J., *The Hitler of History*. New York: Random House. 1997.

Lukas, R.C., *The Forgotten Holocaust. The Poles under German Occupation. 1939–1945*. Kentucky: University of Kentucky Press. 1986.

Macartney, C.A. and Palmer, A.W., *Independent Eastern Europe*. London: Macmillan. 1962.

McLellan, D., *The Thought of Karl Marx*. Second Edition. London: Macmillan. 1980.

Madajczyk, C., *Zamojszczyzna – Sonderlaboratorium SS*. Warsaw: Ludowa Spoldzielnia Wydawnicza. 1977.

Madajczyk, C., *Die Okkupationspolitik Nazideutschlands in Polen 1939–1945*. Berlin: Akademie Verlag. 1987.

Maier, C., Hoffmann, S. and Gould, A. (eds), *The Rise of the Nazi Regime. Historical Reassessments*. Boulder, Col.: Westview. 1986.

Mann, T., 'Bruder Hitler' in Koebner (1989).

Marx, K., *Capital. Volume I*. Moscow: Foreign Languages Publishing House. 1959.

Marx, K. and Engels, F., *The Communist Manifesto*. London: Penguin. 1985.

Maschmann, M., *Account Rendered. A Dossier on My Former Self*. New York: Abelard-Schumann. 1964.

Maser, W., *Hitler*. London: Allen Lane. 1973.

Maser, W., *Hitler's Letters and Notes*. London: Heinemann. 1974.

Mason, T.W., 'Arbeiteropposition im nationalsozialistischen Deutschland', in Peukert and Reulecke (1981).

Mason, J.W., *The Dissolution of the Austro-Hungarian Empire 1867–1918*. London: Longman. 1988.

Mechanic, D., 'What are Mental Health and Mental Illness?' in Grusky and Pollner (1981).

Meissner, O., *Staatssekretär unter Ebert-Hindenburg-Hitler*. Hamburg, 1950.

Mercalowa, L.A., 'Stalinismus und Hitlerismus – Versuch einer vergleichenden Analyse' in Jesse (1996).

Merkl, P.H., *Political Violence under the Swastika*. Princeton, NJ: Princeton University Press. 1985.

Michaelis, H. and Schraepler, E., *Ursachen und Folgen. Vom deutschen Zusammenbruch 1918 und 1945 bis zur staatlichen Neuordnung Deutschlands in der Gegenwart*. Berlin. 1965–1968.

Michalka, W. (ed.), *Deutsche Geschichte 1933–1945. Dokumente zur Innen- und Außenpolitik*. Frankfurt am Main: Fischer. 1996.

Michalka, W. and Niedhart, G., *Die ungeliebte Republik. Dokumentation zur Innen und Aussenpolitik Weimars 1918–133*. Munich: DTV. 1980.

Milward, A.S., 'Fascism and the Economy' in Laqueur (1976).

Mohler, A., *Die konservative Revolution in Deutschland 1918–32: Grundriß ihrer Weltanschauungen*. Stuttgart: Friedrich Vorwerk Verlag. 1950.

Mommsen H., 'National Socialism: Continuity and Change' in Laqueur (1976).

Mommsen, H., 'Hitler's Position in the Nazi System' in Mommsen (1991), pp. 163–88.

Mommsen H., 'The Realization of the Unthinkable. The Final Solution and the Jewish Question in the Third Reich' in Mommsen (1991), pp. 224–53.

Mommsen, H. (ed.), *Weimar to Auschwitz*. Cambridge: Polity Press. 1991.

Mowrer, E., *Germany Puts the Clock Back*. London: Penguin. 1938 ed.

Müller, K.-J., *Armee und Drittes Reich 1933–1939*. Paderborn: Schöningh. 1989.

Neocleous, M., *Fascism*. Buckingham: Open University Press. 1997.

Nicolai, H., *Mein Kampf ums Recht*. MSS 109. Munich: Institut für Zeitgeschichte. 1950.

Noakes, J. and Pridham, G., *Documents on Nazism, 1919–1945*. London: Jonathan Cape. 1974.

Nolte, E., *Three Faces of Fascism*. New York: Mentor. 1969.

Orlow, D., *The History of the Nazi Party. Volume 1. 1919–1933*. Newton Abbot: David and Charles. 1969.

Overy, R., 'Germany, "Domestic Crisis" and War in 1939' in Overy (1994), pp. 205–32.

Overy, R., 'Hitler's War Plans and the Economy, 1933–1939' in Overy (1994), pp. 177–204.

Overy, R., *War and Economy in the Third Reich*. Oxford: Oxford University Press. 1994.

Palme Dutt, R., *Fascism and Social Revolution*. London: Martin Lawrence. 1934.

Payne, R., *The Life and Death of Adolf Hitler*. London: Jonathan Cape. 1973.

Payne, S.G., *A History of Fascism 1914–1945*. London: UCL Press. 1995.

Peukert, D., 'The Genesis of the "Final Solution" from the Spirit of Science' in Crew (1994).

Peukert, D. and Reulecke, J. (eds), *Die Reihen fast geschlossen. Beiträge zur Geschichte des Alltags unterm Nationalsozialismus*. Wuppertal: Peter Hammer. 1981.

Phelps, H., 'Hitler als Parteiredner im Jahre 1920', *Vierteljahrshefte für Zeitgeschichte* (1963) pp. 274–330.

Phelps, H., 'Hitler's "Grundlegende" Rede über den Antisemitismus', *Vierteljahrshefte für Zeitgeschichte* (1968) pp. 390–420.

Pipes, D., *Conspiracy. How the Paranoid Style Flourishes and Where it Comes from.* New York: Free Press. 1997.

Pohl, D., 'Die Ermordung der Juden im Generalgouvernement' in Herbert (1998).

Pollock, J.K., 'The German Reichstag Elections of 1930', *Americal Political Science Review*, 24 (1930), 989–95.

Pospieszalski, K.M., *Documenta Occupationis. VI. Hitlerowskie 'Prawo' Okupacyjne w Polsce. Czesc II. Generalna Gubernia.* Poznan: Instytut Zachodni. 1958.

Präg, W. and Jacobmeyer, W. (eds), *Das Diensttagebuch des deutschen Generalgouverneurs in Polen 1939–1945.* Stuttgart: Deutsche Verlags-Anstalt. 1975.

Price, G.P., *I Know These Dictators.* London: Harrap. 1937.

Quine, M.S., *Population Politics in Twentieth Century Europe.* London: Routledge. 1996.

Radziwonczyk, K., 'Akcja Tannenberg Grup Operacynych Sipo i SD w Polsce Jesienia 1939 R', *Przeglad Zachodni*, 5 (1966), 94–118.

Rajai, M. with Phillips, K., *Leaders of Revolution.* London: Sage. 1979.

Rauschning, H., *Germany's Revolution of Destruction.* London: Heinemann. 1939. [a].

Rauschning, H., *Hitler Speaks.* London: Thornton Butterworth. 1939. [b].

Redlich, F., *Hitler. Diagnosis of a Destructive Prophet.* Oxford: Oxford University Press. 1999.

Reid, A., *Borderland.* London: Phoenix. 1998.

Remme, T., 'Life with Hitler and his Mistress', *Daily Telegraph*, 23 September 1997.

Rich, N., *Hitler's War Aims. Ideology, the Nazi State, and the Course of Expansion.* New York: W.W. Norton. 1992 ed.

Riefenstahl, L., *The Sieve of Time. The Memoirs of Leni Riefenstahl.* London: Quartet Books. 1992.

Röhl, J.C. and Sombart, N. (eds), *Kaiser Wilhelm II. New Interpretations.* Cambridge: Cambridge University Press. 1982.

Rose, P.L., *German Question / Jewish Question. Revolutionary Antisemitism from Kant to Wagner.* Princeton, NJ: Princeton University Press. 1990.

Rycroft, C., 'Psychosis' in Gregory (1987).

Safrian, H., *Eichmann und seine Gehilfe.* Frankfurt am Main: Fischer. 1995.

Sandkühler, T., 'Judenpolitik und Judenmord im Distrikt Galizien, 1941–1942' in Herbert (1998).

Schlau, W. (ed.), *Die Deutschbalten.* Munich: Langen Müller. 1995.

Schleunes, K., *The Twisted Road to Auschwitz. Nazi Policy toward the German Jews 1933–1939.* Urbana: University of Illinois Press. 1970.

Schoenbaum, D., *Hitler's Social Revolution.* New York: Anchor. 1967.

Schöllgen, G., 'Der außenpolitische Kurs Hitlers' in Studt (1995).

Schramm, P.E., *Hitler. The Man and the Military Leader*. London: Allen Lane, The Penguin Press. 1972.

Schuschnigg, K. von, *Austrian Requiem*. 1947.

Schwaab, E.H., *Hitler's Mind. A Plunge into Madness*. New York: Praeger. 1992.

Schwartz, M., 'Euthanasie-Debatten in Deutschland (1895–1945)', *Vierteljahrsheft für Zeitgeschichte*, 46 (1998), 617–67.

Sereny, G., *Albert Speer: His Battle with Truth*. London: Picador. 1995.

Smelser, R. and Zitelmann, R. (eds), *The Nazi Elite*. London: Macmillan. 1993.

Smith, B.F., *Adolf Hitler. His Family, Childhood and Youth*. Stanford, Calif.: Hoover Institution Press. 1967, 1979

Speer, A, 'Neuplanung der Reichshauptstadt' in *Der Deutsche Baumeister*. Munich. 1939.

Speer, A., *Inside the Third Reich*. London: Sphere Books. 1971.

Speer, A., *Spandau. The Secret Diaries*. London: Collins. 1976.

Stachura, P.D. (ed.), *The Nazi Machtergreifung*. London: Allen and Unwin. 1983.

Steiner, J.M. and Freiherr von Cornberg, F., 'Willkür in der Willkür. Hitler und die Befreiungen von den antisemistischen Nürnberger Gesetzen', *Vierteljahrsheft für Zeitgeschichte*, 46 (1998), 143–89.

Steinweis, A.E., 'Weimar Culture and the Rise of National Socialism: The Kampfbund für deutsche Kultur', *Central European History*, 4, 24 (1991), 402–24.

Stern, F., *The Politics of Cultural Despair*. Chicago: University of Chicago Press. 1961.

Sternburg, W. von, *Warum Wir? Die Deutschen und Der Holocaust*. Berlin: ATV. 1996.

Sternhell, Z. with Sznajder, M. and Asheri, M., *The Birth of Fascist Ideology. From Cultural Rebellion to Political Revolution*. Princeton, NJ: Princeton University Press. 1994.

Stierlin, H., *Adolf Hitler. Familienperspektiven*. Frankfurt am Main: Suhrkamp. 1995.

Strang, G.B., 'Once More unto the Breach: Britain's Guarantee to Poland, March 1939', *Journal of Contemporary History*, 31 (1996), 721–52.

Strasser, O., *Mein Kampf. Eine politische Autobiographie*. Frankfurt am Main: Heinrich Heine. 1969.

Strawson, J., *Hitler as Military Commander*. London: Batsford. 1971.

Studt, C. (ed.), *Das Dritte Reich. Ein Lesebuch zur deutschen Geschichte 1933–1945*. Munich: Beck. 1995.

Taube, A. von, Thomson, E. and Garleff, M., 'Die Deutschbalten – Schicksal und Erbe einer eigenständigen Gemeinschaft' in Schlau (1995).

Taylor, R.R., *The Word in Stone. The Role of Architecture in the National Socialist Ideology*. Berkeley: University of California Press. 1974.

Taylor, S., *Prelude to Genocide*. New York: St. Martin's Press. 1985.

Taylor, T., 'Introduction' to Hitler (1961).

Teut, A., *Architektur im Dritten Reich. 1933–1945*. Frankfurt am Main: Ullstein. 1967

Thies, J., *Architekt der Weltherrschaft. Die 'Endziele' Hitlers*. Düsseldorf: Droste Verlag. 1976.

Thies, J., 'Nazi Architecture – A Blueprint for World Domination' in Welch (1983).

Thompson, D., *Harper's Magazine*, December 1934, pp.12–14.

Toland, J., *Adolf Hitler*. New York: Anchor Doubleday. 1976.

Torke, H.-J. and Himka, J.-P. (eds), *German–Ukrainian Relations in Historical Perspective*. Toronto: Canadian Institute of Ukrainian Studies. 1994.

Trevor-Roper, H.R., *The Last Days of Hitler*. London: Macmillan. 1947.

Trevor-Roper, H.R. (ed.), *Hitler's Secret Conversations. 1941–1944*. New York: Signet. 1961.

Trevor-Roper, H.R., *Hitler's War Directives 1939–1949*. London: Pan. 1966.

Trevor-Roper, H.R., 'Hitler's War Aims' in Koch (1985).

Trial of the Major War Criminals before the International Military Tribunal. Nuremberg. 1947.

Turner, H.A., *German Big Business and the Rise of Hitler*. Oxford: Oxford University Press. 1985. [a].

Turner, H.A. (ed.), *Hitler – Memoirs of a Confidant*. New Haven, Conn.: Yale University Press. 1985. [b].

Tyrell A. (ed.), *Führer befiehl. Selbstzeugnisse aus der 'Kampfzeit' der NSDAP. Dokumentation und Analyse*. Düsseldorf: Droste. 1969.

Tyrell, A., *Vom 'Trommler' zum 'Führer'*. Munich: Fink. 1975.

Vogelsang, T., 'Neue Dokumente zur Geschichte der Reichswehr 1930–1933', *Vierteljahrshefte für Zeitgeschichte* (1964), 434ff.

Waite, R.G.L., *The Psychopathic God. Adolf Hitler*. New York: Da Capo Press. 1993.

Warlimont, W., *Inside Hitler's Headquarters 1939–1945*. London: Weidenfeld and Nicolson. 1964.

Weber, E., 'Revolution? Counter-Revolution? What Revolution?' in Laqueur (1976).

Weinberg, G., *Germany, Hitler and World War II*. Cambridge: Cambridge University Press. 1995.

Weinstein, F., *The Dynamics of Nazism. Leadership, Ideology and the Holocaust*. New York: Academic Press. 1980.

Weissmann, K., *Der Weg in den Abgrund. Deutschland unter Hitler 1933–1934*. Munich: Herbig. 1997.

Welch, D., *Nazi Propaganda: the Power and the Limitations*. London. 1983.

Welch, D. (ed.), *Propaganda and the German Cinema*. Oxford: Oxford University Press. 1985.

Welch, D., *The Third Reich. Politics and Propaganda.* London: Routledge. 1993.

Welch, D., *Hitler.* London: UCL Press. 1998.

Wippermann, W. (ed.), *Kontroversen um Hitler.* Frankfurt am Main: Suhrkamp. 1986.

Wulf, J., *Die Bildenden Künste im Dritten Reich. Eine Dokumentation.* Gütersloh: Rowohlt. 1963.

Zaborowski, J., *Generalplan Ost. Koncepcje i Plany Polityki Wschodniej Adolfa Hitlera.* Warsaw: Ministerstwo Sprawiedliwosci. 1977.

Zitelmann, R., 'The Führer – Adolf Hitler' in Smelser and Zitelmann (1993).

Zitelmann, R., *Hitler. Selbstverständnis eines Revolutionärs.* Munich: Herbig. Fourth Edition. 1998.

Zoller, A., *Hitler Privat. Erlebnisbericht seiner Geheimsekretärin.* Düsseldorf: Droste. 1949.

Index

Abyssinia 98
Anglo-German Naval Agreement 96, 119
anti-Semitism 18, 19–21, 23–4, 27–8, 29–31, 32, 51, 78, 86–90, 131–2, 140–1, 162–3, 168, 170, 172–3, 174–5, 177, 178, 192, 194, 196; see *also* Holocaust
Arendt, Hannah 18
Aristotle 10
army 60–1, 83, 85, 117, 118, 123–4, 139–40, 184–5
Austria 96–7, 101, 108–10

Baltic States 37–8, 39, 102, 122–3, 124
bans, on speeches 59
beer hall putsch 54–6
Berlin 149–53, 159
borderline personality 177–8
Boxheim 61–3
Brest-Litovsk, Treaty of see Treaty of Brest-Litovsk
Brinton, Crane 11, 12
Broszat, Martin 18, 106
Bullock, Alan 2
Burckhardt, Jakob 122

Calvert, Peter 11
Charles II 11
Close, David 11
Coburg 52–4
Commissar Order 131–2
Communism 2–4, 5–6, 31–2, 43, 44, 65, 78, 79–82, 131–2, 195–6

Communist International 6–7
conscription 97–8
conservative élites 2, 64–5, 76–7
'Crystal Night' 89–90
Czechoslovakia 38, 105, 108, 110–11, 113–14

Danzig 118, 122
decorations, military 42
Disarmament Conference 97
Dollfuss, Austrian Chancellor 96
Drexler, Anton 26, 45
drugs 167–8
'drummer', Hitler as 70–1

Egypt 10
Ehrhardt, Captain 43
Eisner, Kurt 42
electoral campaigns 63
Enabling Act 82

family 166–86
fascism 6–8
Feder, Gottfried 19, 45
Fleming, Gerald 42, 178
Four Year Plan 106–7, 117
Frank, Hans 78, 95–6
Fromm, Erich 175–6

gassing 173, 178
General Plan East 138
German Socialist Party 27
German Workers' Party 24–6, 45, 46

German Workers' Party programme,
   24 February 1920 24–6
Goebbels, Josef 75–6, 78, 89
Goldhagen, Daniel 135, 195
Great Britain 102–3, 104, 111–13, 115,
   119, 121, 129–30
Greene, Thomas 11, 13
Grossraumwirtschaft 114, 125–7
Guevara, Che 15

Hanfstaengl, Ernst 46–8
Hanisch, Reinhold 147, 174, 183–4
Harrer, Karl 45
heart condition 167
Henlein, Konrad 110–11
Hindenburg, President Paul von 50,
   64–5, 76, 82
history 32–3
'Hitler Myth' 58
Holborne, Hajo 40
Holocaust 132–6
'Hossbach' memorandum 107–8
Hugenberg, Alfred 77
hypocrisy 102–3

ideologue 19
ideology 17–41, 104–06, 194–95
industrialists 8–9, 10, 39–40

Jarman, J.T. 103

Kershaw, Ian 18, 26
Kubizek, August 143–8, 172–3, 177,
   180–2

leadership 66–91, 194–95
Lebensraum 36–9, 104, 106, 131,
   154–6, 173
Liebenfels, Lanz von 22–3
Linz 143, 145–7, 153, 154, 172
living space *see Lebensraum*
lottery 180–1
Ludecke, Kurt 48–9
Ludendorff, Erich von 39, 55, 57

Lueger, Karl 22
Luitpold *Gymnasium* 43, 45

Mann, Thomas 17
Marx, Karl 5–6
Marxism *see* Communism
Mein Kampf 21, 30–2, 35–6, 57, 71,
   93, 101, 106, 171–2
mental illness 177–86, 197
Merkl, Peter 18
Meyer, Captain 19
middle classes 58
models, architectural 149–50
modernisation 192–3, 196, 198
Mohler, A. 17
Mommsen, Hans 18, 103, 194–5
monorchid, Hitler as 171
Munich 42, 43, 44, 54, 55, 69, 147
Munich crisis 111–13
Munich University 19, 44

'Nuremberg Laws' 87–9
Nuremberg trials 198

Oedipal syndrome 14, 173, 177
Operation Barbarossa 130–3, 134–5,
   137, 167
Ostara 22–3

Palme Dutt, R. 7–8
Parkinson's disease 167
parliament 4, 32, 57
party reorganisation 57
Pasewalk hospital 42, 168, 178, 183,
   185
Poland 101, 118–20, 121, 123, 125–8
Pollock, J.K. 17
Potempa 63
prison 57, 58–9
Protocols of the Elders of Zion 30
psychosis 178–80

racism 17–41, 162–4, 192–3; *see also*
   anti-Semitism

Rajai, M. 13–15
Rathenau, Walther 93
Raubal, Geli 177
Rauschning, Hermann 17, 37–9, 71,
    101–2, 106, 110, 195
reading, Hitler's 166
'Reichstag Fire Decree' 81
resettlement 124–5, 138
revolution, definition of 12
revolutionary, definition of 16
Rhineland 98–100, 105
Ribbentrop, Joachim von 99–100,
    102–3, 123
Riefenstahl, Leni 75–6, 86
Röhm, Ernst 82–5
Russia 92–3, 121–2; see also
    Operation Barbarossa

Saarland 95–6
Schiemann, Theodor 39
Schönerer, Georg von 22
school, Hitler at 170
Second Book 36–7, 104–6, 163
Secret Book see Second Book
seizure of power 76–7
Slavs 32, 39, 123, 125–7, 136–8, 192
speech-making, Hitler's technique of
    50–1
Speer, Albert 78, 140, 149, 150, 151,
    153, 166
Stalin, Joseph 2, 3, 10

Stefanie 181–2
Stern, Fritz 18
Stresemann, Gustav 93
Sturm Abteilungen 51–4, 63, 72–4, 80,
    81, 82

Thule Society 45
Treaty of Brest-Litovsk 93
Treaty of Versailles 93, 95, 97, 98,
    101
Trevor-Roper, Hugh 17
trial of 1924 56–7
Turner, Henry Ashby 10
Tyrell, Albrecht 26

Ukraine 39
Ulm trial 60–1
United States of America 132, 138,
    193
'urban plan' 59–60

V-Mann 44–5, 195
Versailles, Treaty of see Treaty of
    Versailles
Vienna 21, 22, 110, 147, 148, 161,
    170, 174, 183–4

Wagener, Otto 33–4, 72, 74
Wagner, Richard 144, 196

Zitelmann, Rainer 2–4, 195